MW00617442

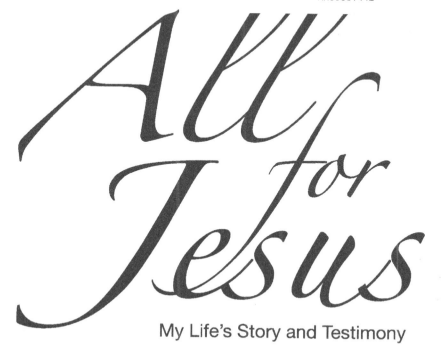

My Life's Story and Testimony

Wesley L. Duewel

OTHER TITLES BY WESLEY DUEWEL

Touch the World through Prayer (Zondervan, 1986)

Let God Guide You Daily (Zondervan, 1988)

Ablaze for God (Zondervan, 1989)

Mighty Prevailing Prayer (Zondervan, 1990)

God's Great Salvation (DLT, 1991)

Measure Your Life (Zondervan, 1992)

Revival Fire (Zondervan, 1995)

God's Power Is for You (Zondervan, 1997)

More God, More Power (Zondervan, 2000)

Heroes of the Holy Life (Zondervan, 2002)

Christmas Is for You...and the World (DLT, 2010)

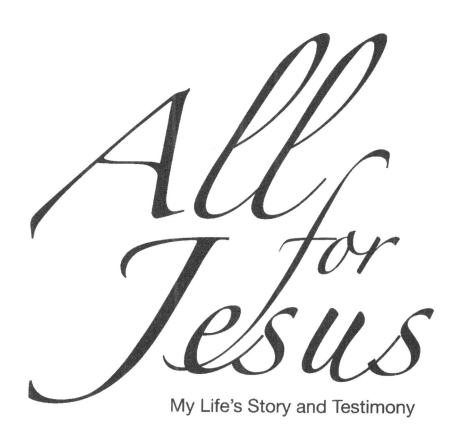

All for Jesus

My Life's Story and Testimony

Francis Asbury Press
Wilmore, Kentucky

The Francis Asbury Society, PO Box 7, Wilmore, KY 40390
www.francisasburysociety.com

Published in association with:
Duewel Literature Trust, Inc. (DLT), 980 Duewel Dr, Greenwood, IN 46142
www.duewellliteraturetrust.org

DLT titles may be purchased in bulk for educational, business, fund-raising, or sales promotional use. For information, please email duewellliteraturetrust@gmail.com

ISBN 978-0-915143-39-9
First edition, second printing
Printed in the United States of America

Dedication and Acknowledgments

Presented posthumously on behalf of Wesley L. Duewel by Mrs. Hilda M. Duewel and Dr. David E. Dick

How can one compose a dedication of one's autobiography without acknowledging the role and impact of loving parents? Rev. Louis and Mrs. Ida Duewel raised me in the fear and admonition of the Lord, and they never ceased providing their loving prayers on my behalf. I will always be deeply indebted to them.

Similarly, I dedicate this autobiography to my dearly beloved first wife, Betty; our children John Wesley, Ruth Christine, and Esther Darlene; and their spouses and children. Perhaps unbeknownst to them, God has blessed me in so many ways through their faithful love, obedience, and sacrifice throughout my life and ministry. Their constant presence in my heart and prayers has been like a wisp of fragrant aroma rising continuously in intercession before the Lord. My family has given me reason to live a life worthy for the Lord.

I also dedicate this autobiography to all those who prayed so faithfully over my life and ministry. Those prayer partners, many of whom I came to know personally and became friends, inestimably influenced my life. I also dedicate this volume to all my past and present colleagues and coworkers within the OMS worldwide family, as well as to the greater members of the body of Christ with whom we labored, loved, and reached the world for the cause of Christ around the world.

Among those who lent value and worth to this book is a local businessman, George Allen. As an experienced author, he graciously gave many tedious hours proofing and correcting the manuscript, making it more attractive and readable. Thank you, George, for all your assistance.

Without a doubt, I also dedicate this autobiography to Hilda M. Johnecheck Duewel, my faithful and dedicated secretary and second wife, without whom none of this would have been possible. She may have been the only one who co-labored beside me long enough to be able to interpret and translate my handwriting, and then reproduce, compile, and edit this work comprehensively and clearly enough to make sense to any who may find it helpful after the fact.

Finally, and above all others, I dedicate this autobiography to Jesus, my Savior and Lord. He gave me meaning and purpose in life, and he became my best Friend, faithful in all circumstances and situations. His Word has guided me, his Spirit has comforted me, and his Father has blessed me with a long life and fruitful ministry. I have simply been his instrument, so any good that came out of my life and ministry was all his doing. For all the mistakes, missteps, and miscalculations that caused any harm or regression or hindered the growth and glory of his kingdom, I accept full responsibility.

I did what I could, *all for Jesus.*

Contents

Foreword

What you hold in your hands is special—the story of a godly man who lived his life relentlessly and uncompromisingly for Christ and others. Dr. Wesley Duewel was a missionary of the Oriental Missionary Society (OMS) to India, where he compellingly demonstrated how prayer makes a difference in the advance of the church of Jesus Christ. He authored ten books, with a combined global distribution of 2.5 million copies in fifty-eight languages, and for thirteen years he served as the president of OMS, which became OMS International, now One Mission Society. He was a missionary statesman, an engaged intercessor, an author, a teacher, a sought-after speaker, a discipler, and a leader.

When I arrived at OMS in 2014, I was amazed by this man in his nineties who still came to the office every day wearing a suit and tie. I marveled at his sharpness and passion for King Jesus. I appreciated his love of the Scriptures and teaching on Wesleyan holiness. And I was moved as visitors, many of whom were from other countries, wanted to be sure they spent some time with Dr. Duewel, inviting him to pray for them. When facing overwhelming challenges on several occasions, I asked for his counsel and prayer. We were all greatly encouraged and blessed by spending time with this revered man of God.

Dr. Duewel was just weeks away from his one-hundredth birthday when God called him home. When my wife and I received the news of his passing, we knew OMS, along with the broader church of Jesus Christ, had lost a great leader and warrior of the faith.

Soon after his passing, Dr. Duewel's widow, Mrs. Hilda Duewel, and Dr. David Dick, using notebooks of material Dr. Duewel left to share his story, began working tirelessly to complete this autobiography. Celebrating this major accomplishment with them, I rejoice that you have a copy and plan to read it. You'll be challenged, blessed, and encouraged as you do.

And with so many Christian leaders not finishing well, may you be inspired by this story of one who did, living his life for the advance of the glory of Jesus—literally around the world!

Robert L. Fetherlin, President
One Mission Society Global
October 2020

Dr. Wesley Duewel was *all for Jesus. He* gave dignity to everything he touched. He was *All for Jesus.* His conduct was above reproach, and his life and ministry were a testimony of what God can do with an individual totally surrendered to Jesus Christ from a young age. He was about serving the King of Kings, and his Spirit-filled life never wavered from total obedience to Jesus Christ, seeking to always please his Lord. Dr. Duewel's desire was for every person on earth to know the peace in their hearts only Jesus can give.

He was a great prayer warrior, encouraged everyone to pray more, and told us, "You can stand beside any preacher or missionary anyplace in the world in prayer." He also passionately challenged and reminded us, "Our greatest work is prayer." Perhaps of the many volumes he wrote, *Touch the World through Prayer* is the most widely read. As I read it, I was on my knees several times because of God's anointed words from the pen of a godly man. Manuscripts of Dr. Duewel's heart and the heart of God are scattered all over the world.

Dr. Duewel never accepted any royalties for the books he wrote; he gave all that money away so more copies could be printed to give the people in China, India, and many other countries. By giving from his own resources, he was the largest contributor to the Duewel Literature Trust. He was about helping everyone he could.

As president of the Oriental Missionary Society (now One Mission Society—OMS), Dr. Duewel led with godliness, intelligence, prayer, and a call to holiness for the missionaries he led. He was a man of integrity.

With the assistance of Mrs. Hilda Duewel, Dr. David Dick, a missionary statesman and president of the Duewel Literature Trust, has spent countless hours with this book from a mountain of copious notes from the pen of Dr. Duewel. He is the most qualified person to complete an autobiography for one of the saintliest men of the last century.

In reading the first fifty pages of *All for Jesus,* I was amazed at the detailed history of the Duewel family and their ministry. Because of their commitment to holiness, they had hearts of obedience to Christ, deep prayer lives, and a determination for intellectual excellence.

I am positive Dr. Duewel would desire all the readers of this book to go into battle with Satan for those without Christ. Our battle cry: *all for Jesus.*

Warren G. Hardig, Chairman, Board of Directors
Duewel Literature Trust, Inc.
July 2020

Editor's Note

An encounter with Dr. Wesley L. Duewel was an unforgettable experience, for anyone who ever met him soon learned he was a man of the Word and prayer. He outlived his peers, but those subsequent generations who knew him or heard him speak reflect an almost universal response: he was, above all, a man with a passion for Jesus, ever ready to lift a prayer for everyone and anyone outside the realm of faith.

Dr. Duewel loved everyone—most of all Jesus—and he was not a complicated person. His outward plain and simple faith was founded on an inward depth and passion that most mere mortals envy yet few achieve. He lived his life singularly focused on knowing and doing God's will, and he did so by immersing himself in the Word for personal freshness and revitalization at every opportunity. He also kept meticulous records. Some might call it journaling, but his diaries are filled with details far exceeding most journals. His prayer times assumed the nature of one friend conversing with another friend.

While he was working on his autobiography, he said to me, "David, I can't decide what to include or what to leave out." I think he felt omitting anything would be shortchanging the marvelous provision and blessings God bestowed upon him throughout his life. But I knew that completing his autobiography as a viable publication would mean making the deliberate and often difficult choice of omitting rich portions of his material.

Growing up an only child in a devout family, Dr. Duewel early on acquired the kind of spiritual discipline and character most people spend a lifetime aspiring to achieve. Subsequently, as an adult, he cultivated an encyclopedic mind and passionate heart that poured forth in unquenchable flame in his public speaking and published writings, all reflecting the devotion and intimacy originating in the *imago Dei*, the mind of Christ.

Dr. Duewel would be embarrassed by much of the first-person narrative used in this book, but even an autobiography completed posthumously has no other option. Nonetheless, he endeavored to give God the glory and to praise him for every aspect of his life and work, and so the reader will see many italicized phrases that do just that throughout the book. He gave glory to God for everything accomplished through his ministry, and he wanted everyone to understand his ministry only in that context.

While keeping his voice, this work has been edited for greater consistency, clarity, and readability—just as it would have been if published during his lifetime. This includes slight edits to notes, letters, diary entries, comments, and various other communications. Last, the footnotes throughout this book not only provide content sources but often offer further explanation, clarification, information, or detail.

In conclusion, several emphases in Dr. Duewel's life and ministry characterized him. One was a genuine love for, and unflinching belief in, the Word of God, from which an authentic burden for the lost and unsaved originated. That in turn, stirred a desire that Christ should increase in a believer's life through a second work of grace and recurring infillings of the Holy Spirit. These two multiplied with essential prevailing prayer and intercession for God's will to be done, including prayer for divine healing for the physically, emotionally, and spiritually needy in the world.

David E. Dick, President
Duewel Literature Trust, Inc.
July 2020

Introduction

The prayer and desire of my heart is to live and serve *all for Jesus*, and this was my parents' deep commitment as well. Mother was a godly, spiritually hungry, and spiritually obedient woman whose prayers covered all my life. Father was a godly, humble, Bible-loving pastor who lived, taught, and preached holiness. They were the earliest, primary, and most decisive influences in my life. From my youth on, their characteristics and examples attracted me, blessed me, and guided me.

My other spiritual heroes included Charles and Lettie Cowman and Eugene Erny of OMS, and of tremendous blessing and challenge were the lives and ministries of Adoniram Judson, Charles G. Finney, Jonathan Goforth, and John Nelson Hyde (known as Praying Hyde). They, too, were marked by the same commitment and holy consecration—*all for Jesus*. "To him who loves us and has freed us from our sins by his blood, and has made us to be a kingdom and priests to serve his God and Father—to him be glory and power for ever and ever! Amen" (Rev 1:5b–6).

All for Jesus
You know, Lord, that this heart of mine
Is first and absolutely thine.
'Tis consecrated to Your will.
Your plan alone I would fulfill.

I have no will, Lord, of my own
I seek Your will, Your will alone.

I only have one life to give
So I for You alone would live.

I would not waste a single day;
In nothing dare I miss Your way.
This is my hunger and my cry,
Oh let my life You glorify.

I do not ask for self, for ease;
I only ask Your will to please.
It is joy to have You my path choose;
Just take me, please anoint and use.

Each day I all to You confide;
You are my Counselor and Guide.
I want to love You more and more
To give You sweet joy o'er and o'er.

Your holy heart I long to thrill
As I Your own desires fulfill.
Oh holy Jesus, You are mine
And all I am and have is Thine.[1]

---

1   Composed en route to Gadag, India, January 17, 1963.

1
The Early Years

On Easter Monday, April 12, 1852, my great-grandfather, Henry Duewel, and his family left Germany for America—the land of their dreams—on the sailing ship *Olland*.[1] After forty-five days of eventful sailing, they reached New Orleans. In mid-America it was still possible to purchase property and invest one's life in the uncrowded land of freedom and hope. On the heels of an already precarious voyage across the Atlantic, they started up the Mississippi River by steamboat, arriving in St. Louis, Missouri, on Independence Day, July 4, 1852. But then six days later, after several days of sickness and with the strains of the long journey, Great-grandmother Duewel died. Her last words to my great-grandfather were, "Keep yourself in touch with God."

Grandfather was a lay minister and preacher in the local German Methodist Church. If the Methodist circuit rider wasn't available, he and a local doctor took turns conducting the services and preaching. My relatives, including my parents, are buried in the graveyard adjacent to the Zion German Methodist Church near Truxton.

Father

My father, Louis J. Duewel, was born on April 15, 1884, in Truxton. He was a quiet, studious, and serious young man responsive to spiritual reality. When at age seventeen he read *God's Revivalist*

---

1   Information in this section was synthesized from the small fifty-six-page booklet, *One Hundred Years of Duewel History (1852–1952)* compiled by Dr. Duewel's father, the Rev. Louis J. Duewel, in 1952.

published by God's Bible School (GBS) in Cincinnati, Ohio, he was definitely born again.

He also read a German book on sanctification by John Wesley, the founder of Methodism.[2] Through reading both *God's Revivalist* and this German book, he realized that a born-again Christian could be sanctified holy. In 1905, at age twenty-one, these resources led him to experience entire sanctification, which is described on page 24.

Afterward, he felt God's call to the ministry and enrolled at Methodist Central Wesleyan College in Warrenton, Missouri. But the college did not provide the spiritual nurture for which he longed or the encouragement of the John Wesley–type experience, so he started in ministry without the strong, clear, inner-witness, and assurance of sanctification. He received special teacher training courses and taught in country schools for two years. Providentially, he was my mother's teacher in Sunday school and grade school.

Louis and Ida Duewel, circa 1935

Mother

My mother, Ida Luelf Duewel, was born December 22, 1887, at Hawk Point, near Truxton. She was the second youngest daughter of August and Johanna Winter Luelf, who had emigrated from Germany. They were also hard-working and reverent believers.

Mother yielded her life to Christ at the altar when the invitation was given in a revival service. Suddenly, she was granted a vision of angels ascending and descending a ladder that reached to heaven! The evangelist said, "God is in this place," and Mother thought, "Of course God is here. Can't you see his angels?" She was the only one to whom God gave this vision. From then on, she possessed the inner assurance

---

2   Sanctification is an instantaneous and radical work of the Spirit that takes place in the moment when the believer offers his or her life as a living sacrifice and the Holy Spirit purifies the believer's heart by faith and fills with his fullness [Wesley L. Duewel, *More God, More Power*, 120].

and confidence that she was born again, but she heard no preaching on being filled with the Holy Spirit.

From childhood, Mother had been bothered with an uncontrolled temper, and her sisters would purposely try to goad her to anger. For example, after she'd scrubbed the kitchen floor, they would deliberately walk through mud outside, and then walk across the newly cleaned floor. At times Mother got so angry that she chased them with a broom. When she realized how anger had controlled her, she would run to her bed, fall on her knees crying, and ask God to forgive her, promising to never get angry again.

Before long, though, her sisters would provoke her once more. Several times she heard her mother praying and crying on the second floor of their home and moved to listen at the foot of the stairs. "O God," her mother prayed, "deliver Ida from her terrible anger." Mother felt so ashamed, and again she told the Lord she would never, never get angry again.

Mother's Infilling of the Spirit

As a teenager, Mother hungered for the kind of experience she read about in the book of Acts. After she went to live with her older sister, who had married a German Methodist minister and needed help with their several children and housework, she approached her brother-in-law and asked, "How can I have an experience like this?" "Oh, that is not for you," he replied. "That was just for the apostles."

With no one to guide her, Mother began praying every spare moment throughout the day. One night she lay in her bed and prayed, "Lord, I'm not going to sleep until I know You have filled me with Your Spirit." But after working long hours, she fell asleep as she prayed. When she awoke in the morning, she was so ashamed. "Lord," she prayed, "how can You ever fill me with Your Spirit if I don't want it more than this?" All day long she maintained a praying heart. Then when she went to her room that evening, she told the Lord she would pray all night if need be. She would not go to sleep until she knew she was filled with the Spirit. But again, she fell asleep from sheer physical weariness.

Her household chores included rising each morning before the family, lighting a fire in the stove, going to the barn to milk the cow, and then preparing breakfast. The cow she milked had a mean disposition and often rebelled, kicking vigorously. Mother was a frail person physically, and she often thought, "I know I'm a child of God, but I also know I'm not ready to go to heaven and meet Jesus, because I'm not holy like I ought to be. If that cow kicks me just right, I'll die without being ready to meet Jesus."

On the third morning, after again failing to stay awake all night in prayer, she was still hungry-hearted with no one to explain the role of consecration and faith to her. Nevertheless, she prayed, "O Jesus, fill me with Your Spirit," and, as she lit the morning fire, her faith touched God. Instantly, he filled her with his Spirit. She was flooded with joy and inner assurance, and from then on she was completely delivered from her evil temper!

When she started out to the barn to milk that kicking cow, she skipped along, swinging the milk bucket and thinking, "If that cow kills me this morning, I'm ready to meet Jesus. I know he has cleansed me and filled me with his Spirit." After that, Mother was always such a spiritual, prayerful, and victorious person. If she had not told me herself, I would never have suspected she'd previously had such a sour disposition.

CHILDHOOD AND YOUTH (1916–1934)

Father's pastorates, first in the German Methodist Church and subsequently in the Fire Baptized Holiness Church, meant my early life was characterized by frequent moves—every two or three years, no less than seven times during my early childhood and youth.[3] But rather than his allowing me to feel deprived, the Lord was gracious and helped me experience much personal growth, both physically and spiritually.

---

3   Cecelia Luelf Douglas and Ruth Smith Taylor, *The History of the Bible Holiness Church*, 320. Articles on Wesley and Betty and his father, Louis J. Duewel. (See DLT Library.) Dr. Duewel marked all paragraphs of the unabridged edition.

As an only child, I was mostly surrounded by adults, which in retrospect probably spared me from youthful temptations and a multitude of heartaches. God often uses a praying home to prepare his children for life. My parents, especially my mother, lavished much love and prayer on me, from my birth until God called them home. They gave me a wonderful Christian heritage.

St. Charles, Missouri (1911–1916)

In 1911, when Father was twenty-seven, his first church assignment was at the German Methodist Church in St. Charles, Missouri. He preached there in German each Sunday for six years and so retained fluency in the language.

I was born in St. Charles on June 3, 1916. One of my earliest memories is of Mother placing her chair in the middle of the kitchen floor each morning, then kneeling for her private devotions.

Wesley with parents

I pulled my little red chair beside hers, knelt, and quietly prayed to Jesus, too. I remember making my prayer lists as soon as I was able to write. Mother also taught me the table grace, "O give thanks unto the Lord; for he is good: for his mercy endureth for ever" (Ps 118:29 KJV).

We practiced evening family prayer time each day, when my parents also both read from God's Word. Mother prayed generally and wept for China, and Father tended to pray more comprehensively. Both prayed for church needs. I cannot emphasize strongly enough how indebted I am to my parents for our Christian home.

Unknown to me at the time, Elizabeth Dolly Raisch (later known as Betty) had been born on June 11, 1915, on a farm in Bevis, Ohio. She was the third of William and Margaret Raisch's ten children. Life for the Raisch family also centered on their church. Little did Betty and

I know that, later in life, we would meet, marry, and serve the Lord together halfway around the world.

Springfield, Illinois (1917–1919)

When I was six months old, the bishop transferred Father to the German Methodist Church in Springfield, Illinois. The church and parsonage were just one block from the state capitol building and only a few blocks from the historic Abraham Lincoln home.

In Springfield, I first felt God's saving grace as a small child of two or three years of age. Before Mother tucked me into bed each night, she knelt beside me to pray. One night when she was finished, I said, "Oh, Mama, don't stop praying. It's doing me lots of good." And then I jumped off the bed and hopped around. "Oh, Mama, I can't stop jumping, I'm so happy. Jesus has come into my heart." From then on, with childlike faith, I began to follow my parents' prayer example, like kneeling beside that little red chair.

After I received Jesus as my Savior, Mother began to tell me of heaven. She told me later that I cried for joy, and said, "Oh Mama, I want to go there. I want to go there."

Wesley as young child

"Yes," she answered, "one day you can go there. Not now, but one day."

"But, Mama," I said, "I want to go right now!" Mother patiently taught me God's time is the best time.

Nashville, Illinois (1919–1923)

After his two-year pastorate in Springfield, Father was transferred to Nashville, Illinois, where he was appointed to pastor for four years. Mother became ill with acute appendicitis, and surgery would cost nearly a thousand dollars. She hesitated, praying, "Oh Lord, I'd rather not have to pay all that money to a hospital and doctors. If You will just heal me, I'll give that money to the Oriental Missionary Society for China."[4] God instantly healed her, and she sent the money, which she had been able to save. OMS responded, giving the name of the province where the money was used in evangelism and for literature for evangelists.[5] Her prayer burden and faithful example resonated in my heart and carried with me into adulthood.

In Nashville, we had a sandbox under a tree in the yard. One day when I was about five years old, I was making roads in the sand for my little toy cars. Suddenly, with a strong impression that God was calling me to India, I ran into the house. "Mama, Mama," I said. "Jesus just told me that when I get big, he wants me to go to India and tell people about him." I didn't know where India was, but I wanted to go there because Jesus had told me to go there.

Wesley as young child on church steps, circa 1920

"Mama," I added, "I want you to go with me!" What else would a five-year-old boy want, but for his mother to go with him! Indeed, Mother did go with me—through her daily prayer times, often weeping, until her death in 1962.

To underscore my sense of call, Father was not conducting any special missionary services at the time, no missionary had recently visited our church or home, nor can I remember any vision or voice. It was an ever-deepening impression, and my parents never knew why this call came upon my heart. But from then on, I always held a deep conviction that it was God's will I be a missionary in India, and as a child, I began praying for that country. Several times later in life, when he surprised me with a new step of guidance, I also suddenly knew in

---

4   Regardless of the rebranding efforts, it has been continuously referred to by the abbreviation, OMS.

5   One thousand dollars in the twenties would be equivalent to about $12,250 in twenty-first century value.

my heart what God wanted me to do. I never lost that assurance of God's call to India.

Father's Sanctification Experience

Nashville had two small Methodist churches. One was a rural church, and the other was a rather lowly and despised Southern Methodist Church, characterized by its dilapidated entrance steps. The church was pastored by a man who had never finished his formal education, and he endured various forms of ridicule and opposition. Stones were even thrown through the church's windows. Nevertheless, he planned revival meetings and called a well-known former missionary, Dr. Mingledorf, to preach. Out of courtesy, Father felt he should attend one service.

Dr. Mingledorf preached on 1 Thessalonians 4:3, "It is God's will that you should be sanctified." He gave no invitation at the close, but he said if anyone wished to pray, they should remain after the benediction. My father had lost his clear witness to sanctification, and he said to Mother, "Let's stay." They both went forward for prayer.

As he often testified thereafter, that night Father experienced the reassurance of sanctification "through and through" (1 Thess 5:23). As a result, our home was tremendously blessed by both my parents' experience of entire sanctification. I did not understand all that had happened, but I could feel the presence of God in our home in a new way.

Wesley: 3 yrs, 5 mo

Edwardsville, Illinois (1923–1925)

After four years in Nashville, the bishop transferred Father to Edwardsville, Illinois, just outside of St. Louis, where he pastored Emmanuel German Methodist Church. Because of the church's prominent location, as well as its stateliness and beauty, many couples from St. Louis stopped at our parsonage next door and asked my father to marry them. I often sat quietly in the room or nearby where I could listen as my father went through the marriage ceremony. I heard him repeat it so many times that, even as a young lad, I memorized a large part of it.

Run Over by a Model T Ford

I attended the second and third grades in Edwardsville, walking about seven blocks to a corner fire station, and then turning left for another long block to the school. One rainy day the red brick streets were wet and slick, and when I got to the corner, for some reason I didn't check to see if a car was coming. I ran into the street in front of a high school student driving a Model T Ford. He slammed on the brakes, which immediately locked the wheels and sent the car into a skid. The front bumper struck me in the back, knocking me flat. But Model T Fords were higher off the ground than vehicles are today, so when the car spun around in a circle over me, it broke my umbrella but missed me completely. The children who saw the accident picked me up by the arm and walked me home. I felt guilty for not looking before crossing the street, so I hid in embarrassment behind the church. The children called Mother outdoors and said, "Don't worry, Mrs. Duewel, don't worry. Please don't worry." She replied, "No, I'm not worrying." Just a short time earlier, she had been in prayer and felt an unusual nearness of God's presence. They told her I had been run over by a car and led her to where I was hiding. She took me into the house and reassured me of her love, and then she told me how Jesus had watched over me.

Wesley on running board of vehicle

Healed of Scarlet Fever

Scarlet fever made its rounds while we lived in Edwardsville, infecting a little girl in my Sunday school class who subsequently died.

Not long afterward, I, too, fell sick and broke out with red eruptions all over my body, accompanied by a high fever. The doctor examined me, determined I had scarlet fever, and said to my father, "Anything you want from this house in the next couple of weeks, take out of the house immediately, tonight. According to government law, I must post a quarantine sign on your house the first thing in the morning, and once that sign is posted, you will not be allowed back inside. If you do come back, you, too, will be quarantined. You will not be allowed to go out and carry on your pastoral ministry."

My parents hurriedly brought a cot from upstairs to the dining room so I could rest on it. Then my father set up another cot in the garage, strung a twine rope there, and then carried out his clothing to hang. Mother would put food on a plate on the back porch, and he could pick it up from there. As Mother tucked me into bed that night, she said, "Wesley, don't worry. We'll just trust Jesus." Of course, I didn't know how serious a disease scarlet fever was, so I understood her to mean, "We'll just pray and trust Jesus, and God will heal you." She asked God to take care of me. I simply prayed for Jesus to heal me.

The next morning, I was completely free from all symptoms. The doctor came and asked, "Well, how's my little patient today?" He opened my pajamas and saw that all the red eruptions were completely gone. Then he said, "Open your mouth." He looked into my throat, and all the red blotches had cleared away. He put his hand on my forehead, and my fever was completely gone too. He turned to Mother and demanded, "What's happened here?"

Mother was a bit timid by nature, but she stepped up to my cot and said, "You see, Wesley, it pays to trust Jesus."

"Why," the doctor said, "it must be wonderful to have a faith like that."

"No," she replied, "it's wonderful to have a God like that."

"I didn't know you could know there was a God. I'm an agnostic."

Mother testified and explained her faith in Christ. "Oh, yes," she said, "you can know there is a God. You can talk to Jesus." That precipitated an extended discussion with the doctor, who sat down and asked Mother question after question.

Nokomis, Illinois (1925–1928)

In those days, it was not uncommon for pastors to be classified by the amount of salary they received. Each time he was about to be transferred, Father pleaded with the bishop to send him to the most conservative church available.

"Why," the bishop repeatedly said, "you will lose the status of the salary level you have received."

Father replied, "I don't care one thing about that. Send me where I can preach John Wesley Methodism."

In 1925, he was moved to Nokomis, Illinois, to pastor Grace Methodist Church for three years. But there he experienced something new.

Father's Unrest

Father began experiencing a spiritual unrest because of the denominational Sunday school literature. It contained so much liberalism that he didn't use it, and Mother suggested they leave the ministry of the Methodist Church because of increasing liberalism. The issue came to a head when Father planned an annual revival service with three other Methodist churches. In one evening service, two pastors argued with the evangelist about the doctrine John Wesley taught. My father, broken-hearted, tried to reason with them.

Father felt a great loyalty to the Methodist Church, and he hoped he could somehow build up the evangelical minority within it. In every pastorate, he always requested a Methodist missionary for his missions meetings. The climax came one year, when the missionaries who'd been sent scoffed and ridiculed the blood of Christ. "How can I ask my members to support such missionaries?" he asked.

Mother's Sudden Extended Illness

When I was in the sixth grade, one Sunday evening Mother became suddenly and severely ill. I still remember peeking through the curtains of the front door window as the ambulance pulled away with my parents, headed for the hospital thirteen miles away in Pana. Questions turned over in my mind: *Will I ever see Mother again? What will happen to Papa and me?* I remember feeling extremely alone, wondering what was going to become of us.

Mother had developed double pneumonia, which became pleurisy. She experienced partial paralysis and a heart condition, and when she returned home, her nervous system had become so unsettled that she was extremely sensitive to light and sound. We could not receive visitors in our home.

She was ill for about five years. At times she was slightly improved, and at times she was worse. She also experienced severe depression, times when she could not sense the love of God. Sometimes she wept uncontrollably when she knew no reason for it. Her deep desire was to play the piano and worship the Lord through praise one more time, singing the gospel song, "The Lily of the Valley," which describes Christ as "the fairest of ten thousand" to our souls.

Truxton, Missouri (1928–1933)

Because of mother's illness, we moved to be near Grandmother's house in the little town of Truxton. We stayed for four years. During those years, I would kneel to pray in the little mission hall, called the Truxton-Bellflower Mission, which was out in the country near my uncle Herman Luelf's farm. Some of the other boys laughed, made jokes, and shook my chair, but I remained faithful in my walk with the Lord—until I was about in the seventh grade. Then I succumbed to these boys' influence, became ashamed of the Lord, and quit kneeling and praying. I didn't commit open sins, but I was backslidden in my heart. I knew I was not walking faithfully with Jesus.

The next year, on the first day in high school, the principal handed each of us a piece of paper and told us to write down what we planned to be in life. Instantly, I had a mental block. All I could think was *missionary*, but I did not want to write that down. I raised up somewhat in my seat so I could look over the shoulder of the student in front of me and saw he'd written *aviator. Oh*, I thought, *I'll put that down*. That was the only time I ever copied from someone else's paper. As we left school that day, the teacher looked at me and said, "So you intend to be an aviator, do you?" as though he didn't believe it. Neither did I as I hung my head in embarrassment and shame.

My mother was physically unable to attend church during the Truxton years, so when Father was speaking at another church, I rode to Truxton-Bellflower Mission with one of my relatives or friends. But during our first year in Truxton, my father asked for a one-year leave of absence from the Methodist ministry to care for his mother and her sister, Caroline.[6] Father was his mother's last surviving child, and she was in her eighties and in poor health. Caroline, who had spent her life with my parents, was also in her eighties and bedridden. Regretfully, they both died within the year, but Father cared for both of them until the end.

Father was always sweet-spirited and gentle in his speech. He was not bombastic, nor was he argumentative. He was a Bible-teaching minister, quiet, and loving, and he referenced his Greek New Testament until he went to heaven. During this leave of absence, he decided to look beyond the Methodist Church and seek alternatives. He forthrightly told the bishop he was looking for another denomination that preached the Methodist doctrine of John Wesley. The bishop lamented this decision, saying, "Brother Duewel, I make your pastorates my example throughout the conference. You have revivals wherever you go. You promote missions wherever you go. You pay all your conference apportionments. The official board always has a few members who don't like your type of preaching, but if you ever come back, I will be the first one to again give you the right hand of fellowship." My father had been a faithful and humble pastor in the Methodist ministry for eighteen years.

---

6   Rev. Louis J. Duewel requested a leave of absence in 1928 from the Methodist Church, and within the year he was serving again as pastor with the Bible Holiness Church. See Douglas and Taylor, 312.

Father's Bible Holiness Church Ministry

Several small churches grew out of the ministry of Rev. Floyd Martin, an evangelist of the Fire Baptized Holiness Church.[7] Since most of these churches were without a pastor, they said of my father, "Why, here's a Methodist preacher without a pastorate, and he believes the same things we believe. Let's use him."

Before long, my father had a four-church circuit—preaching in one church each Sunday of the month. We began to live by faith, receiving only small offerings for Father's supplying these pulpits. My parents gladly adopted a simple, humble lifestyle, and they never once complained. For two years, our home had no electric lights and we relied strictly on a wood-burning stove for heat. To save money on matches, Mother rolled a scrap of paper and lit it at the kitchen fire, then lit the kerosene lamp.

Mother's Miraculous Healing

Because of her extended illness, Mother ventured out of the house only once or twice a year in the car, wrapped with a black cloth around her neck and head, so that she looked almost like a mummy. We tried to protect her from the light and any possible breeze.

Then, when she developed new symptoms, she was taken to a doctor in Troy, Missouri. After years of physical, emotional, and spiritual debilitation, she was diagnosed with cancer, which required immediate exploratory surgery that seemed imperative. But Mother was too weak to undergo such an operation, and my parents returned home and prayed.

Her healing took place as she sat in the living room of Uncle Herman's farmhouse. She couldn't turn her head to either side because of the excruciating pain it caused, nor could she move her eyes from side to side. Her nerves were so frayed that she longed for someone else to carry her prayer burden and to pray through for her healing. Seven family members and friends had gathered, and they prayed for

---

7   Initially known as the "Fire Baptized Holiness Church," it was eventually known simply as the "Bible Holiness Church" and is referenced as such throughout the remainder of this book.

several hours. As they were praying, she suddenly opened her eyes and looked straight ahead, where Herbert Lockhart was kneeling, with a real prayer burden on his face. Mother suddenly exclaimed, "Oh, praise God, someone is carrying my burden for me!"

She shut her eyes and continued praying silently. Then in her heart she heard the words, "Look, the windows of heaven have opened for you." She opened her eyes and saw angels' feet leaping for joy near the floor in front of her. "Oh," she said, "the windows of heaven have opened, and even the angels are rejoicing."

The next moment, she leaped to her feet, declaring over and over at the top of her voice, "I'm healed! I'm healed! I'm healed!" All the others arose, and Mother went from person to person exclaiming the same words in praise to God. For nearly a half hour, she could not stop shouting them, over and over. When my parents came back from the farm, she walked into the house, went straight to the piano, and began to play and sing "The Lily of the Valley," just as she had yearned to do for so long.

Her illness began on March 13, 1927, and she was healed on January 19, 1932. After five years of intense suffering, Mother had been gloriously and instantly healed. What a transformation it made to our home! She'd been frail as a young girl, in her youth, and in her early marriage. She was also a retiring, timid-natured person. But despite all that, she was active in every kind of ministry, and she was radiant as the sanctified wife of her husband, who was a pastor, Bible teacher, and finally college president. She lived another thirty-five years with better health, except for a more endurable colitis condition. Her physical turnaround and healing occurred through prayer, and I never forgot the power of prayer for healing.

Mother died at the age of seventy-five. Among those who knew her, she was considered one of the godliest people they had ever known.

Recommitment to Christ

Mother's instant healing had a profound spiritual effect on me. Our home was transformed to a place of joy and light. We could talk, sing, and use our chiming wall clock. People could visit us. Life was dramatically different.

Two months later, during my second year of high school, I was convicted by the Holy Spirit, and I rode my bicycle out into the country to a field. Behind a haystack, I knelt, recommitted my heart to Jesus, and trusted him for the forgiveness of my sins. I had precious times walking the bank of the creek that summer, praying to the Lord, loving him, and having blessed fellowship with him. At times I was so blessed that I hardly knew where I was walking. I was so enraptured by his wonderful, magnificently sweet and real presence that I can still recall the blessedness of those summer days on the farm.

From that time onward, I was systematic in reading the Bible from Genesis through Revelation, which I have continued throughout my life. I also renewed the habit of occasionally finding a quiet place alone to pray, whether out in a field, beside a stream, down a railway track, or later in life while on the mission field, on a mountainside, or in a borrowed room in the home of friends, uninterrupted for a few hours.

Humboldt, Nebraska (1933–1935)

After Mother's healing, we moved to Humboldt, Nebraska, where Father served as the pastor of a Bible Holiness Church. He soon discovered that this small spiritual movement was basically unorganized, and he gradually prepared a church manual for them, patterned after the Methodist manual. They nominated him as their president, a patriarch among them. Father also developed their missions program, serving as the founding chairman of their first board of missions.[8] (When Betty and I sailed to India, the board partially supported us during our first term there.)[9]

Eventually, the Bible Holiness people in Tabor, Iowa, requested that Father serve as president of their Bible school, editor of their denominational paper, *The Flaming Sword*, and founder of their

---

8   Douglas and Taylor, 314, "There were thirty-six mission halls."
9   Wesley and Betty Duewel sailed to India on December 31, 1940.

bookstore.[10] I was inspired with ideas for tracts on missions, and I encouraged the committee to insert them in their mailings. I also collected illustrations they could use to make *The Flaming Sword* more attractive. Father wrote the Sunday school lessons for their periodical, became founding president of their Christian day school in Independence, Kansas, and was always interested in youth ministry.[11]

Early Vision of India

I often went into my father's empty church building to pray. As I was kneeling between two rows of seats one afternoon, God opened a vision before my eyes. I seemed to be standing before lines of Indian village people going to their judgment on judgment day (Matt 25:31–46). As they neared me, they raised their arms and pointed their fingers at my face. Each one seemed to say to me, "If you had been more faithful, maybe I would have had a chance to be saved." I wept and wept and never forgot that vision.

I never wanted to attend the high school assemblies because I didn't want to be affected by the worldliness of some of the programs. So, I bravely asked Principal Weber for permission to sit in a classroom and study. Because he respected our family, he was cordial and allowed me to remain in the study hall.

Once during our church revival meetings, Mr. and Mrs. Weber attended an evening service. I played a tenor banjo for several years, plucking the melody, and that night the church pianist and I played a special number. It was a secular song, "When the Old Man Died," but Christian words had been substituted. Mr. Weber was so impressed that he immediately invited us to come to the high school and play for an assembly.

---

10   Douglas and Taylor, 318. According to this history, there were two previous denominational newsletters, one called *Two Fires* published in 1908 through 1938, and a second called *The Flaming Sword* in 1938 with two previous editors prior to Rev. Louis J. Duewel, who is credited as editor for a ten-year period from 1940 through 1950.

11   Ibid., 287. This history records that "for sixteen years Bro. and Sis. Duewel were engaged in Christian Education. He served as President of Missionary Bible College, Tabor, Iowa, 1942–1949. He then became founding President of Independence Bible College, serving until 1958."

The church pianist was Miss Viola Clough, who was a number of years older than me. We played music together during church services for two years. She had also been the pianist for several evangelistic tent meetings, where I played my banjo and helped as part of the evangelistic team. Viola's mother and my mother did house-to-house visitation together in Humboldt, praying with people. Since I had no sister of my own, I called Viola my big sister.

After the death of my mother in 1962, Father asked my permission to marry Viola, and she became my stepmother. Immediately after their marriage, they went to Granada, West Indies, where they served together with the Bible Holiness Church for one year, and Father served as field superintendent.[12]

COLLEGE YEARS (1935–1939)

Charles and Lettie Cowman had been associated with God's Bible School (GBS) before they went to Japan and formally established the Oriental Missionary Society.[13] One of Charles Cowman's close friends was Rev. Martin Wells Knapp, a fiery Methodist evangelist, who emphasized evangelism, revival, and publications. He founded the independent holiness paper *God's Revivalist* in 1888, and GBS in 1901 in Cincinnati, Ohio.

Since my parents were subscribers to *God's Revivalist*, I grew up regularly reading it and learning about GBS and the Cowmans. My first personal contact with the school came during my senior year of high school, when Rev. Fred Abel, a missionary to Japan, visited the church my father pastored in Humboldt. A young Japanese man, Sueki Urano, a new graduate from GBS, came with Brother Abel. We were visiting in our home when Brother Abel noticed Brother Sueki Urano wasn't there. We found him out on the sidewalk witnessing to

---

12   Ibid., 287. This history records that Louis J. Duewel married Viola (Clough) Duewel in November 1962 and "immediately went to Granada, West Indies, serving for one year as field superintendent."

13   For additional information regarding GBS, refer to Moser and Smith, 455; Smith, 174; and *God's Revivalist*—back issues.

people. I said to myself, "If students at GBS become that committed to the Lord, that's where I want to attend."

The Oriental Missionary Society

During the summertime, my family would go for a week, or ten days, to the interdenominational holiness camp meeting held in Bonnie, Illinois.[14] That's where we initially became acquainted with OMS. Because my parents contributed to the missionary society, they also received its monthly magazine, *The Missionary Standard*. Over time, I was persuaded that OMS was faithful to the gospel, and I was convinced of their threefold emphasis—evangelism, church planting, and the training of national leaders to carry on the ministry. I came to know OMS missionaries who were examples of great personal faith and holiness. I also met an international representative of OMS, Robert Chung, one of the Korean OMS national workers who were studying at a Methodist college.[15] He was a classmate of and had graduated from Asbury College with Eugene Erny. Robert Chung deeply influenced and blessed Eugene, who eventually became my coworker, close companion, spiritual guide, and mentor at OMS. In the 1932 issue of *The Missionary Standard*, Rev. Erny shared his testimony of how God called him to the Orient using Robert Chung to invite and challenge him.

Enrolling in God's Bible School

After high school, in September 1935, I enrolled in God's Bible School. Father had loaned some money to the school years before, and my tuition was covered by applying the money they owed him. I enrolled at age nineteen, and although I was eager to be there, I had one inner hesitation: would GBS really be as spiritual a place as I desired?

I was assigned a dormitory room (in the old building over the dining room, which had the engine room on the bottom floor), and as

---

14   Bonnie is in Jefferson County, southeast of Nashville just south of I-64 and on state route 57 (today I-57).

15   Asbury College, today known as Asbury University.

I stood on the grounds after supper that first evening, I heard "There Is Power in the Blood" sung by some of the students returning from their regular street meetings. Every Saturday and Sunday evening, a student group went out into the city for practical evangelism. A college-owned stake bed truck filled with students went all over the city. They sang as they went, chaperoned by Mrs. Julia Shelhamer, wife of a well-known Free Methodist evangelist, Rev. E. E. Shelhamer. I determined that, from then on, I would be a part of that group.[16] Our truck driver went up and down the main streets in the center of Cincinnati, past the theaters, taverns, nightclubs, and people walking on the streets, back and forth, as we shared our testimony by song and occasionally called out a memorized Scripture verse appropriate for the occasion.

We sang gospel songs, such as "Tell Mother I'll Be There," "Since Jesus Came into My Heart," "Love Lifted Me," "There's Not a Friend Like the

Wesley with parents, circa 1935, just before GBS

Lowly Jesus," "Tell It to Jesus," "Wonderful Words of Life," "Down at the Cross Where My Savior Died," and "Nothing But the Blood." The driver went slowly and planned to reach a corner while the traffic light was red so the people there would hear more of our message.

Someone would preach in the open air. Then we sang another song, and the evangelist began again, with a slightly different approach. We spent about three hours for the Lord each trip. What a special joy it was to be on the city evangelism teams!

---

16   Elmer Ellsworth Shelhamer (1869–1940) was an American evangelist with the Free Methodist Church who wrote many tracts, pamphlets, and a few books. One in particular caught Dr. Duewel's attention: *How to Get Healed and Keep Healed* (1929).

Testimony of Entire Sanctification

My first year at GBS, I took the Christian Worker's Course, preparing for work in India. I did not want to take college classes, because I thought a desire for a degree was worldly. I wanted my only ambitions to be knowing Christ and his Word, completing my studies as quickly as possible, and then going on out in missionary service.

During my first year, nearing the end of the first semester, I had been sincerely testifying to other Christians that the Lord had both saved and sanctified me, cleansing me by his Holy Spirit's infilling. Then as I entered my dorm room one noon, Stanley, one of my two roommates, asked, "Wesley, when you were in high school, what kind of grades did you get?" With some satisfaction, I told him about the good grades I received. But after about an hour, this thought came to me: "Was I proud when I answered Stanley's question about my grades?" I had merely told the truth, but was there pride in my heart when I told him? "No, no," I thought, "I could not have been proud because the Holy Spirit has cleansed me."

A little later, a student from down the hall came to me, "Wesley, can you help me with my New Testament Greek? I can't make heads or tails out of it." Our semester exams were scheduled for the next week, and I said to him (but only in my heart), "You lazy boy. You haven't been disciplining yourself to study during the semester. You love the Lord, but you're too lazy." But without complaining, I spent the rest of the afternoon trying to help him understand his Greek. When supper time came, he thanked me and left.

Wesley, circa 1935, just before GBS

I had wanted to spend that afternoon reviewing some of my own class work, but instead I had spent all that time with him. So, although I'm sure he never dreamed what I was thinking, I was still undergoing an inner conflict with him: "You are so ready to testify that you love the Lord, but you've been wasting your study time. I'm spending extra time to help the dean get his work done (more about this work later), and then when I finally get time to review my own work, you come and waste my time. What kind of spirituality is that?"

As I was about to hurry to supper, I wondered if what I was feeling toward this fellow student was anger. So, I decided to take time to examine my heart before the Lord. After my meal, when both roommates went to the college library to study, I took my Bible and went to my knees. As I prayed, I turned to 1 Corinthians 13. Never have I heard a message on love from any preacher that so searched my heart as the Holy Spirit did with that passage. As I came to verse 5, I read that love "doth not behave itself unseemly" (KJV). The NIV says, "It is not easily angered."

Suddenly, the Holy Spirit shined his searching light into my heart through that verse, and I began to recall incidents since I had become a Christian. How un-Christlike it was for me to be proud in any way or to be tried by the laziness or weakness of others when God had been so patient with me! Then I remembered times when I had been impatient with my godly mother. I could still see myself standing before her on one occasion, feeling impatient. I was absolutely ashamed and horrified as I thought of it. I had never seen my godly father impatient with anyone or heard him utter one impatient word. As the Holy Spirit searched me, my heart seemed even darker to me than I imagined an unsaved sinner's heart appeared in God's sight. But I was not discouraged. "Is that how my heart appears to God?" I asked myself. "Well, I know what the answer is!" I answered. That gave me hope and joy, because I knew the Doctrine of Entire Sanctification. If I didn't have it, I knew what the remedy was.

I began to carefully search my whole heart and life, and I prayed for God to cleanse me. I confessed my need as fully as I understood it. I consecrated my life anew to him as thoroughly and in as detailed a way as I knew how, point by point. I continued to search my heart carefully and prayerfully until I had fulfilled all of God's conditions, as I could understand them. The promise of 1 John 1:7 became my promise: "If we walk in the light, as he is in the light, we have fellowship with one another, and the blood of Jesus, his Son, purifies us from all sin."

After the library closed, my roommates returned. So, I took my Bible and went to the restroom, where a light remained on all night, and I could be alone with the Lord. Once, someone came in and saw me sitting there on the floor. "What are you doing?" he asked. I answered, "I'm getting sanctified."

I knew I had fulfilled God's conditions fully. I had walked in every bit of light I understood. I had been obedient in every way I knew how. I told God if he gave me more insight on anything, I would gladly walk in it. Therefore, I had every reason to believe his promise and by faith claim his purifying me from all sin. The word *sin* in 1 John 1:7 is in the singular, and I knew that meant the sin nature within me, not only my committed sins. I had long before taken them to the cross.

I felt no special emotion, and I felt no special witness of the Spirit at the moment. But I knew I had fulfilled God's conditions, and, by faith, I claimed for myself God's promise. At midnight, I went back to my room and dropped off to sleep.

My first morning class was Theology. I stepped up to the teacher and asked if I could say a word before the class began. He permitted me to do so, and I asked the students to forgive me. I said, "I have been testifying that I was both saved and sanctified, but last night God searched my heart and showed me it was not yet pure in his sight. By his grace and help, I opened my heart to him, confessed every need I could see, and consecrated myself point by point as fully as I know how. Then according to 1 John 1:7, by faith I claimed God's promise of cleansing."

As I sat down, my soul was instantly flooded with the presence of God. I had the witness of the Spirit in my heart that I was sanctified and cleansed by the infilling of the Holy Spirit. After class, one of the students hurried up to me. "Wesley, when you testified, God showed me my own need. Will you pray for me?" We arranged a place to meet that evening. Another student came to me. "Wesley, when you testified,

God showed me my need. Pray for me." I promised I would, and that night as I prayed with him, the Lord wonderfully sanctified him. As I quoted 1 John 1:7 to him over and over, I felt so clean "through and through," just like 1 Thessalonians 5:23 says. I had never in my life felt so clean in my soul.

God began to use me in a new way. Within twenty-four hours of my sanctification, he had given me my first soul. Then I began to notice the absence of any irritation in my heart. I had always thought that was a normal human reaction. Now I realized that irritation had been carnal. Now, at last, I was clean. Of course, we don't like some things, but they need not bring any irritation to our soul.

Praise God for his cleansing blood! Praise God for the Spirit's work of cleansing and empowering us through and through! I thanked God for his promise in 1 Thessalonians 5:23–24: "May God himself, the God of peace, sanctify you through and through. May your whole spirit, soul and body be kept blameless at the coming of our Lord Jesus Christ. The one who calls you is faithful, and he will do it."

That experience still holds, at the time of this writing, so many years later. What's more, I long to grow more and more in grace and Christ's likeness!

Second Year at GBS

I had known God's call to India since childhood, and I knew it as certainly as I knew I was saved. I just supposed I would be an evangelist, and, in my youthful zeal, I also thought I would go to the farthest place in India—someplace no one else had gone. That was still my mindset going into my second year at GBS.

Each student was required to work one hour a day. My first work assignment was helping in the kitchen. I washed the utensils; pots and pans; big thirty-gallon, two-inch thick electric cookers; big two-by-three-foot trays in which our macaroni was prepared; and other equipment used in preparing the evening meal. The big vats in which soup, stew, and similar dishes were prepared for 450 to 500 people were heated by gas, and I had to clean them as well. But all my life I have detested and been somewhat allergic to onions and garlic. On the nights when they prepared food with onions, I took a deep breath, held it, and then dove my head and arm into the vat and rapidly washed around the sides. I did that again and again until I had the whole work done. With such a deep aversion to onions, that was not a particularly pleasurable job!

But then, as I was sitting in the library, a man who was obviously one of the staff, sat down across the table from me. He turned out to be Professor James D. Robertson, academic dean of the college. He asked how well I had done in English in high school, and I replied briefly. After asking another question or two, he invited me to fulfill my required work hour a day as his personal secretary. When I agreed, he arranged this with the administration. From then on, I worked in his office, and he put a lot of confidence in my work.

At the time, Dean Robertson was working on his master's degree at the University of Cincinnati. Later, he worked on his doctorate. He used me for many different needs, and I got all kinds of educational experience. For example, I typed the revisions for each chapter of his master's thesis, then typed the final draft. He also assigned me more and more academic experiences when he was increasingly involved in working on his doctorate at the university. He even had me prepare and grade examination papers and basically put me in charge of student registration, classroom assignments, class schedules, and student social privileges. Little did the faculty know all my involvement, but God gave me all kinds of experiences I would later use in missionary service.

Studies and Academic Classes

When I registered students for their following year's college classes, I decided to register myself for some extra classes. I'd realized I was to pursue a degree after all, and the college had given me some credit for the Christian Worker's Course I had taken the year before. One class was English Literature, primarily designated for seniors. So, in my first year as a college student, and I was taking an advanced class.[17]

Eventually, Dean Robertson said to me, "Mr. Duewel, how many classes are you taking this semester?" I told him.

"Why," he said, "you can't take that many courses."

"But many of my courses are under you this year," I said. "Do you have any complaint about my work? Am I doing creditably well? Are you satisfied with my work?"

He was speechless for a moment. "Well," he finally said, "please don't tell anybody you're taking this many."

From then on, I had no problem, and I followed through with the extra classes.

Calling and Anointing to Teach

One day while I was in the dean's office, his phone rang just as the bell sounded for the five-minute intermission between classes. He said to me, "Sister Standley (wife of the president) has just asked to consult with me for a minute. Go and start the class with prayer, and by the time you're finished, I'll be there." It just so happened this was the senior English Literature class. I went to the classroom, and when the bell sounded to begin, I stepped to the teacher's table and started with prayer. When I was finished, the dean was not there, and I explained that he should arrive in a minute or two. But the moment I sat down in the teacher's chair, I felt as if an anointing of the Holy Spirit came upon me from heaven as truly or more so than I have ever had anointing in preaching the gospel. The dean never arrived for that class, so I taught the entire period.

As we went out the door at the close, one of the senior classmen, Bert Goodman, said to me, "Don't tell the dean, Wes, but we got along just as well as if he had been here." No one but me knew what that meant. God had not only called me to teach but had anointed me to teach, even affirming it through this senior's statement, thus sealing

---

17   Dr. Duewel was not enrolled in the college courses his first year at GBS, but enrolled in the Christian Worker's Course, a practical-oriented ministry course. He was, however, subsequently given college credit for this study.

his guidance to me. I had dual confirmation: the anointing from the Holy Spirit and my fellow classman's affirmation.

I eventually moved to a room next to the dean's office to be more readily available to him. I was working overtime by typing his thesis and grading his class papers, even his examinations, so I was almost always a bit sleepy. Students' lights went out at 10:00 p.m. and came on at 5:00 a.m., but I often worked till eleven or twelve, or even later, so I left my light switch on. That way, when the lights came on at 5:00 a.m., they would automatically awaken me. My nights were short, and my days were long.

One morning, at 4:00 a.m., I was instantly wide awake. That was strange, for I always slept till the lights came on. I began to feel the Lord's presence around me, and I was puzzled. Why was his presence so near and real? I prayed, "What is it, Lord? Why are You so sweetly near me? Why have You awakened me?"

An awareness came over me. I heard no voice, nor did I see a vision, but in my heart, I instantly knew God's call to teach in a Bible school in India. I had never even taught a Sunday school class or thought of teaching in a Bible school in India.

Two days later, I received a phone call from Dr. W. W. Holland, dean of the School of Theology. He said, "The doctor just told me I have pneumonia, so I can't teach my two Bible classes for several days. Would you please teach them?" I was a student in the one class, but not the other.

In another day or two, Miss Grace Burkholder, a teacher in the GBS high school, called me. "I'm taking graduate classes at the university, and I can't teach my Friday afternoon high school classes at GBS." Before I knew it, I was teaching four high school English classes each Friday.

Until that day filling in for Dean Robertson, I had never taught a class of any kind in my life. But now, just after the Lord called me to teach in India, I was temporarily teaching two classes a week in the college and four each week in the high school!

In my mind, I had never considered any form of missionary service other than evangelism. And again, in my zeal, I wanted to go to the farthest, most spiritually dark place unreached in India and do pioneer missionary work. But God guides us to the center of his will. By the end of that school year, I had taught ninety classes in the GBS high school and college. Who but God could work that out?! "As for God, his way is perfect" (2 Samuel 22:31).

University of Cincinnati Summer Classes

Enrolling in summer school at the University of Cincinnati, College of Education, in 1937, I took psychology and education classes, which could be transferred to my record at GBS. As a result, in 1938, at the conclusion of my third year in college, I received a Bachelor of Arts degree, *summa cum laude*.

I decided to take classes to also earn a Bachelor of Theology degree that God's Bible School, School of Theology, offered. Since I had been taking advanced classes to prepare myself for India, I fulfilled the entrance requirements.

Before the next school year began, President Standley asked whether I would be willing to teach two missionary courses. He offered me one hundred dollars, which I now realize was a ridiculously small amount for a year of part-time teaching. But that didn't bother me. I said, "Well, I will do it under the condition that you will give me staff social privileges—not a student's." (Little did I realize how this arrangement would eventually become so beneficial!) He agreed, so during my last year, while I took classes halftime in the School of Theology to complete my Bachelor of Theology requirements, I also taught two missions courses: History of Missions and Missionary Methods and Problems.

Introduction to Betty Raisch

Elizabeth Dolly Raisch had a real desire to live for the Lord, and when she was eighteen years old and enrolled at GBS, she experienced personal salvation by placing her faith in Jesus Christ. Betty, as she became known, wrote that her salvation experience was a wonderful milestone in her life. She knew without a shadow of a doubt that she had been reconciled with her Father in heaven and had received the gift of eternal life. Soon after that, he showed her the importance of living a life fitting for a child of God, with a clean heart through the indwelling of the Holy Spirit. She demonstrated that holy life to people all around her and around the world for the rest of her days.

After studying at GBS for three years, she and a girlfriend felt led to evangelistic ministries and took time out of school to work mainly in New York State. Practical ministries for the next two years included hospital visitation and helping in the homes of terminally ill patients. Then, she returned to GBS to finish her studies.

During my first two years at GBS, I kept my eyes open but never felt God leading me to date or even contact anyone. When Betty reenrolled at GBS, I was beginning my third year of college. She caught my eye, and since I was working for the dean and had access to all the students' records, I looked up her grades and discovered she had been away from GBS for two years as part of an evangelistic team. She was a part of a girls' trio. The group consisted of Miss Charlotte Beagle (Christian and Missionary Alliance), the main evangelist; Miss Ruth Hamilton, a disabled young woman who got around with the aid of crutches; and Betty. I think her holy lifestyle and practical outreach was part of what attracted me to her.

Betty was not enrolled during my first two years, so by the time I had established my friendship with her, I was one academic year ahead of her at GBS.

Social Relationships

GBS had strict rules, particularly about social relations between young men and women. The dean was the head of the committee that dealt with discipline and social privileges, but he was often busy and didn't want to be bothered with that responsibility. Now with staff status, I was often put in charge of social privileges. One night a month, students could have social privileges, if they signed up with the dean, including taking a walk around the block, etc., off campus as part of a date.

Betty was an attractive, intelligent, and spiritual girl, and I admired her, but I never felt free to contact her. Somehow or other, I was always providentially blocked. I became somewhat discouraged and disgusted with myself. I thought, "I can't trust my own decisions or emotions. I could easily make a mistake."

Then, I told the Lord one morning, "I'm through. I will never try to date a girl. If You want me to establish a friendship with and eventually marry someone, then You cause her to approach me." It was a foolish thing to do, but I threw myself across the bed in prayer as I wrestled it out with the Lord. That day, I got a letter from my mother. She wrote, "I have been praying much about God's plan for your life and for a companion for you as you go to India, and I feel you are on the verge of establishing a very wonderful friendship."

I thought to myself, "How strange. How odd. I have just given up on dating unless a girl herself approaches me, and here I get a letter like this from my mother."

That night was when students with permission could take walks with dates. I had observed Betty on different occasions, and because I was president of the Literature Society, I had appointed her to a committee so I could observe more carefully how she reacted with other people and so on. I knew she had excellent grades, and I could tell she was a spiritual girl, but as I said earlier, I was afraid to trust my emotions or judgment.

That afternoon, a fellow student, Fred Fike, came to me and said, "Did you know Betty Raisch would like to have a date with you tonight?"

I replied, "Betty Raisch!" I didn't want to let on that I had been especially observing and wondering about her. But I thought, "That's just what I told the Lord this morning—that the girl would have to take the initiative."

In the meantime, Fred's girlfriend, Grace Murrell, went to Betty and said, "Did you know Wesley Duewel would like to have a date with you tonight?" Betty was thrilled because she had also prayed about and wondered about me. Our friends were the ones who finally got us together!

Toward evening, I went to the dean and said, "You'll have to take charge of permissions to the couples tonight."

"Why? What's wrong with you?"

"Well, it just could be that I would like to date someone myself." "And who would that be?" he asked. I didn't like to tell him, but finally I did.

"Brother Duewel," he solemnly said, "are you sure that is God's will?"

I was shocked that he spoke so directly to me, but I answered, "I'm not absolutely sure, but I am praying about it." Not until later did I learn he had his own eyes on Betty and was thinking of eventually asking her for a date!

That evening, Betty and I took that walk and got some ice cream at a nearby pharmacy. Then, we went to the high school principal's office, for which I had a key. We took along our Bibles and had a time of reading and prayer together. I don't remember who it was, but one of us said, "I'll read you the verse God specially gave me for my life." To our amazement, we discovered that both of us had the same life verse —Isaiah 54:2, plus the first part of verse 3: "Enlarge the place of your tent, stretch your tent curtains wide, do not hold back; lengthen your cords, strengthen your stakes. For you will spread out to the right and to the left."

Each month afterward, we had a date.

Special Arrangements

Betty and I had no problem seeing each other between dates because of a secret method. Only faculty members were authorized to enter the reference room of the GBS library from the back door into the hall. Behind the librarian's desk was a small room with reference books—one shelf for each faculty member. Very naturally, I used the faculty door because I was teaching two missions courses. I also had a shelf for reference books for my classes.

Betty worked as a librarian in the reference room and agreed to use a secret signal between us. When I entered the library wishing to talk with her, I didn't have to look at her. I just touched my nose with my hand while examining my books, and she knew I had something to tell her. She would then meet me in the hall or in the storage room, where additional library books were kept. So, we had no problem seeing each other.

I didn't think our meetings had been discovered, but at the end of the school year, the junior class had a fun evening roasting the senior class. They listed a number of things as being willed from one of the seniors to one of the juniors. Among them was Wesley Duewel's ability to get Betty Raisch out into the library hallway! We laughed. Though they weren't sure what our secret system was, they knew we had one worked out.[18]

Betty as a Student

Dean Robertson had suggested to Betty that she take mission courses since she planned to be a missionary. But the question on both of our minds was, should she take the missions classes I taught? We started praying about it. Then, when the dean asked Betty if she was going to enroll in my classes and she said she didn't know, he told her not to hesitate, even though by that time, it was common knowledge we were planning to be married. So, like my father who once taught my mother, I had the privilege of having my future fiancée and wife as one of my students for my History of Missions and Missionary Methods and Problems classes.

Missionary Call

During the winter revival meetings at GBS that last year, the evangelist gave a wonderful message, and at the invitation, many students went forward to pray. As I moved to pray with some of the seekers, I felt checked by the Spirit and impressed to instead go to my dorm room. I thought, *God must want me to carry some prayer burden tomorrow*

---

18   Dr. Duewel originally omitted this information, perhaps hesitant to reveal this aspect of his social life.

night. Perhaps I will be praying with people into the night hours, or maybe all night long, and that's why he wants me to rest now.

I went to my room and dressed for bed. As I crawled under the covers, I felt the Lord's presence so near. He began to speak to me with no audible voice, and I felt led to apply for acceptance as a missionary of the Bible Holiness Church. But I could not understand this since they had no work in India. Nor would they likely be able to fund a work of the size to which I felt called, including the establishment of a Bible school. I noted six different points the Lord seemed to suggest to me as I lay there praying. I got up and wrote them down, and then I went back to bed and was instantly asleep.

I also felt impressed to write a letter to my father, whom the Bible Holiness Church had just chosen to be the founding chairman of the foreign missions board they had decided to form. So, the next morning, when I had a free period between classes, I wrote to him and included those six points. At noon I mailed the letter.

That afternoon, I received a letter from Father. He said he and Mother both felt it was time for me to apply to the Bible Holiness board of missions to go as a missionary. They added that they realized I was called to teach in a Bible school and that the Bible Holiness Church would be highly unlikely to establish that kind of work in India, but somehow, they still felt I should apply.

To my amazement, in Father's letter to me, I found the same six points I had included in my letter to him! Also in the envelope was a letter from India, addressed to me. The author had asked Father to forward it. Rev. F. B. Whisler wrote that he understood I was called to be a Bible teacher and that inasmuch as it was reported that another missionary organization was about to establish a Bible school in India, maybe I would want to contact them.

I was amazed that at that very time and from the opposite side of the world would come a seal upon what God had said to me. I sent for that organization's missions application, but then I immediately felt checked so strongly that I could not return the application. So, I never followed through with a further letter to them. I now know they did not plan to establish a school in India. But at the time, I continued to pray daily about those six points.

Fulfilling My Call

Twice during my years at GBS, I met representatives of OMS, of whom I inquired if OMS would ever enter India. In both cases, they cordially laughed and said, "Why, of course not. OMS has such a big job in China that it could never consider entering another field." Both replies suggested that if they were in my place, they would ask God for another field, and then join OMS. I protested, "But I know I'm called to India. What can I do?" One of them replied, "If I were you, I would not dictate to God." I felt a bit crushed because I knew that, instead, God was dictating to me. So, I just left the matter in God's hands and kept on praying.

Prayer for India

Night after night for about two years, I waited until the library closed at 9:30 p.m. Then, when I was sure it was empty of people, I slipped inside but did not turn on the lights. Instead, I switched on the low dim light of a world globe for a private prayer time. I knelt beside the globe and placed my hand on the image of India. I prayed for God's will concerning my ministry there, often for an hour or two, always concerning the same six prayer requests. Lord, I prayed:

1. Call some spiritual mission agency to begin work in India with the same doctrine, threefold ministry priority, passion, and burden as OMS.

2. Speak to some leader of that mission and put the burden of India on his heart.

3. Cause some donor to give a large financial donation, designated for India, which will then serve as Your seal that You do want that mission to enter India.

Wesley at World Globe, Missionary Standard Back Cover 1969

4. Call other members for the first team of missionaries to go out under that agency to India so I will not have to go alone.

5. Prepare national coworkers, so that when the missionaries of that agency reach India and still need to learn the language, these coworkers will be available, without taking them away from another agency and hindering their work.

6. Guide that agency where to begin its ministry in India.[19]

For those two years, I prayed these requests as I knelt alone beside the lighted globe. I didn't worry because I knew God was in control. I also went to the Cincinnati Public Library and found an old copy of the National Council of Churches of India directory. It listed all the societies and denominations working in India and their missionaries, by district, giving the address where each was located, and told about the work of each group. From that I could tell no mission agency doctrinally compatible with my theological convictions was at work in India. I found none were nondenominational in character, Wesleyan in doctrine, and emphasizing the threefold priority of OMS. But again, I was not worried, for I felt sure of God's guidance and trusted him to send the agency of his choice. I knew he would work out his own purposes.

Considering OMS

One day in my last year at GBS, I was in my fourth-floor dormitory room during a free period between classes. I heard a knock at my door, and when I opened it, to my amazement, there stood one of the godly, senior faculty members, Rev. E. G. Marsh. He was a teacher in the Christian Worker's Course and a brother-in-law to Rev. Paul E. Haines, an OMS trustee and OMS treasurer. He seemed awkward, fumbling a handful of papers, as he asked, "Brother Duewel, would you please put these examination papers in Dr. Robertson's office?"

He knew I was no longer assigned to help Dean Robertson, so I thought that was an odd request. I immediately replied I would be

---

19 Dr. Duewel stated, "Somehow I sensed that whatever mission agency began its ministry in India would become my agency."

glad to do so, but I wondered why this elderly teacher had climbed three flights of stairs to ask me to take papers back downstairs to the dean's open office.

For another moment, Rev. Marsh stood awkwardly outside the door and didn't seem to know what to do next. I'd never had a faculty member visit my room, but I asked, "Would you like to come in and sit down?"

He replied, "Oh, I guess I will for just a few minutes." He came in and sat down on a chair, then suddenly said, "You're called to India, aren't you, Wesley?"

I immediately affirmed that I was. "Yes, the Lord called me to India when I was a child."

He continued, "Did you know the Oriental Missionary Society may open up work in India?"

I almost jumped from my chair and exclaimed, "OMS! No, I didn't know that!" I was almost overwhelmed.

Then Brother Marsh said, "Well, I guess I better be going."

I bade him goodbye, and as he left the room, I knew in my heart that God had sent him to my door to give me this news. But then I thought, "Just because OMS may go to India, does that mean God wants me to apply to them?" I fell on my knees and began to pray, but I added, "Oh, Lord, don't let me make a mistake. Don't let me apply to OMS if You don't want me to go under that organization."

I continued praying until it was absolutely clear in my heart that I was to apply to OMS. And then I wrote a long letter to their office in Los Angeles, telling of God's call on my life to India, my agreement with their doctrine, and my two years of praying those six requests every night. Were they interested in me? I felt led to send my letter airmail, and I was told they had not received a letter like mine for a long time.

I received an immediate response, also by airmail. One OMS missionary in the USA on furlough felt a burden for India. His name was Rev. Eugene A. Erny. He would be passing through Cincinnati that very week, and they had immediately sent word asking him to stop by the Bible school and speak to me.

When Rev. Erny and his wife, Esther, arrived at GBS with their two young sons, I carried their toddler, Edward, as I escorted them to the guest room at the school. Their older boy, Bob, who was perhaps four or five years old, walked beside me. That night Rev. Erny met with Betty and me for that important meeting. I testified to my call to India, about my full agreement with OMS doctrine and practice, and how I had been praying for India.

Rev. Erny said, "OMS never enters a new field unless it's the unanimous decision of its board of directors, and as far as I know, I am the only missionary in OMS who feels led that we should open work in India." He explained the whole situation to us, then said, "You pray, and I will pray, and if this is of God, He will open the door. If He does not, I can guarantee that OMS will never enter India." We prayed together, and the Ernys left campus the next day.

GBS Graduation, Our Wedding, and a Transition Period

Graduation day was a special joy for Betty and me. She was the valedictorian of the Bachelor of Arts degree students, and I was the valedictorian of the Bachelor of Theology degree students. Betty led the column of College of Liberal Arts students, and I led the School of Theology students. The Lord had helped me complete both my Bachelor of Arts (1938) and Bachelor of Theology (1939) degrees in four years by carrying heavy class loads and doing summer school-work at the University of Cincinnati.

When Betty and I graduated from GBS, my parents drove from their pastorate in Troy, Missouri, to Cincinnati, and then I went back to Missouri with them. We then returned to Cincinnati for our wedding on June 29, 1939.

The wedding reception was held at the Raisch home on their farm, just a few miles from the ceremony location. We spent our wedding night in a hotel, and the next day we drove back to Missouri with my parents. Somehow, I'd developed a quinsy sore throat the night of the wedding, so after we arrived in Troy, I spent the next day or two in bed. We had to cancel our honeymoon plans—staying in a cabin in a Missouri state park.

Betty and I lived in my parents' guest room for several weeks. While there in Troy, we began to go out in deputation meetings, sharing the speaking responsibilities. A number of youth were in Troy, and we formed them into a Soul-Winners' League. Each member was required to daily read God's Word and list at least five unsaved people for whose salvation they prayed each day. In August, we went to the Bible Holiness Church Central Camp Meeting in Independence, Kansas. There, Betty and I were active in the young people's meetings before the evening services in the main auditorium.

Bible Holiness Church Approval

The Bible Holiness Church did not practice baptism or Holy Communion, and in this respect, it was much like the Quakers. I was aware that abstaining from baptism and Holy Communion was quite an issue among the membership. Conversely, it was widely known that I *did* believe in baptism and Holy Communion. Another evangelist friend, Rev. Jackson Crane, heard about my convictions and drove many miles to my parents' home in Troy to inquire into this matter. He asked me point-blank whether it was true that I believed it was scriptural to practice baptism and Holy Communion. I admitted that I believed it was.

After the camp meeting, the Bible Holiness Church held their annual business meeting on Monday. I was asked to be the secretary, and I sat on the platform at a small table, taking the notes in shorthand, and recording the actions. The issue of baptism and Holy Communion came to the floor when Rev. Elliott Hodge, an evangelist of the church, rose to his feet and said, "Are we going to send out missionaries who don't believe our doctrine?" Many of these people loved me, and my parents were loved and accepted. Father's reputation was sterling, and he was looked upon as a patriarch in the Bible Holiness Church with all that he had contributed to the denomination. But I knew rumors that I believed in water baptism and Holy Communion had circulated.

Several hours of discussion about the whole issue of the kind of candidates a denomination should send forth took place. Everyone knew this was about me, although no one mentioned my name. Finally, I rose to my feet and said I would like to make a statement. I spoke with tears and requested that the people, whatever they did, not turn their backs on their missionary vision. "The Lord told me to apply to the Bible Holiness Church," I said, "but he has never assured me that I am to go out to the mission field under the Bible Holiness Church." I emphasized that when I applied to the mission board, I put in writing that I could not understand why I was led to apply, because I knew they would never be able to establish the kind of work in India to which I was called, and yet I felt sure God had called me.

I also said maybe God had just used my application to help place missions on the heart of the church, and it would be tragic for them, having been in existence for more than forty years, to come to the verge of a missionary outreach and then turn back. I begged them to find some candidates called of God in whom they could freely have confidence and support. I told them to forget Betty and me, and that if we were really called of God, he would have a way to get us to the mission field. I then added that I had no proof whatever, but there was a slight possibility OMS might open up work in India, and, if so, we might be accepted and serve under that agency.

When I sat down, Rev. Hodge, the leader of the opposition, jumped to his feet, inspired by the Spirit, and moved that the board of missions contact OMS and ask if the Bible Holiness Church could support us under OMS in India. I got back on my feet and begged them to realize there was no evidence at that time that OMS would enter India, but someone else jumped to his feet and seconded the motion.

People began to shout God's praises across the conference, and the motion was unanimously passed, amid much weeping and praising the Lord. Some of our friends threw their arms around me and said they had made up their mind. Whatever the church decided, they would stand beside us. Some actually lifted me up off the floor, almost as if I were some kind of military or athletic hero.

OMS Votes to Enter India

As we returned from camp meeting and arrived at my parents' home, we found a stack of mail on my father's table on the back porch. Among the mail was a cablegram from Seoul, Korea. I opened it immediately. It was from Rev. Erny and said, "OMS votes unanimously to open work in India. If interested, apply at once." Still interested? We had been praying for two years!

Betty and I immediately applied as the first applicants for India. Part of the call God gave me was to have the same threefold priority as OMS, and he had used our prayers to help lead OMS into India. Several months later, while pastoring a small church in Barnsdall, Oklahoma, we received word of our formal acceptance as OMS missionary candidates. As much as possible, we continued serving in camps and churches, traveling out of my parents' home in Troy, until the end of the year.

BARNSDALL, OKLAHOMA (1939–1940)

We left Troy to pastor the Bible Holiness Church in Barnsdall for about a year, and our deepest desire and goal was to do our utmost for the salvation of souls. We knew the hope we received from Jesus was not just for us but for all those we came to know. No sacrifice was too great for Christ. We spent long hours in prayer throughout that summer, seeking God's face and seal as guidance.

No salary was promised, but we were given whatever came in the church offerings. We lived economically and managed to survive. Gasoline for cars was much cheaper in those days. I remember once filling my tank with gasoline at eleven cents a gallon!

This was a small congregation, with an average attendance

Newlyweds, circa 1939, Barnsdall, OK

of thirty to thirty-five people when we arrived, all new to us. How could we get the church to grow? I took a phone book and began to pray for the people of Barnsdall, name by name. By December, four had been saved, one had been sanctified, and attendance had increased to sixty-five, with forty-five faithful souls attending the mid-week service.

World War II—Battleship *Graf Spee*

I was tremendously burdened about World War II. My heart cried out to God as Hitler overran one small European country after another. All war is a call to prayer.

I was specially burdened by the accounts of the German pocket battleship *Graf Spee*. It had a removable facade that covered and disguised its torpedo tubes. It would sail in the merchant fleet lanes, and then suddenly remove the facade and torpedo one or two merchant ships, with all lives lost. Then it would steam away, put up the facade, and disappear, perhaps for some weeks before it would again attack somewhere and sink more merchant ships. I felt this was so wrong and evil. For a battleship to attack another battleship—that was war. But for a battleship to attack a peaceful merchant or even a passenger ship—that grieved me deeply. So, I prayed against the *Graf Spee* day after day, for months.

One night while in Barnsdall, I had just gone to bed when the Lord acutely burdened me. I did not pray out loud, for I did not want to awaken Betty. But my soul cried out to God, over and over, "Lord, stop the *Graf Spee*. Stop it. Stop it." The Lord lifted the prayer burden from my heart, and I went to sleep. It was December 12, 1939.

The next morning, the radio news announced that the *Graf Spee* had entered the harbor of Montevideo, Uruguay. Like Switzerland, Uruguay was neutral during the war. After some hours, the German captain felt he must leave. He took his ship just outside the harbor, where he commanded all the crew to don life jackets, get into the lifeboats, and pull away from the ship. They had dynamite stored throughout the ship, and he blew it up just outside the harbor, choosing to go down with the ship.[20]

Many people prayed for God to deliver innocent travelers from such unnecessary loss of life. I was sure God answered those prayers, and later in life, he introduced me to living evidence of an answer.

Candidate Interview

OMS wrote that Rev. Edwin L. and Mrs. Hazel Kilbourne were going to stop by Barnsdall to interview us, and they gave us the date. Since we were living in a tiny house with no room for guests, I arranged for someone in our congregation to host the Kilbournes instead. I also planned an evening service, and to make as good an impression as possible, I urged our entire congregation to be present.

When their car pulled up in front of our home the evening the Kilbournes were to arrive, to my amazement, the back door opened and out jumped "Uncle Jimmy" Williams. We first met the Williamses when they lived next door to GBS. We'd had such cordial and warm fellowship at GBS, but I had forgotten Uncle Jimmy was Hazel's father.

He almost fell all over me, hugging me, then said, "I've been telling Bud and Hazel all about you." We planned to be on good behavior and hoped to make a good impression on the Kilbournes, but they had already been told all about us! They were so friendly that we nearly forgot Rev. Kilbourne, "Uncle Bud," was the vice president of OMS.[21]

From then on, I had no worry as to whether we would be acceptable. I knew and felt the loving heart of the Kilbournes, and I knew Uncle Jimmy had paved the way for us. Also, it was interesting (and hadn't hurt any) that Betty's sister, who had been a student at GBS, had been assigned to help Uncle Jimmy's late wife with housework during her final illness.

---

20 This story is told in *Touch the World through Prayer* by Wesley L. Duewel, 81.

21 Rev. E. L. Kilbourne, or Edwin, was known within OMS as "Uncle Bud," and Mrs. Kilbourne was known as "Aunt Hazel."

We had a great time with them in our tiny home, and we had a good service that evening. I asked Uncle Jimmy to play a solo on his harmonica.

OMS Orientation

The Kilbournes were the OMS missionary representatives at the GBS camp meeting, and there, they gave us general orientation. One day a dear sister who had founded her own independent missionary society was standing by her table with its literature and a chart, sharing how funds were needed for her orphanage. As she pleaded for the needs of her work, Brother Kilbourne took me to one side and said, "You see that? That is what we don't do." He spoke the word *don't* with a verbal emphasis and a downward thrust of his finger, then said, "We had to get rid of a brother who was our treasurer because he hinted and talked about money too much. He still loves us, though, and he often mows our lawn in Los Angeles."

I understood that Betty and I were to trust God for our support needs, but not always be emphasizing our need of money. I learned that our main emphasis was to be the need of missions and prayer. We were to emphasize evangelism, soul-winning, spiritual harvest, and revival.

Leaving for India: Farewell, Troy

It was time to leave for India, and a large crowd attended our farewell service in my father's church in Troy, Missouri. At the close, Betty and I stood with my parents as people lined up to shake hands, say goodbye, and assure us of their love and prayers. Some asked my mother why she was smiling and not in tears. "Oh, God has called Wesley, and he will take care of him," she joyfully responded.

The wife of my friend Wesley Schwartz handed me a piece of paper and said, "When you get to California, I hope you'll have time to visit my uncle. This is his address." I thanked her, putting the paper in my pocket.

We spent an hour or two at my parents' home, then packed up our luggage and drove to the small train station at Moscow Mills. At

1:49 a.m., the train arrived, and we were on the way to India! Only then did Betty and I discover that our life verse, Isaiah 54:2–3, had also been the life verse God gave Charles Cowman, founder of OMS. Later on, when I reached India, I discovered it had also been William Carey's life verse. He was the famous missionary to India who was often called the father and founder of modern missions. Based on this verse, he composed his famous motto, "Expect great things from God; attempt great things for God."

Letter to Mother

Neither of my parents ever underwent an operation. Father hardly had a sick day in his life, apart from contracting the Spanish flu during the pandemic in 1918, colds, and a bout with kidney stones. But as Mother's health deteriorated, we were uncertain of her longevity. Others were trained and prepared to take over the work in Granada, West Indies, and Father returned to the pastorate.

With Mother's health uncertain and Betty's and my pending departure to India looming in the near future, I wrote a letter to my mother, expressing my deep sense of indebtedness to her for all she poured into my life. Later, I was so glad I did.

2
The India Years

When we arrived in Los Angeles, we were met by Mrs. Cowman's secretary, Frances Black. She told us, "We're going to have you stay with a German couple who gave a large sum of money to help launch OMS in India." We were taken to Mr. and Mrs. Bruenimeyer's home, and to my total and utter surprise, theirs was the address Mrs. Wesley Schwartz had given me at the Troy farewell!

THE BRUENIMEYERS' HOME

The Bruenimeyers took us to the OMS headquarters church for the farewell service and prayer rally for the India team of seven. Then we enjoyed Sunday dinner at their home. Brother Bruenimeyer was full of love for the Lord and missions. When I mentioned my grandfather's name, he suddenly asked, "Heinrich Duewel was your grandfather? Why, he was my best friend when I was a young man in Missouri." He laughed and laughed with joy. Then he asked, "Who was your grandfather on your mother's side of the family?"

"My mother's father was Anton Luelf."[1]

He repeated the name several times, and then he laughed again. "He was my guardian when I was an orphan boy. He walked with me to the train when I left for California!" Again, he laughed and laughed, and his daughter said, "I haven't seen Dad so happy for a long time. You've reminded him of happy childhood memories."

---

1   Some notes indicate Dr. Duewel's maternal grandfather's name was "August" Luelf.

NBC STUDIOS, HOLLYWOOD

Brother Bruenimeyer said, "I have to show you my old farm!" After lunch, his son-in-law drove us to Hollywood. "There is where the well was, where the barn stood, and where our house stood," he explained as he pointed. He had sold his farm, which was part of the city of Hollywood, to the National Broadcasting Company (NBC) for their studios and production buildings. He sent a large portion of the proceeds to OMS to help launch our work in India. I realized that was God's answer to one of my six nightly prayer requests lifted before the Lord for at least two years as a college student!

How amazingly God answers prayer! What an amazing example of divine orchestration! The Lord used Mr. Bruenimeyer, a friend of both my grandfathers, to supply a large gift to begin OMS work in India! Together in heaven, we three will have to celebrate how God answered prayer. *What a joy that will be!*

I don't know what Mr. Bruenimeyer harvested before he sold his farm, but it facilitated a miraculous spiritual harvest in India. The Evangelical Church of India (ECI) currently has three Bible seminaries and ten Bible schools, each in a different language area, and more than ten thousand national churches with more than a million people in attendance on

First seven missionaries with Mrs. Cowman, in L.A.

Sunday mornings![2] What a harvest from his little farm! Praise the Lord! You never know the eternal results when you obey God! All six of the requests I had prayed were answered, and God kept answering prayer after we got to India. *Never give up! God answers prayer!*[3]

---

2   According to the official newsletter of the ECI called *The Church Planter*, December 2019, a total of 22,740 congregations were then affiliated with the denomination.

3   See page 50 for the first mention of these six prayer requests.

MRS. COWMAN'S HOME, HOBART BOULEVARD

The evening before we sailed from Los Angeles—Monday, December 30, 1940—after speaking to a youth group, our seven-member team hurried to the Hobart Boulevard home of Brother and Sister Cowman, the founders of OMS. Charles had been in heaven for many years, and Lettie was serving as OMS president.

A few OMS missionaries, who had evacuated from Korea, were there as well as several on furlough from China and some headquarters staff. We gathered

Sailing to India

around Mrs. Cowman's piano as she played and sang "Lead on, O King Eternal, the day of march has come," "The Son of God Goes Forth to war, a kingly crown to gain," and "At the Battle's Front, I've enlisted for life in the army of the Lord."

Mrs. Cowman explained how OMS was a faith-based mission from the beginning. She opened her heart and told of miracle after miracle and how marvelously God had led OMS over the years, supplying all their needs. She told how hundreds and hundreds of souls had been saved and sanctified. "God has told me he wants to do more in India than he has done thus far in the other OMS fields," she said.

Then she told us how God was opening the way for us. She urged us to lay a deep spiritual foundation in India, have much of the Holy Spirit, be separate from the world, and be an example to missionaries of other groups in India. She added, "You will be a marked people, and others will be watching you, but God will give you grace!"

We could have listened to her for hours. We each testified, and then we sang again. OMS trustee Dr. Roy Adams, an anointed Bible teacher, admonished us to keep our spiritual life strong, take everything to the Lord in prayer, and take care of our physical bodies. It was nearly midnight when we left, "feeling nearer to God and stronger in the Lord than when we came."

SAILING ON SS PRESIDENT TAYLOR

December 31 was busy with departure details. Then Sister Cowman, other OMS staff, and Christian friends stood on the dock, while seven new missionaries stood at the ship railing. We sang "God Be with You till We Meet Again" and "Jesus Never Fails." As was the custom in those days, rolls of colored streamers were tossed from the ship to the shore. As we held one end, Mrs. Cowman and the others on the dock held the other. Then as the tugboats pushed us to deeper water, the rolls of paper unrolled, tightened, and eventually broke, severing us physically, but not spiritually.

We were just getting into our cabins when we heard a shout, "Where are the missionaries?" We went back on deck and saw that two friends from our home denomination had rented a little motorboat and followed the ship out of the harbor. We shouted farewells, then they tossed us several oranges, and we were on our way.

Overnight, we sailed to San Francisco, where we spent several days doing some final shopping. The *SS President Taylor* had a crew of 176 and about a hundred passengers, including twenty-five missionaries from various groups. Our party of seven included: Rev. J. T. and Mrs. Ruth Seamands;[4] Miss Mary Ella Taylor, a teacher God had called to India when she was twelve; and Rev. Roy and Mrs. Dewdrop Davis.[5] Betty and I completed the team. It was the stormy season of the year, so the sea was rough; the route to Hawaii the roughest part. A young Baptist couple, recently married, were dreadfully seasick and never changed their clothes or left their cabin till they reached Hawaii!

---

4   J. T. (John Thomas) grew up in India, where his parents, Rev. Dr. Earl Arnett (aka E. A. or more affectionately, "Thatha," meaning "beloved and honored grandfather") and Mrs. Yvonne Seamands were veteran Methodist missionaries. "Thatha" had been engaged in village evangelism for years. Ruth Seamands would later write *Missionary Mama, House by the Bo Tree*, and others.

5   Roy Davis and Dr. Duewel were roommates for two years at God's Bible College. Betty and Dewdrop Davis had been close friends, and Betty was praying with Dewdrop when God called Dewdrop to India.

Singapore

When we reached Singapore on February 17, we sensed we were nearing the mission field. I walked around to see the life of the people. Betty thought the rickshaw pullers worked like beasts. Here we had our first contact with Hinduism. Visiting a Hindu temple, one of our ladies said, "Oh, it's so dark here"—not physically, but spiritually. The Hindus observed the Festival of Thaipusam while we were there. Thousands of Hindus were fulfilling vows made during the year, presenting offerings in the temple.

Many of them were flagellating themselves, torturing their almost-naked bodies. Some had studded their chest, cheeks, and other body parts with what looked like double-ended fishhooks—one end hooked to half a lemon or lime and the other end hooked into their flesh. Some had several inches-long spikes driven through one cheek, through the mouth, and out the other cheek, with half limes on each end of the spike. Others had a similar spike holding their tongue tip out of their mouth. Still others carried a heavy metal contraption like an umbrella frame with lengthy iron staves fastened to a central and heavy top of the device, then branching out. The ends were implanted into the skin on their chest and back—fifteen to twenty staves on one person. The weight of the device held it close to their body.

The eyes of some had a strong, glazed stare. Obviously, they were enduring pain. To torture their bodies like that, some were likely demon-possessed, others demon-motivated. Some men as well as some women—and some children—were fulfilling vows they had given to their god or goddess when they wanted help from them. The entire journey to the destination temple at the end of their ordeal covered several miles.

Some walked and some dragged themselves along. Others ran as they neared the temple. Some collapsed along the way—physically and emotionally exhausted by observers, excitement, pain, and effort to fulfill their vows. To them it was a duty of religious desperation, a masochistic attempt of deprivation to satisfy their gods. We will never forget it. Later in our time in India, we saw many other processions of

Hindus or Muslims, and numerous forms of self-torture and self-mutilation, especially on the "sacred" days of their demonic religion.

Penang

In Penang, Malaysia, the temples reminded me of what the apostle Paul said when in Athens: "As I walked around and looked carefully at your objects of worship, I even found an altar with this inscription: TO AN UNKNOWN GOD" (Acts 17:23). Paul used this illustration to motivate the prayer burden he carried for the lost and to illustrate his preaching. God can use such scenes to break your heart and transform your prayer life. Keep the memory before you and maintain regular prayer habits. Blessed are those who do not let their prayer burden slip away and be forgotten.

FIRST TERM (1941–1948)

We arrived in Bombay (now Mumbai) Harbor on February 19, 1941. As the ship eased alongside the wharf, two American missionaries were walking on the quay beside the ship. They were Nazarene missionaries, the John Andersons Sr., and one of our OMS team, Miss Mary Ella Taylor, who had Nazarene background, recognized them. So, we called back and forth as the ship glided to a stop.

First OMS India Missionaries

Culture Shock

The first nights we stayed at the Inter-Mission Business Office (IMBO) guesthouse with Rev. and Mrs. Blickenstaff. They were assigned to IMBO by the Church of the Brethren and helped missionaries of all denominations with Bombay business matters. Since thirty-three missionaries had been on our ship, Rev. Blickenstaff was busy. He provided us with a small amount of Indian cash, and the next day we visited the American Express office, which served as a bank, and changed our USA currency for Indian rupee. American Express also transferred our ship baggage to their office for us to clear through customs.

The next day, we purchased bedding rolls, mattresses, mosquito nets, and pith helmets with wide brims. We were exhorted by veteran missionaries to always wear these stiff, broad-brimmed hats to shield our heads and necks from the sun. Several times on that trip, when the train stopped at a station, I jumped off, forgetting to put on my *topee* (pith helmet). When I realized what I had done, I hurriedly retrieved it and put it on, asking the Lord to forgive me for being so forgetful and careless. I was grateful I had not suffered sunstroke!

The third day, we cleared our baggage through Indian customs, and then the baggage handlers wanted their *baksheesh* (tip). Roy Davis thought that was bribery and refused to pay, but Brother Seamands knew we wouldn't consider it bribery after we understood the country better.[6] He said, "Boys, you just let me clear your things through customs and pay your duty, and then I'll figure out your portion and each of you can just pay me." What a blessing to have someone with experience and wisdom to help us!

Rail Travel to Raichur

To take the train to Raichur in the evening, we went to the railway station early. If you got on the train at an ordinary station, you often had to force your way into the rail car, so we wanted to reserve space. Each person with a ticket was assigned a railway car by number as well as his berth in that car. In those days, the missionaries traveled third-class, and the hand basins in both second-class and third-class were often not clean enough to use, except to let the water run through. In the lavatory, the toilet was simply a hole in the floor through which one could see the ground below!

---

6   After culture shock wears off, one realizes that these financial transactions are simply compensation for services rendered.

We found our assigned car and spread out our baggage. Each car had a hinged padded board halfway between the seats and the ceiling. This provided extra space for baggage, and, if there was enough room, you could make it your upper berth. We men let our wives use the lower berth. It was generally understood and accepted that, if you had a reservation, you could organize your own compartment sleeping arrangements. The ceiling light bulb burned nonstop, so we had fun trying to find a way to fasten an umbrella to shield our eyes. Finally, J. T. Seamands slid one of his socks over the bulb, making the light bearable.

The train stopped every hour or so, and various food and drink hawkers called through the windows to sell their wares, such as *pän*, a betel nut mixture used for chewing that stained the mouth red, and *biri,* cigarettes and various other forms of tobacco. Weary, we managed to sleep intermittently most of the night.

Mrs. Yvonne Seamands' Snake Stories

When we reached the Raichur railroad station the next afternoon, Mrs. Yvonne Seamands met us with a hired flute player and an Indian drummer to lead us "in triumphant procession" a mile or so to the Seamands' home in the Methodist mission compound. "Mission compounds" were well-defined living spaces commonly established to provide some environmental controls to safeguard health with some modicum of sanitation through isolation from the general populace. Eventually they became locations for various mission institutional settings, which led to employment opportunities for new believers. The downside was that these new believers were "extracted," or cut off, from their natural culture and social context and were unable to effectively share their new faith within their spheres of influence.

Betty and I were assigned to the women's compound, a half-mile down the road from the Seamands. Our first night there, Mrs. Seamands regaled us with snake, scorpion, and plague stories. Some I remember to this day. For example, she said the snakes lived in pairs. If you killed one, its mate could trace you by the odor of your body and would often seek to kill you. She told how one of their coworkers had killed a snake, and then when the family was asleep on the floor, the snake's mate slithered its way around the others to bite the one who had killed the first snake! (Not very reassuring or comforting thoughts with which to start out. Obviously, she was toying with us. Or was she?)

While waiting for Rev. Erny to arrive and clarify our assignments, I attended the graduation of four men from the National Holiness Missionary Society (NHMS) school in Bangalore.[7] I also stayed at the NHMS home one week, studying language with a young Muslim man.

During this time, the U.S. government canceled all passports, so that in the event they were lost or stolen, no one could sell them on the black market. That was apparently happening frequently. To apply for replacement passports, we headed for the capital city of Delhi. We took the train there from Bombay, a distance of about nine hundred miles, requiring almost a full day. On the return trip, we witnessed to Hindus, some wiping tears from their eyes as we told of healing and how God answered prayer. Betty traveled in the *zenana* (women only) coach alone for a while, but I spoke with the train officials, and they allowed me to ride with her until another woman boarded very late in the night. We reached Bombay Easter Sunday morning, where the IMBO staff met us and took our heavier luggage. We stored our main trunks at the home of the Blickenstaffs until we relocated to Allahabad.

Language Study

Our first assignment was to learn the language at a school in North India. We were thrilled to be able to enroll in language school, but we felt alone traveling there. At Dehradun, we boarded an Indian bus to go the last eighteen miles, up a winding road with many hairpin turns. The bus was full, and on top, a canvas tarpaulin spreading over all the suitcases, bags, and baskets was roped tight. The windows were open, and sometimes people got nauseated from all the twisting and turning along the roads. Some were vomiting out the windows—not a pleasant experience.

---

7   Today known as the "South India Bible Seminary" of World Gospel Mission (WGM), headquartered in Marion, Indiana.

The "Hill Station"

The hottest temperatures in India were from April through July, at the end of the school year. Universities on the plains closed during the summer heat, and all life slowed down. So, during those months, we and other missionaries traveled by train five hundred miles to a "hill station" in Landour-Mussoorie in the state of Uttarakand in North India. It was usually twenty degrees cooler than on the plains.

This area had been built by the British years before, in Himalaya south of Nepal, and missionary societies had established a western hospital, an international school with a worship center, and a language school. Missionaries from many parts of India came there, and we had as many as four hundred language students enrolled during the first years. The "hill station," then, became a "colony of missionaries," and we accomplished so much more there than we could have in the heat of the North India plains.

The language school in Landour was an outlying village, higher up the mountain than Mussoorie. The school was formerly the property of "Kellogg Memorial Church," the Union Church of the missionaries. So, our address temporarily became: Mr. and Mrs. Wesley Duewel, Tipperary, Landour, Mussoorie, Uttar Pradesh, India.[8] We were there four months, and we walked to and from language school on a fairly level, unsurfaced road, around the mountain twice a day.

Days of Prayer

Several times during this "hill season," I felt the Lord wanted me to retreat for a day of prayer. I got up about daybreak on Saturday, or any other free day, and in a bag on my shoulder, I took a small rug, my Bible, my hymnbook, my typewriter, a number of theology books, and writing paper. I hiked miles on the mountain road to a quiet spot where I could be with the Lord and pray out of sight, as well as read and prepare notes for my future classes.

---

8   Formed on April 1, 1937, during British rule as the United Provinces of Agra and Oudh, after Independence in 1950, this state was renamed *Uttar Pradesh* (the Northern State), retaining the abbreviation of U. P.

I often went to a place called "the tollgate," where British India ended and a native state of India began.[9] There I leaned across "the tollgate" and prayed for the mountain people beyond, an area then closed to the gospel witness. Another of the various hideaway places I found was a house in Mussoorie called the "Haunted House." Very few people—maybe two or three per day—would come. I'd read and prepare notes for my future classes. What

Wesley on mountain

a wonderful view and peaceful place to worship the Lord! These were times of great "mountaintop" experiences spiritually as well as physically. Along with much wrestling in prayer, victories claimed by faith, and new guidance about many matters, I always spent hours feasting on the Word of God.

Woodstock School

Studying language in Landour was also an answer to prayer when we had children. We served in India before today's home-schooling movement, with its proliferation of teaching materials, and English-speaking children of missionaries needed a Christian school. The Union Missionary children's school, a boarding school known as Woodstock School, was God's answer to prayer for missionaries who served in India from many denominations and English-speaking nations. Missionary children boarded there while their parents served all over India. The school had been founded a century earlier, but at that time, it was operated by an interdenominational board. I was given the privilege of serving as a member of the executive committee and the responsibility of serving as vice-chairman for a number of years, until we left India.

---

9   Prior to India's independence, India had two sections. Most was "British India," but many small "Indian States" were under the rule of Indian princes, then in subsidiary roles.

Union Missionary Hospital

A Union Missionary Hospital was in Landour, and because Woodstock School was only a half-mile away, it served the several hundred children there. A missionary doctor and nurses were always present except in the bitter cold of winter, so we could usually receive necessary treatment from nine to ten months each year.

The school medical doctor was Dr. Bethel Fleming. Her husband, Dr. Robert Fleming, taught high school classes and engaged in the hobby of collecting butterflies. He collected new species and sent them to overseas museums. He was world-renowned for his collections from the Himalayas, and he had exhibits in American museums of nature history. Several varieties were named after him. This couple were key in expanding ministry outreach into Nepal.

"Dandy" Dysentery Treatment

It was not long till we had our first symptoms of a problem we experienced repeatedly during our India days—amoebic dysentery, which we also called "hill" dysentery. The actual term is giardiasis, or giardia. The only boarding house with vacancies in Landour was operated by an older Anglo-Indian lady. We later heard it was nicknamed "Dysentery House" because so many who stayed there (including us) came down with amoebic dysentery. Perhaps everyone contracted the disease through unsanitary food preparation.

When I came down with it, I was put on a ten-day course of medicine and had to be carried in a boat-like reclining chair, called a "dandy." Those suffering from dysentery had to be carried because the medicine was so strong that it could be hard on the heart if they overexerted themselves. They were not permitted to even walk to the bathroom. Bedpans were brought to their cots. While four men carried me around, I'd practice my new language by sharing the gospel with the Hindu men.

Throughout our time in India, from the first summer in 1941 at the "hill station" in Landour, we had repeated health problems. But none seemed more common to the missionaries than amoebic hill dysentery. Over the years, we sent several hundred stool specimens to one clinic or hospital after another, depending on where we were. We were prescribed many kinds of strong medicine.

We nicknamed the most drastic form of treatment "the missionary uplift." The typical twenty-one-day treatment included ten days

Bhutia Dandy Bearers, circa 1880s

of oral medication, one day of rest, and then days of the same medication in retention enemas nine hours at a time each day. To enable us to hold in the enemas, the feet of our beds were elevated about ten inches. So, when we went to the Union Missionary Hospital during the "'hill season'" and saw missionaries with their feet elevated on their cots, we'd joke, "Oh, I see you're getting the 'missionary uplift'!"

Studying Hindi and Urdu

Betty and I took language study as our priority assignment from the time we were able to enroll at the language school until we completed our second-year Hindi exams. The more than four hundred missionaries enrolled were studying Hindi or Urdu, and many classes had four to eight students. Fast learners could move ahead from class to class, while slower learners were given help to improve their proficiency. In addition to group classes, we each had a private hour with a tutor, before or after the school day.

At first, we concentrated on the Urdu language since it was preferred in Christian churches in the Uttar Pradesh state and used by the British for government and the military. However, during our first year at Allahabad, we realized we'd need Hindi more than Urdu, because when India became independent in 1947, Hindi would be the official language. So, for a year and a half, we gave about nine hours a day to Hindi language classes, plus private study and preparation.

God gave us a splendid *pandit* (tutor) to whom we owed much, Mr. Inayat Mull. We employed him for nine hours a day. Then Betty and I had one hour of individual time with him. He emphasized pronunciation and often had us repeat a word or phrase after him over and over—even ten to twenty times to perfect our pronunciation. It was tedious as we strove to pronounce it just like he did, but he was so invaluable that we took him with us when we later went south to Babatpur for the winter.

When I went for my second-year language exams, the examiners were so amazed at my success that they asked who my teacher was. I gladly answered, "Mr. Inayat Mull." God helped me pass in first division, which was not all that common, in both Urdu and later in Hindi! After the school season was over, we stayed an extra month and had private tutoring from other teachers at the language school.

Once we relocated to Allahabad and opened the Bible school, we used our new language constantly. In order to be better equipped, and of course to bless my own soul, I read chapters in my Hindi Bible during daily devotions and became increasingly aware of what a treasure we have in God's Word. In Allahabad, seminary students, a few local Christians, and often some missionary language students attended Sunday worship services. While preaching, I would speak in English, then Hindi, and then repeat the theological and more technical terms in Urdu. In that way, all three language groups could get the message, and second-year language students could listen to how the English words were translated, which helped their language comprehension.

Language Coordinator

Later, I was asked to serve as a coordinator for the language exams at the main North India center in Allahabad. The winter session for the language school was conducted a half-mile from our seminary. We began to teach and preach in the language to some extent in one year, and we kept up our language study for a year and a half—seven hours a day, and during several concentrated times a year. When we began our seminary classes, we had to teach one course a day that first year. We also retained a pastor-helper who assisted the older missionaries with interpretation.

If you're serious in obeying God's call on your life in another country, you make language learning a priority, and keep adding new words to your vocabulary as long as you are in the field. How long does it take to "learn" an Asian language? Our answer: All your life!

Initial Adjustments

At Christmas, Mr. Inayat Mull went home to Punjab, another state of India, to be with his family. Alas, he never came back. What could we do for a language teacher? We heard a teacher was available in Allahabad, where we were going to start our Bible school. Early that summer, Rev. Erny had rented a property in Allahabad. We moved there and sent for our personal belongings from the IMBO office in Bombay.

Babatpur

After leaving the higher elevation of Landour and arriving at the lower elevation of Allahabad, Betty and I were assigned to nearby Babatpur, until the Landour language school opened again the first of May. We arrived there with our suitcases and trunks in October 1941. Babatpur was twelve miles outside of Benares,[10] which was renamed Varanasi when India became independent.

The Pilgrim Holiness Church mission work had been centered in the village of Babatpur in an area that had been "occupied" by the London Missionary Society for seventy-five years. Across the road from their property was a small Christian cemetery with several graves of Indians and children of former missionaries. Their mission-aries had labored there twenty-five years with almost no harvest. As a result, their mission board decided to close the area and not appoint any more missionaries. But when they heard OMS was opening work in India, they transferred everything to OMS and offered their one remaining missionary, Miss Beatrice VanVranken, to serve with OMS.

We were assigned part of the missionary bungalow where she lived. She had a small, adopted Indian daughter, Kalawati Singh, who was about one-and-a-half years old. She'd been abandoned on Miss

10   There are variant spellings for "Benares" or "Banares."

VanVranken's doorstep. We all lived in Babatpur until just before Christmas that year.

The Babatpur railway station was across the railroad tracks from the mission bungalow, just a hundred yards away. To us, the railway station was the symbol of modern civilization as well as the primary means of traveling and exploring our new homeland. Some thirty trains passed through daily, including some of the express trains that traveled the country. We lived one hundred yards from our primary means of connection to civilization!

Prayer for India

When we arrived in India in 1941, I gave up the prayer list I had used in the States. Each day, I had prayed for every one of the Bible Holiness Churches by name. And I had added to the prayer lists several hundred names of Bible Holiness people who promised to pray daily for missions. But now I made a new list with a number of the larger cities in India, praying for God to help OMS open outreach in these places and give us a harvest of souls. When traveling on the train, if not reading, I prayed for people in cities or villages in the areas we passed through, but especially for the cities. Then, I changed my prayer list again and began to pray specifically for the ministry in which we were already engaged and the section of the country where we were already working or planning to work.

Beginning my day by feasting on God's Word, reading twenty-five to fifty chapters, was such a joy! Sitting or kneeling on my prayer rug, I'd fast and pray throughout the main part of the day for the various aspects of our missionary work, for spiritual harvest and breakthrough in our outreach, for revival in India, and for whatever God put on my heart. Sometimes the Lord gave important guidance. I'd not trade a million dollars in exchange for the guidance he gave during those prayer times.

After about a year or two of such praying, it suddenly occurred to me how foolish I was to think that OMS would be in all those cities across India. Undoubtedly, like other missions, we would be located in only a certain section of the country. Other missionary societies were in other parts of India, and India was such a huge nation. With nearly four hundred million people in India at that time, how could we ever hope to spread all over the country?[11]

Uninvited and Unwanted House Guests

Some of our early adjustments included uninvited and unwanted "house guests." The wet season was worst for snakes. In one week, three cobras were killed. One was on the porch and another in the house! One poisonous "jumping snake" was also killed on the porch.

A young man who had been bitten by a cobra was brought to the compound, but he died within three minutes of his arrival. He first had been taken to various Hindu *fakirs* (spiritual shamans) and priests who had tried for several hours to cure him with magic spells. Scorpions also were found in homes, and we were warned about their poison. If we had to go to the bathroom during the night, we were to shake out our slippers to make sure none had crawled inside.

Less dangerous, yet more pesky, were quite a number of *chipkili* (common house geckos) in the residence. They ran over the walls, hid behind pictures, and were likely to fall in front of you when you went through a door—even landing on your head! They were non-poisonous, and on the positive side, they were useful in catching, eating, and eliminating many insects and bugs. Another kind of lizard, however, looked almost exactly the same except for a ridge down its back. One had to be keenly aware of it, because it was more poisonous than a cobra!

There were other unwanted visitors—diseases. Every year smallpox appeared regularly. People would say "*Mata Ji* [the

---

11   This particular allocation and apportionment of geographical ministry outreach was called missionary "comity" agreements. It is based on the legal principle that political entities (such as states, nations, or courts from different jurisdictions) mutually recognize each other's legislative, executive, and judicial acts. In the realm of missions, comity agreements primarily defined geographical territories of particular regions (like dividing up pieces of pie) for which specific agencies would assume responsibility and avoid duplication of efforts and wasting of resources. Some comity agreements would also include various resources (e.g., ships) that would be shared in order to be the best stewards possible of resources given to them by God.

honorable mother—smallpox goddess] comes to see us every year."
The government sent a health officer to enforce vaccination or cholera
inoculation, but many people didn't trust foreign medicine. One man
I knew climbed a tree to evade the government officer when he came
to his village. The officer climbed after him and inoculated him there!

The bubonic plague spread through surrounding village areas
every year or two. It was called "Black Plague" or "Black Death"
during the Middle Ages, when it depopulated large areas of Europe.
It's a disease carried by rats and transferred by fleas, which carry the
disease to a new host when the rats die. Our area was one of the worst
sections of India for the plague. Two years before we arrived, a terrible
epidemic continued even when the hot season came, and a multitude
of people died—twenty or thirty every day for a long time. When it
entered a family, generally the whole family would contract it and be
gone in a week.

To be safe in an area where "rats are dying," one evacuated for a
distance of at least two miles. But twenty villages sat in the two-mile
radius around Babatpur, and the average village had more than five
hundred people crowded together in the simple, mostly thatched-roof
mud houses. The rats were in many of those roofs. The village people
trying to escape them would camp just outside our mission fence.

Mercifully, we had only four deaths from the plague during the
hot season that year, two about a half-mile from us. It did its deadly
work mainly in the cool season, because the direct rays of the sun in
the hot season were so strong that they killed off many of the germs.
While this was also a bad section for cholera, the bubonic plague was
our most feared disease. We prayed; God protected us.

God Provides Our Health Needs

Because of the war, American doctors gained much more experience with dysentery. New medicines were developed, and treatment
became more effective. But God helped. Betty was ill during our
first furlough in the States. She was tested and retested for nearly
three years, examined at an Indiana clinic for several days. She was
also at Christ Hospital in Cincinnati for several days, as doctors

tried to determine her problem, testing and treating her for various possibilities.

Finally, a medical laboratory in Cincinnati told Betty to come and provide her stool specimen at the lab. They said a specimen is invalid after twenty minutes. We had never been told that. In India, again and again we had given specimens in containers to hospitals and labs, and often they stood for hours before the doctors got to them. When this new lab tested her specimen, they found she still had amoebic dysentery. I was told by a Christian medical doctor that had we delayed returning home a few months that I might have lost Betty. She was just a shell ready to collapse!

With the new medications they gave her, she was soon free of the disease—but not from the effects. For the rest of her days, she battled lingering symptoms. God was merciful, however, sparing her life. *Praise the Lord!* God helped us survive our twenty-five-year span in India. We had so much for which to thank him. When you pray for your missionaries, pray not only for their ministry but also for their health and safety. *Remember, God answers prayer!*

Hindu Presence

Varanasi is a famed holy city of more than four million people on the banks of the Ganges River.[12] India has many "holy" places, but the most sacred is at Prayag in Allahabad. All Hindus desire to wash away their sins with a ritual cleansing bath in the Ganges. If they live within a few hundred miles of the river, they will attempt to self-cleanse a number of times annually—or, at the very least, once each year.

According to Hinduism, Prayag, this most holy location, is at the junction of two sacred rivers—the Ganges (or Ganga) and the Jamna (or Yamuna). Hindus believe a third unseen and mythical river, the Saraswati, springs up at the exact spot where the Ganga and Yamuna rivers join. It doesn't puzzle them that during the monsoon rainy season each year, when the banks are covered with the swollen waters,

---

12   The estimated population of Varanasi (formerly Benares) ranged from 4.06 million to 4.106 million in 2016–2017.

the exact spot where the two rivers merge is shifted by the silt deposited by the floodwaters. They call this place the Tribeni Ghat, meaning "the three-mouth place," "the three-opening place," "the three-fold sacred passage," or "the three-fold gate." To Hindus, it is the holiest location on Earth. All Hindus want to visit Prayag at least once in their lifetime, and if they could not go while alive, some relative or friend will take a small quantity of their ashes after death and have them cast into the Ganges.

Because it is such a holy Hindu site, numerous celebrations are conducted there annually. The Magh Mela (Grand Festival) is held there in January or February, depending on the lunar month, and the gathering area is transformed into a sacred tent-city. Usually several thousand *sadhus* (Hindu holy men) camped there for the month. Annually, on the holiest day with the new moon, more than one million people were in attendance. There's also a celebration of the Amavasya at nearby Sangywayi, with about two million bathers.[13] Every twelfth year, the population at the Kumbh Mela (Special Grand Festival) can reach into the millions.[14] The most I witnessed was seven million people. At one of the more recent Maha Kumbh festivals, seventy million were present on the main day.

Evangelism at the Mela Festival[15]

Every year on the three most sacred days of the mela festival, we closed the seminary so everyone could go witness, pass out gospel literature and thousands of tracts, and sell hundreds of Gospel portions and small evangelical books to as many people as possible. With the

---

13   "Somvati Amavasya" is the "no moon day" that falls on a Monday in a Hindu lunar calendar. It is a rare occurrence and considered very auspicious. Devotees pray for the souls of their departed ancestors during the occasion. Wednesdays are also considered auspicious days, but any Amavasya days are appropriate to perform various rituals to appease ancestors and to ward off various forms of evil, illness, and other calamities. Mantras are often connected with these rituals, and repeating them as many as eighteen thousand times is encouraged.

14   Every twelfth year is the Kumbh Mela (Pitcher Festival), and the 144th year is the Maha Kumbh Mela (or the Great, or Supreme, Kumbh).

15   Taken from an article Dr. Duewel wrote for *The Flaming Sword*, a publication of the Bible Holiness Church, July–August 1944.

festival only three miles away, no other Christian seminary in India was so favorably located for such an effective gospel witness. If the heart of Jesus yearned and wept over Jerusalem (Matt 23:37), how often his heart must yearn to save those millions at the mela festivals in Allahabad.

Wesley with bicycle and boxes of literature

Once, as we neared our destination by boat, we could see hundreds of people along the bank vainly attempting to wash away their sins before they went to the temple of the goddess of the volcano. The boat had pushed in between the bathers to the bank, when suddenly the students shouted to me and pointed to the one side. There—amid the men and women bathing in the murky water, which was thick with withered flower petals, leaves, and other items left by the worshipers as an offering to the sacred river—to my horror I saw a baby's head. The body had been devoured by the crocodiles, and there, floating amidst the bathers was the head—still covered with flesh and skin. I quickly left the boat, turning my back on the painful sight, then scrambled up the sloping bank.

We decided to scatter among the people, choosing a certain tall tree as our place of rendezvous. Each student had a bag of Gospels and food strapped over their shoulder. We sold Gospel portions for the smallest India coin, because people valued them much more if they purchased them, making them less likely to simply discard them. Greater good by far was accomplished in the long run.

Another young man and I struck out along a back road skirting a village, then came to a larger road where people were passing in a constant stream. Many could not read, and many had no time to stop and listen to the "despised" Christians. Others mocked us when they learned what we had was Christian literature, but, in spite of all, we emptied both our bags and sold a New Testament in less than two hours' time.

I was a short distance from the main temple of the smallpox goddess when one of the students hurried to me and said, "I just saw a demon-possessed person turning handsprings on the surface of the Ganges" (obviously through demonic power). In a while, another student came and reported, "I just saw a small child bathing in the river, and a crocodile seized it, pulled it into the river, and ate it!"

Many of the villagers came to the temple with offerings of a coconut wrapped by a wisp of red cloth, held before them in their hands. As they neared the temple, their arms and hands began to shake, and the nearer they came, the more violently they shook. Village groups arrived—twenty to thirty people in a group, all holding coconuts, all shaking tremendously, controlled by demonic power. A villager explained, "You see, they are possessed by the goddess!"

India village evangelism was quite different from holding revivals in churches in our homeland. Often there is long, hard seed-sowing before the reaping comes. But we praised God that he gave us strength and grace to reach multitudes of those who would in no other way receive the message. We prayed that his Word would not return to him void. We scattered the Word far and wide among the people who lived under the sway of false gods and goddesses. The true Light was entering. *All praise to our mighty Savior!*

The "Volcano Goddess" Mela Festival

Once each year comes the day for the mela festival in honor of the volcano goddess, Jwala Mukhi Devi (a volcano-faced goddess). The main festival is held in a distant district of Uttar Pradesh, but small auxiliary temples sit in several places. One is located at Manikpur, a short distance from where we camped for the winter evangelistic season. I was unable to learn why people worship the goddess in places where a volcano has never been seen, but this much I did ascertain: every village Hindu male child in this area had his head shaved for the first time at this annual mela festival on the banks of the Ganges.

During a visit to Allahabad in October 1983, I took Betty and my secretary, Hilda Johnecheck, to the mela grounds to show them where the event is held. Only a small encampment of sadhus was there. We were just ready to leave when I felt strongly drawn to go back. I asked Nathan Krampitz, our missionary colleague and driver, to park the car just outside the area. Then I got out, praying, "Lord, what do You want me to do?" I felt drawn to the area down the embankment, where some fifty or more sadhus were camping.

Suddenly, my name was called out. "Duewel Sahib! Duewel Sahib!" One of the sadhus came hurrying to me. "Do you remember me?" he asked. "Allahabad Bank! Allahabad Bank!" That was where our mission conducted business. When I had previously visited the bank, I had given him a copy of the New Testament, and I had not seen him for fourteen years. Now, according to Hindu belief, he was giving his post-retirement years to seek God, and he was worshiping at this Hindu holy place.

"I still have the book you gave me," he said. "And I still read it!" We were speaking in Hindi, and the other sadhus gathered around us. I exhorted him to not only read the New Testament but to trust in Jesus. "It won't be long!" he said as he pointed upward. I told him I wanted to pray with him one more time. He bowed his head, and the other sadhus gathered closer. I poured out my heart in prayer to Jesus, asking him to save this man and all those sadhus.

Sadhus often wander from place to place and temple to temple. God had this man there at the exact time—and probably the last time I'd ever be there—and he caused him to recognize me. Will I ever meet that "holy man" in heaven? I did what I could with the guidance and help of the Lord. *Praise God!*

Initial Survey

While in Babatpur, one day I decided to study my vocabulary words and model sentences as I rode my bicycle, checking out the surrounding area to see how adequately it had been evangelized. I made a one-day bicycle survey trip, starting out in a large circle on dirt roads, going into Benares from the west side, and then coming back on the regular Benares road. My cyclometer measured about sixty miles by the time I returned home.

After riding some miles, I came to a central town and entered the bazaar area with typical open-front village shops. Each had a sign advertising its wares, such as Eveready flashlight batteries, Standard Oil, or Cal-Tech (subsequently known as Texaco) kerosene. In one shop, a tailor was making shirts out of Indian cloth on a Singer hand-cranked sewing machine.

When I reached the village school, the children came running out to see this strange, white man. I asked, but none of them could remember having ever heard the name "Jesus." We had sent them light for their path, but no light for their soul. We had supplied a machine to sew clothing for the body, but nothing to clothe them spiritually.

I crossed India's highway No. 1, the national road that went from Calcutta to Delhi, then stopped by an open-front shop and asked the shopkeeper if he had ever heard the name "Jesus." "Yes," he replied, "about twelve years ago a car came along this road and stopped at my shop. The people sang a song to us, and they mentioned that name, *Yishu Masih*. They must have spent a half-hour here."

I spoke to a number of people that day, but no one else could remember having heard that name. At one place, three men were walking along, carrying goods on their heads.[16] I asked if they had ever heard of Jesus. One of the men turned his head slowly, so as not to unbalance his load. "No," he replied, "I have never heard that name. Right on ahead is a crossroad, and if you turn to the right and go one mile, there is a police station. Ask them. Maybe they can tell you where he lives." They had no idea who I was talking about!

I came to where a farmer and his adult son were irrigating their field by hand. I got off my bicycle and asked the man if he had heard the name "Jesus."

"No," he replied, "I've never heard it."

I told him to think a bit. Had he never heard that name?

"No!" he said.

---

16   The common Indian way to carry various commodities.

Because this was my last stop, I decided to try once more. I was speaking in his language. "*Yishu! Yishu!* Just think. Can't you remember ever having heard that name?"

The farmer stopped his work and looked at me. "No, I have never heard of him! I don't know where he lives. I don't know what he eats. I don't know what he wears. I don't know anything about Yishu. He has never been to our village!"

I knew he spoke the truth. Only once in sixty miles could someone remember having heard the name of Jesus, and on that occasion, only once in his life, when a passing car stopped for a few minutes. To their knowledge, Jesus had never visited their area! This experience confirmed to me that God had sent us to India to proclaim the good news of salvation through *Yishu Masih*!

Wesley Duewel with bicycle in India, circa 1943

Allahabad Bible Seminary

We opened the Allahabad Bible Institute, as our Bible seminary was called for the first several years, in July 1942. After spending more than a year in language study, we applied our new skills there with a small student body. We had no previous work from which to draw national coworkers; therefore, we had to offer student tuition scholarships for the three-year course, depending on the referrals and recommendations of pastors of other denominations. Our agreement with the students was that, after graduation, they would serve with us for at least as many years as they had received a scholarship.

The first of our students arrived with little clothing and no bedding. Cloth was rationed, but I managed to obtain ration permits, often standing in a line, waiting my turn to see the official who could grant the cloth permit. Then, I'd take the permit to a shop and buy the cloth by the yard to make two bedsheets per student, shirts, simple trousers, and so on. There was no ready-made clothing then, so you had to go to a tailor in the bazaar.

The second semester brought more students. We had been working hard at the language (again, seven to nine hours per day), so we began to use it in many roles. Betty taught New Testament classes and served as the dean of women. Assisting with *Revival Magazine*, she also taught Sunday school classes and women's Bible studies, as well as serving as mission hostess for the many guests who visited our home. She was known as a quiet, sweet-spirited missionary. She loved and prayed for our family, coworkers, students, and friends. She was always faithful in reading God's Word and in loving the ministry of OMS.

The students were patient, and we found our language skills developed rapidly. We knew we must get them deeply established in their Christian experience and walk with the Lord, so we had three series of special, spiritual, revival-type meetings the first year. God met with us, and many students experienced a new infilling of the Holy Spirit. These annual spiritual emphasis weeks became a tradition of the school and are continued today.

NOTE: Today the Allahabad Bible Seminary (ABS), located directly across the street from the city hospital, is the oldest and largest OMS-established seminary in India, with over 165 residential students and hundreds more nonresidential, or distance education, students. Other buildings have been built, or rebuilt, to accommodate classrooms, a library, a dining hall, and other faculty residences, including the "Wesley and Betty Duewel Faculty Residence" constructed in honor of Betty and me in April 2006.[17] On another

New Faculty Housing

17 Overseas Council for Theological Education International (OC International), founded by Dr. Charles Spicer, who originally served with OMS in the development department, partnered with OMS in constructing the "Wesley and Betty Duewel Faculty Residence." In 2006, there were about

section of the overall property, the "Erny Memorial School" was built in honor of Dr. and Mrs. Eugene Erny. Partial income from this Christian day school contributes to the operational budget of the seminary. *Praise the Lord!*

Practical Evangelism

In the early years, bicycles for our students to use in their practical evangelism had to be assembled from scratch. New bicycles were not obtainable, so I purchased secondhand bicycle parts at junk sales, got new parts when available, and then assembled them. Often, the students had to learn to ride.

By the end of the first term, I had assembled enough bicycles for half the students. During our field term of village evangelism, we devised a plan whereby, in the morning, half the student body went out on the bicycles, going as far as eight to ten miles away to more distant villages, while the other half walked to the villages in a radius of up to three miles away. In the afternoon, they switched.

Wesley with students on bicycles

Villages in our province were everywhere, but they did not occupy a large area. Roads were eight or ten feet wide. Fields for agriculture were, of course, much higher valued and preserved. Many homes had only one or two rooms, and most were mud-walled, with no yard except perhaps a few feet in front and located in the most inauspicious grounds. Each morning, every housewife not only swept her mud floor but any space in front of her house.

The average village nationwide was said to have five hundred people. When we lived in Babatpur, I counted twenty villages within

187 students, and the ABS president at the time was Rev. Sundara Raj. Allahabad was originally considered part of the Delhi Diocese of the Evangelical Church of India, but Allahabad became a separate diocese in 2020.

a radius of about two miles. Every village had its own Hindu temple, set apart from the residences, and every Hindu home had a worship shrine, either built into a wall or buried along the edge of the floor inside of the house.

Hidden in a wall or under the ground were "sacred objects," or spiritual fetishes, thought to be endued with special powers—maybe a coin, a stone, or a simple ring. From time to time after the Hindu worship, the householder, or a member of his family, would momentarily stop by the sacred shrine and drop a few drops of milk, a handful of rice, or flower offerings, and then make a hand gesture of reverence.

Sometimes, a householder who accepted Jesus would have a house-cleaning ceremony. Normally we removed our shoes in a person's home, but when we participated in a house-cleaning ceremony, we just entered the house and located the sacred shrine, or fetish. It was usually found in some corner of the dirt floor. Then we dug up the items of spiritual bondage, removed them, replaced the topsoil from some other area, and compacted the ground while intentionally singing "Victory in Jesus!"

If *Dalits*, the lowest caste in India's traditional caste system,[18] were living in the village, they usually lived in one corner or along the perimeter of the village. Before India's independence, *Dalits* often were not permitted to use the same water well as higher caste people. If they wanted to buy cloth, they were not permitted to touch it before they purchased it. The shopkeeper would hold up several kinds of cloth, and they'd point to the piece they wanted, not daring to defile the unsold cloth by their touch.

Christmas Evangelism

Just before Christmas, 1943, some of my seminary students and I were evangelizing in an area where the people had never heard the message of Christ—a village twenty-five miles from our seminary in Allahabad. It was the last night of our field term of evangelism. Among

---

18 *Dalit*, meaning "broken/scattered" in Sanskrit and Hindi, is a term mostly used for the ethnic groups in India that have been kept repressed (often termed backward castes, or other backward class, aka "OBC").

the villagers, sitting cross-legged on the ground around us and under the stars, was an old white-haired man without a shirt or anything on his chest. He was listening carefully. We had sung several gospel songs in their language, and I picked up the large Hindi Bible and began to read the beautiful Christmas story of good news for all people from Luke 2.

As I began to tell the story of Jesus and his birth, the old man looked up and interrupted me. "How long is it since that great day when God's Son was born?" he asked.

I knew most of the people in the area could not read or write, but I said, "Can you read? Have you ever received a letter in the mail from the post office? What is the number the government puts on the outside of the letter at the post office? Or if you go to the courthouse, what is the number they put on your papers?"

The villagers talked back and forth among themselves for a minute or two, and then someone answered, "1943."

"That's right," I said. "We call that the date. It says it's been approximately that many years since God's Son was born. It is nearly two thousand years ago."

Pointing his finger at me, the old man asked, "Then why has the news been so long a time in reaching us? Who has been hiding that book all this time? Why has no one ever come to tell us before?"

What could I answer? What would you have answered? I dodged his question, for what could I say? But then I replied, "I don't think anyone has been trying to hide it. You see, this world is a big world. We have been going from place to place telling people, and tonight we have come to your village to tell you."

He became quiet, and we finished the service. The villagers lapsed into silence, then one by one they returned to their homes.

The students went to their tent, and I went to mine and lay down on my pallet. Others were probably soon asleep, but I turned and twisted this way and that as I kept hearing that man's question, "Who has been hiding that book all this time?" Finally at 2:00 a.m., I got my flashlight, paper, and pen, and wrote the poem: "Are You Hiding the Word of God?"

Revival Magazine

A year after we arrived, one of the great burdens of OMS in India, from the time Dr. Eugene Erny arrived in North India, was for revival in the church there. This burden for revival extended to the whole world. Dr. Erny began first with revival prayer meetings in the mountain area among the missionaries. In July 1945, he got permission to restart *Revival Magazine*. The first year, he sent a monthly copy to every Protestant missionary in India. In the next year or two, editions were printed in three languages. Our colleague and coworker, Rev. Meredith Helsby (aka "Med") continued as editor through 1954. Then I succeeded as editor, furnishing the main editorials and series of Bible studies on prayer and revival. We also increased the publications in English, Chinese, Japanese, Spanish, Portuguese, Greek, Korean, and five Indian languages.

Because of my *Revival Magazine* editorials, articles, and role as editor, I received many requests to hold special spiritual-life retreats, revival campaigns, and so on at various mission stations and Bible schools throughout India. One of my heartaches was constantly having to turn down many requests; I just had too many other responsibilities. Later, when I was transferred to our USA office in Los Angeles, my colleague and fellow missionary, Rev. Rudy Rabe, continued publishing nearly ten thousand copies of the magazine in multiple languages each month.[19]

---

19   The *Revival Magazine* editors: Eugene Erny, 1942–1950; Meredith Helsby, 1950–1954; Wesley Duewel, March 1954–December 1968, though Rudy Rabe began writing the editorials in January 1967. The Duewels returned to the USA in 1964 and were assigned to the L.A. office in 1965. Dr. Duewel continued as editor of *Revival Magazine* through December 1968; however, his last series of articles ended in the August 1966 issue. Beginning March–December 1968, editorials included the writings of various people. *In These Mortal Hands*, written by Robert Wood, gives incomplete information about the magazine, because it only covers the first fifty years of OMS history (1901–1951).

Family Additions and Answered Prayer

On February 2, 1944, I took Betty, who was expecting our first child, to a local physician. Dr. Barrar was an American Presbyterian missionary who had married an Indian college professor and lived about a half-mile from us. She was superintendent of a large Presbyterian hospital run by the Presbyterian mission, and she became our dear friend and medical advisor.[20] Betty had become exceedingly tired, and Dr. Barrar began injections to help induce labor. Our OMS nurse-teacher, Miss Beatrice Van Vranken, who frequently helped Dr. Barrar, was present to help. They were so busy that they forgot to pull the curtain, so as Esther Erny and I waited just outside the window, we watched the whole birth procedure. John Wesley Duewel, often called John Wesley, was born at 10:38 p.m., weighing six pounds, six ounces. We soon discovered that he had contracted a form of dysentery at birth, but God spared his life, and he quickly recovered.

On the nearby island nation of Indonesia, three weeks later, on February 22, John's future wife, Retno Sumarmi Jakti, was born into an aristocratic Javanese family whom we would come to admire, appreciate, and love many years later.

Only five days after John recovered, Edward Erny, son of Eugene and Esther Erny, was found to have frightening symptoms of infantile paralysis polio. He was the toddler I had carried to the guest room when the Ernys came to interview Betty and me back in our GBS days. This was before the Salk vaccination, and polio usually meant almost certain doom or, at least, severe crippling. Our small family went to prayer, and eventually God's gracious hand began to show on little Edward's life. His previously contorted face could whistle again, and he was left with only minimal physical limitations.[21]

On June 20, 1946, God gave us our "second blessing" with the birth of Ruth Christine Hope Duewel in Landour, Mussoorie, Uttar Pradesh, whom we've come to call Chris in her adult years. We were

---

20   The Presbyterian hospital was where John Wesley and, later, Darlene, were born.

21   See also Erny, *This One Thing: The Story of Missionary Leader Eugene Erny*, 176–77.

thrilled with our daughter and Betty poured herself into caring for her and helping her to grow in the Lord.

In the same year, on the other side of the world, on December 11, Chris's future husband, Edward DeFrance Zahniser, was born into a fine Free Methodist family whom we would also come to admire, appreciate, and love many years later. *Praise God for answered prayer!*

Our first four-year term stretched into eight years before help arrived so we could take our first furlough. John Wesley and Christine were born into our family during our first term, which proved to be difficult, because we faced much illness and discouragement due to little response to the gospel message. Our greatest sacrifice was made each year when our children, when they were older, returned to Woodstock School up in the "hill station." Because of its location five hundred miles away and our heavy schedule, our visits were limited to once during the school year, if we visited at all. Finally, in 1948, after eight years in country, we were able to return to the States for our first furlough. But our first reason for leaving India was our concern for John Wesley's health.

As an infant, John Wesley's chest bones stuck out till he looked like a famine waif. His problem was digesting the available milk. We tried everything we knew to get pure milk he could digest. We tried cow's milk, goat milk, water buffalo milk, and, at times, a small quantity of foreign milk that became available in three or four elite food stores in Allahabad. For short periods, we were able to get tins of condensed Australian, Dutch, or British milk. But no form of pure milk could be purchased in India, and we tried everything. Yet John would repeatedly break out with boils on his head and body.

Dr. Barrar used part of her house as a private two-room hospital. She asked us to bring John Wesley to her house so she could work more closely with him. We didn't realize she feared he'd die and thought it would be more bearable for us if he didn't die in our house.

Finally, she advised us to get him out of the climate. But the British army was pulling out because of India's independence and had priority on all air and ship travel, and the British government reserved all ship passages on British ships for people with British passports. I went to Calcutta, looking for God's answer, but we could get no ticket by ship for two years. The first travel arrangements we could make were to fly to Britain and then go by ship from there to the USA. But air travel was not normally used for missionaries at that time because of the expense.

While in Calcutta again for OMS business, I obtained one air ticket to Holland, promised by KLM, the Dutch airline, and the only ticket available for several months. The plan was to wait a month in Holland and then purchase ship tickets to New York. I discovered that a KLM plane coming from Indonesia had one seat available and would touch down in Calcutta in several weeks. By faith, I booked that seat, the only space available, planning to take John Wesley with me.

After several weeks, our family went to Calcutta by train, trusting God to work out our travel itinerary. To our surprise, when the plane arrived from Indonesia, it had two open seats, instead of one, so Betty and I both had a seat and held the two children on our laps. It was just after the war, and the Dutch government apologized, explaining they didn't have enough money to equip their planes with air conditioning, so they had to fly at low altitude all the way from India to Holland, "because Holland is too poor to pressurize her planes."

When we arrived in Holland, we were able to travel from Amsterdam to Glasgow on a small airplane that carried only twenty-six passengers. From there we traveled by train to Llanfairfechen, North Wales. We experienced reverse culture shock, overwhelmed at how clean everything seemed after India. The men working on the train line were wearing shirts and pants, dressed up compared to what we had grown accustomed to in India! We suddenly realized our excited comments as we looked out the train windows attracted the curious attention of others and embarrassed our British host.

Once we were in England, waiting a month for passage to the USA, British airmen who were formerly stationed in Allahabad and had attended our servicemen's prayer meetings arranged a series of meetings in their local churches. They lived in various parts of Britain, and I was occupied almost every night. During the first five days I was away from Betty and the children, they had to call the doctor three times for John Wesley. We felt crushed in our hearts that he was so ill.

The second week, I had a meeting in London and visited with the pastor of the Salvation Army Gospel Hall, where I would preach that night. The commander asked how the family had gotten on in the extreme heat of India, and I told him about John Wesley's health problem. That night, after my message, the leader rose and asked, "Is there any prayer request?" Then, "Well, if no one else has a prayer request, I have one." Then he recounted my son's health problem. They prayed, and although I didn't realize it at the time, God instantly healed John Wesley.

After that month in England, we had ship passage to the USA on the *M. V. Britannic*. It was May 1948. When departure day came, I was carrying John Wesley in my arms and Betty was carrying Chris as we walked up the gangplank. I didn't have any opportunity to tell the crew about our health problem, and we still hadn't realized God had completely healed our son. As soon as the ship's waiters saw the children, they brought us two tall glasses of ice-cold milk. John Wesley cried and grabbed the glass with his

Wesley, Betty, John, and Chris in Indian dress at camp, circa 1948

hands. I immediately tried to take it away, because I didn't want him to get sick, but he tried to pull the glass back. I was embarrassed to cause a scene at the first meal, so finally I said, "Well, let him have just a bit." He drank it—with no ill effects.

When we got to the States, he seemed to have no further problem with milk at all. John Wesley announced, "I like America, Mama and Papa, best of all." When he grew older and went to school, he still had no trouble with milk. When he came home from college, he'd even buy an extra gallon of it just to make sure we had enough while he was home. He has never had any lactose intolerance or milk allergy since the people at that Gospel Hall in London prayed for him. He was completely healed!

At the time of this writing, to this day, John has a strong, rugged body. For more than forty years, he lived in the villages of Indonesia, supervising irrigation work. *Praise the Lord! Praise the Lord! When God heals, he heals completely!*

Unexpected Call to Study

One day in 1947, before our first furlough and while we were in Landour, I felt led to spend a day alone, as I did from time to time. I went to a place about nine miles back in the mountains. As always, I started early in the morning to plead with God for souls, a greater harvest in the OMS work in India, and his promises.

Suddenly, I inwardly knew that when furlough came, I was to earn a doctorate in preparation for our return to India. I wasn't praying about myself, our family, or our furlough, so this was a complete surprise. It was "out of a clear blue sky." I had not talked it over with others. I had not even considered it before. And I do not believe I had thought about that possibility even once. I didn't understand how it would work out, but inwardly, I knew it was God's will for me. I had no desire for degrees or more study, but the Lord made it so clear to me that I had not the slightest doubt—just as clearly as when God called me to India at age five as I played in my sandbox and when he called me to teach.

After a day or two, I told Dr. Erny what happened. He said, "Wesley, I know you. You'll have such a burden on your heart for India that you will not be able to stay away that long. Just get a master's degree, then return to India." But God had specifically told me to complete a doctorate. My OMS colleagues did not understand me, but that had to be left with God. The time came when they fully agreed, and I never doubted this further call for my life.

I knew if I tried to get a doctorate from most seminaries, I'd have to first get a Bachelor of Divinity degree, then a master's, and then a doctorate. That would take too long. I found that at the University of Chicago, I could rent a missionary apartment and apply for study in the area of church history. I thought there'd be less liberalism in that subject than in any other.

I did not want to set a precedent in OMS that would make it difficult for OMS administration. No one had ever taken a leave of absence to earn a doctorate. So, I informed Dr. Erny I'd resign from OMS, get my doctorate, and then reapply at once. He protested that it might negatively reflect on OMS if I resigned; constituents might misunderstand. "Take a leave of absence," he advised me. So I did, without pay and trusting God to provide for our expenses.

FIRST FURLOUGH (1948–1952)

When we came home on furlough in 1948 and visited Betty's family in Cincinnati, I felt impressed to go to the University of Cincinnati to see what was possible in their School of Education. God opened the door for me. I had taken some summer courses in psychology there during my Bible college days, and I asked Dr. Carter Good, the dean in their Teacher's College division, if he'd accept my credits from God's Bible School. He provisionally accepted them for a six-month trial period.

I did not have funds for the entire first year of university studies, but I enrolled the first semester and trusted God to help me fund the second and onward.

God's Gracious Provisions and Teaching Experiences

As a graduate student, I was assigned a study carrel space in the library, where I could keep my books. One day, a week or so after classes started, I looked up and saw the dean take a seat opposite from me. He said, "Mr. Duewel, I don't know how much your missionary society is paying you during your time of graduate study, but my guess is that you can't afford to rent a large house with quiet study space. You have small children, don't you?"

I said, "Yes, two," but I didn't tell him I was receiving no funds whatsoever from OMS.

"I have an empty office on the faculty row," he went on, "and I'd be glad to assign it to you. You can leave your typewriter there and spread out your books." What a surprise blessing! So, I had an office for my typewriter and books, and I could work there till I completed my doctorate. God had provided for a need I did not realize I had. *Praise the Lord!*

God also provided my tuition costs. A few weeks later, the dean came to the library where I was studying. He looked across the table at me and said, "Our faculty meets together once a week for an hour or so. I need someone to take notes and follow through if there is any assignment for me to do. It may take forty-five minutes, or it may take an hour or two. If you'd care to do the work, I'd be glad to give you free tuition. Don't keep track of the time; just meet with us and do whatever is needed." So, I became secretary of the faculty. *Thank God for this unexpected blessing!*

The Lord helped us financially in other ways. I had asked the OMS for a leave of absence, without pay, to do my doctoral studies. After several months, however, they wrote to say they felt led to send me sixty-five dollars per month, almost covering our eighty-five-dollar-a-month rent at 4226 Delaney Street in Cincinnati.

In the spring, near the end of the school year, the dean said, "Mr. Duewel, I'm making arrangements for this summer, and I need someone to teach child psychology the first term and adolescent psychology the second term. I'd be glad to appoint you, if you will." God not only provided my tuition the first year, but I received a modest income.

Then near the end of the summer, the dean came to me again and said, "I need an extra teacher to teach Education 101 this year. Will you be willing to teach it? In fact, I have several other classes you might teach." I told him I wanted to get back to India as soon as I finished my doctorate, but I was glad to teach one class. Education 101 had a number of sections, and I was assigned Introduction to Education, which covered my tuition the second and third years.

Psychiatry Experience

Before the second year, I told the dean that, in India, I'd have to deal with cases of demon-possession, so I'd like to take classes in psychiatry to better tell the difference between that and a psychological problem. He said he'd arrange for me to take several classes in the Graduate School of Arts and Science, without the required preliminary courses. In psychiatry, our teacher was the national president of the American Psychiatric Association. I took several classes and joined when psychiatric cases were interviewed. I was impressed by how kindly each person was treated. One man was asked his name. "You'd be surprised who I am," he said. "I am Jesus Christ." No one laughed, and the professor treated him with full respect. Another day, a man said he'd thought his girlfriend was the Holy Ghost, but he had become disillusioned after realizing she was apparently an immoral, promiscuous person.

Cases were referred to me by the county for diagnosis and testing, and one day a week a judge assigned me to examine children at General Hospital in Cincinnati. I was given background information to read before each case, and I was touched by one boy about the same age as our son.

I really prayed about this child's case the night before I met him. Psychiatrists had failed to get any proper examination because he would not cooperate with them. But before being sent to an institution, he was given this one final chance.

At our meeting, I had a ball and toy, and, as we played together, I told him I had a boy like him and asked some pertinent questions. Before our time was over, he was cooperating and happy. He was perfectly normal. I submitted a good report, the first anyone had been able to provide for him. Instead of his being institutionalized for the rest of his life, he could be placed in a normal adoptive home. God worked redemptively in the life of that young boy.

God Provided Again

God supplied our needs through many ways. One day in a faculty meeting, two of the professors talked about how much their doctorate cost them—several thousand dollars each. I sat there without any cash of my own, just the Lord. When graduation came, I found my diploma fee was one hundred dollars, but I didn't have the money. Then I received a letter from a man who had been in a service where I'd spoken some months before. His letter said, "I understand you are doing graduate study to better prepare for the mission field. Don't expect to hear from me again, but here is $100 *to help you.*" I wrote, thanking him, and never heard from him again. But God used him to supply my exact need.

When we know we're obeying God, we can depend on his supply. He led me all the way; he supplied my every need, and he deserves all the praise. I now can see how God used those three years at the university again and again in my ministry. God's plan is best! *To him be all the glory!*

Evangelical Fellowship of India

In 1951, evangelicals of various denominational backgrounds formed the Evangelical Fellowship of India (EFI). We were still on our first furlough at the time, but the preliminary formation committee meeting was held at Allahabad Bible Seminary. As soon as we returned to India, the Lord placed me in an active role with the EFI, which was functionally equivalent to the National Association of Evangelicals (NAE) in the United States. I joined in prayer, membership, and attendance at its annual conventions.

The featured speaker at its first official annual convention was American evangelist Dr. Paul Rees, and, under his encouragement, the EFI adopted "revival in the church" as its top priority. God's Spirit hovered over us during those days, and the nightly attendance at the EFI conference grew to around twelve hundred people.

Initially, the EFI was a group of some fifty denominations or missionary societies and hundreds of missionaries and Indian Christians who banded together to support the evangelical cause in India, particularly to make revival their first priority in prayer. Our united conviction was that we could not reach India for God until he visited the nation in mighty revival power.

The EFI was primarily led by Indian evangelicals, but I had the honor of serving on the executive committee, and despite my protest, I was eventually made chairman. The Indian executive secretary said, "It is not a question of nationality, missionary, or Indian. We want the person God wants, and that is you." I remained chairman from 1962 until we ended our time as missionaries to India.

In 1964, I had the privilege of giving the five evening messages at the EFI annual conference. By then, the EFI had expanded and coordinated the missionary activities of a hundred societies and denominations working throughout India. Four thousand were in attendance at those evening sessions. In 1976, as one of the founding members, I was honored to serve as their speaker for the twenty-fifth anniversary conference.

Today the EFI is stronger and more active, and its role and importance are greater than ever before. Our former coworker and ABS president, Dr. Richard Howell, then served as the EFI general secretary and provided leadership for the larger Evangelical Fellowship of Asia (EFA).

SECOND TERM (1953–1960)

When we returned to India, after I completed my doctorate at the University of Cincinnati, I was thrust into the area of teaching theology, and I discovered the former Allahabad Bible Institute's bachelor's level had been elevated to the Allahabad Bible Seminary's master's level of instruction. So, I plunged more seriously into the study of theology. During the next decade, on most days in Allahabad, I devoted three to five hours to theological study, research, and writing theological textbooks on such subjects as the Doctrine of God, the Doctrine of Creation, the Doctrine of Christ, the Doctrine of the Church, the Doctrine of Salvation, and the Doctrine of Scripture. I also wrote shorter compilations on biblical hermeneutics, revisions of introductions to books of the Bible, and more.[22]

Family Additions and Improved Conditions

Praise God that, with improved living conditions, better health care, and more encouragement in the ministry, our second term was slightly less demanding than our first. Into this much more enhanced and tranquil context came our third little gift from God, Esther Darlene, born in Allahabad on November 25, 1956.

With the birth of Darlene, and John and Chris in school at Woodstock, Betty resumed the role of caregiver and family prayer warrior. In the Old Testament, we read that King David spoke with praise of those who "stayed with the supplies," while others went down to engage in battle (1 Sam 30:24). Betty was pleased to "stay with the baby," while supporting me in ministry through prayer, as I taught and traveled far and wide.

Prem Pradhan—The Apostle Paul to Nepal

God put a prayer concern for Nepal in many OMS hearts for years. Prem Pradhan was a young Nepali Gurkha soldier serving in the Indian army and converted in Calcutta. He felt called to preach and became convinced he needed Bible training. He met one of the former students of Allahabad Bible Seminary, and we accepted him as a student in the summer of 1956.

During the two years Prem was in Allahabad, he and I often discussed his burden to reach his nation for Christ, and together we prayed repeatedly for Nepal and about how OMS could become involved and work there. He desired to identify with

Wesley, with Prem Pradhan pointing out Nepal on map

---

22 Copies of the original class notes are retained in the DLT archives.

us and have our prayer backing. We developed a simple church constitution for Nepal, calling it the Evangelical Church of Nepal (ECN), patterned after the model of our Evangelical Church of India (ECI).[23]

Prem went back to his home country to witness, and he won many Nepalese to Christ. Many of the new believers were arrested and sentenced to a year in jail, and Prem was sentenced to six years' imprisonment for having baptized them.[24] I would, however, see him later in my life.

Healing on a Train

Throughout our second term, we still had health challenges and opportunities to lean on the Lord. Once, in my Tipperary office, a room in a shed about ten feet from the house, I was trying to catch up on my work before an upcoming trip. Slowly, I became increasingly weaker, but I didn't want Betty to realize it for fear she'd object to my leaving. The trip would take eight hours by train.

She and our coworker, Elnora Hunter, walked with me down to the bus stand, and I was so sick it was hard not to show it. After I waved to them, I put my head on the back of the seat in front of me. I was almost too sick to hold my head up. When I got on the train at Dehradun that evening, my headache was so severe, and I felt so weak, that I could hardly sit erect. I asked the Lord to please have someone pray.

About nine o'clock, I suddenly felt like a human hand with a cool, wet washcloth was wiping my brow. Instantly, my headache was gone, and I began to feel perfectly well. I knew someone had prayed for me. I later received a letter from a missionary colleague in India, saying,

23 The officially recognized and registered name of the OMS-established national denomination in India was known as the Evangelical Christian Church of India, but since churches are normally associated primarily with the Christian faith, the term *Christian* was considered redundant and unnecessary. Therefore, from early on, the official name was changed to the Evangelical Church of India, or simply abbreviated as ECI. The Prem Pradhan story can be read in its entirety in the unabridged *All for Jesus* autobiography under the heading, "A Decade of Investment in the Apostle to Nepal."

24 Nepal was considered a Hindu kingdom, with laws sentencing anyone who became a Christian and was baptized to three years in prison and anyone who baptized a new convert to six years in prison.

"About 9:00 p.m. the night you left, I felt a heavy burden on my heart for you and prayed." I knew then that my colleague was the answer to my prayer, and I later wrote the poem, "I Felt Your Hand in Prayer." *Thank God for his constant-watch care!*

Witnessing on a Train

Once, I entered an overly crowded rail coach and sat on the only available seat, the edge of my portable typewriter case. Travelers with reserved space stretched out and began to sleep after 8:00 p.m. One man greeted a fellow passenger, and I wondered who he was. It turned out he was the prime minister of Madhya Pradesh in Central India, and I eventually realized all the people in my coach were members of Parliament. For about five hours, the prime minister practically lectured to the other passengers on Indian art, music, religion, comparative linguistics, and history.

A little after 9:00 p.m., he invited me to sit beside him and asked my profession. When he learned I was a theology teacher, he began to question me. From then till midnight, I had the joyous privilege of explaining the gospel to this high government official and three other members of Parliament. The latter all sat up and listened to both his questions and my answers.

I was asked: Is God immanent or transcendent? How could Christ be both human and divine? Why must there be a Holy Spirit in the Trinity? What is the difference between the Holy Spirit and man's spirit? (I soon realized that many of these questions related to the Hindu belief in pantheism.) What do Christians believe about prayer? What is the difference between Catholicism and Protestantism? What is the difference between various denominations? What is the difference between the Catholic mass and the Protestants' Lord's Supper? Why are there various missionary societies?

I testified of God's power in my life, and my heart thrilled with joy at the privilege of explaining principles concerning his kingdom to those respectful Indian leaders. Who was my interested new friend? He turned out to be the speaker of the house in the Delhi Parliament.

The next year, again and again, he used his position to intervene against anti-Christian legislation. It appeared that God had used my testimony and teaching to positively influence his life and, consequently, the lives of many other not-yet Christians.

Evangelism in the Home

A young Muslim university student appeared at our door in Allahabad one evening. His father was a Muslim *maulvi* (Islamic religious minister) and professor of philosophy at an Indian university. He was so discouraged with his life that he had decided to commit suicide. But as he passed along the street and saw the name on our gate—The Allahabad Bible Seminary—something (or Someone) compelled him to stop.

As I invited him into the guest room, he said, "Unfortunately, I have committed many sins, and they are pricking me." He went on to tell how he had seen a copy of the Gospel of Matthew but had never talked with a Christian worker. He repeatedly went to his father, asking him what he should do to find salvation and peace, but his father had always given him the same answer, "Read the Koran." He read the Koran twenty-five times! When he still found no peace, he decided there was no God and became an atheist and communist. Then, at the end of all hope, tired of all, facing futility, but still hungry of soul, he intended to commit suicide.

Me: "Do you believe a man can be saved from his sins?"

Muslim: "Yes."

Me: "Do you believe one can know, with certainty, that a person has been saved from his sins?"

Muslim: "Yes."

Me: "That is exactly why Christ came, so that we could be saved from our sins."

Muslim: "Tell me how!"

I explained to him the necessity of incarnation if we were to have an atonement provided for our sins, so that God could still be just and yet merciful to the repentant sinner. After nearly an hour with the

Bible, we knelt for prayer, and that very moment—the first time he had knelt in the name of Christ—he was saved. He testified how light and happy he felt inside. The burden and heaviness were gone.

I gave him a New Testament, and he left for his rooming house. That night, he devoured the Word of God, which was sweet food to his soul. Before he went to sleep, he had read all of Matthew, Mark, Luke, and John. The very first prayer he prayed after conversion, although he had never even seen the Old Testament, was almost word for word the wonderful verses of Psalm 40:1–3 (KJV):

> I waited patiently for the LORD; and he inclined unto me and heard my cry. He brought me up also out of an horrible pit, out of the miry clay, and set my feet upon a rock, and established my goings. And he hath put a new song in my mouth, even praise unto our God: many shall see it, and fear, and shall trust in the LORD.

The Lord witnessed to me that these verses were not merely a song of David; they were the inspired words of the Holy Spirit, which exactly depict the experience of a seeking soul anywhere in the world. I was moved to ask for prayer for the salvation of many more of India's youth.[25]

The Hindu "Holy Man"

While Betty and I were still living in Allahabad, we were thrilled to receive a phone call from Ray King. He and his wife, Yvonne, were in Delhi and wanted to come spend several days with us.

Ray was an OMS board member and the engineering consultant for our Tokyo Biblical Seminary, under construction at the time. They had received word from Japan that they were not quite ready for his visit, so they decided to take the long way around and come to India first. Visitors were rare in India, so we were happy to entertain the Kings. While they were with us, I took them for a day to Varanasi. It was an experience of a lifetime at the center of Hinduism. We rented a

---

25 Taken from an article by Dr. Duewel in "Missionaries Prayed—He Answered," compiled by Mrs. Charles E. Cowman.

small tourist rowboat used on the Ganges to view the temples from the water. Up a bank, a well-known *sadhu* (Hindu priest), who had taken a vow of silence, had been living in a hut for the past twelve years. On a previous visit, I'd told him I would bring him a New Testament in his language, Sanskrit, which is holy to them.

I said to Yvonne, "I'm taking Ray right up the bank to that hut, and you'll be able to see us. This boatman is the owner of most of the boats on the river here, and he's a friend I've known for years. You'll be quite safe here."

Her response was, "Wherever my husband goes, I go."

"You don't understand. It will be a short visit, and this famous sadhu has taken a vow of silence and never speaks to anyone. He'll be sitting in his hut on a spotted deerskin, and he won't say a word, although he'll listen to all I say. He makes sign language, which is interpreted to me by his disciple. Moreover, as part of his vow, he wears no clothing. To him, that is an expression of holiness."

She insisted, "Where Ray goes, I go."

So, I told her that was fine with me, I just didn't want her to feel offended. We climbed up the bank about a hundred feet and stepped to the door of the hut. A well-dressed man sat inside the door. He looked like a businessman, and the moment he saw us, he sprang to his feet in alarm. "Do you know this sadhu?"

"Oh, yes," I replied, "He's my friend."

The businessman relaxed and said, "I came here all the way from Calcutta, searching for peace. For three days I've been walking the streets of Varanasi, searching. Then someone told me of this famous man, so I'm just sitting at his feet now, waiting for peace."

"You don't have to go anywhere special to find peace," I said. "Jesus came into this world to give you peace."

"May I come with you to find it?"

"You can, but again, you don't need to go to any special place. Jesus can give you peace when you willfully receive him."

I turned to the sadhu and said, "Here is that book I told you I would bring." Using sign language, he pointed at me, moving his finger as if writing, to ask if I wrote it. I replied, "No. It was written nearly two thousand years ago after Jesus, the Son of God, was here on earth. It's the life story of Jesus written by four of his disciples and some important writing by other disciples."

I underlined John 3:16 in red ink and gave him the Sanskrit New Testament. Using motions, he thanked me and handed me his Sanskrit Holy Book, which I looked at briefly, then returned to him. I said, "Before I leave my friends, I always ask God to bless them, and I will now ask God to bless you." I poured out my heart in prayer in Hindi, praying for him briefly and thanking God for Jesus while praying the gospel story of Jesus's love, life, and death for us. Again, I thanked Jesus for coming to earth and giving his life for us because he loved us so much.

Using hand signs, the sadhu profusely thanked me. The business-man listened all that time. Excitedly, he asked if he could accompany me to my home so he could find peace. I explained he was welcome to come, but again, it was not a matter of being in a particular place. All he needed to do was yield his life totally to Jesus. I also gave him a Hindi-language Gospel and my own testimony written in Hindi. My testimony included how Jesus had healed my mother, how he had saved me, and how to receive personal salvation. We said goodbye and returned to the rowboat on the Ganges.

SECOND FURLOUGH (1961–1962)

We returned to the USA for our second furlough on the *RMS Queen Elizabeth*, the world's largest tourist liner. It was not as fast as the *SS United States*, but it could sail 701 miles a day with 2,700 passengers. We docked on the eastern seaboard on May 27, 1961.

FINAL TERM (1962–1964)

In late January 1962, while in Delhi, I attended the annual Republic Day parade and celebration. It was the largest annual national gathering, including a two-and-one-half-hour procession. I received a special permit to take pictures from the official photographers' stand, which was across from the president, prime minister, ambassadors, and officials from many nations. I rejoiced with the Indian people in their recently acquired freedom from Britain as I observed India's leaders, including Prime Minister Jawaharlal Nehru. The experience was deeply moving.

Most deeply moving of all was a group of several dozen wounded veterans marching near the end of the procession. Some had empty sleeves, some had only one eye, and some had artificial wooden legs. As each came by the prime minister's stand, they saluted with their arm stubs or with other symbols of the price they had paid in defending India. Tears filled my eyes as I took photographs. I, too, loved India—the land to which Jesus had called me as a child. India was my adopted motherland!

Our Children Return to Woodstock School

John, Chris, and Darlene started back to boarding school and joined the Woodstock section of a train to Landour. John, student body president, was selected to present a book report on author Pearl Buck when she visited the school. Miss Buck reportedly told the principal that her most outstanding experience was hearing John's speech. At the annual Woodstock award ceremony, Chris received a scholarship award. John, a senior at the time, received the typing award (66 wpm), an athletic letter, a scholarship award, a student government award, an all-around student award, and the salutatorian award.

On the sobering side, John also received word that he was classified 1A by the Warsaw, Indiana, Draft Registration Board, with a month to file an appeal. Since he was accepted for college, following his appeal, he received a different classification and, ultimately, a military deferment.

Mother's Triumphant Homegoing

In God's mercy, in February 1962, we received word of my mother's serious illness. I didn't know if she would be able to understand my message, but I sent a telegram that stated, "Tell her we will always seek to put God's will first regardless of the cost. Tell her that her life continues to minister through us. Tell her that though she has only one child, I am trying to live as fully for God and to love Christ as closely as I know how and that, God helping me, I shall continue to do so as long as I live."

God gave Mother seventy-five years. Wherever Father pastored, she went house to house in personal soul-winning ministry. She was a lifelong student of God's Word. At her request, in lieu of floral tributes for her funeral, an offering was taken for missions. The angels she saw at her youthful conversion were undoubtedly lingering near to escort her to the glory and joys of heaven. She had shared the ministry and love for souls with my father for fifty-one years.

In every family prayer time, Mother prayed with such longing for God to bless OMS ministry in China and elsewhere. When she prayed around the world and came to China, she always wept a heartfelt sob. In my college years, Mother prayed each day for China. She knew God had called me to India, and especially in later years, she faithfully prayed each day for OMS work there, but she never forgot China. Because of her, I learned what it was to truly carry a prayer burden.

Commonwealth Country Ministry

From our first term onward, I was assigned longer periods of ministry in the various Commonwealth countries. Apparently, God used my editing of *Revival Magazine* to open many doors in Fiji, New Zealand, and Australia. It was always my joy to minister for the Lord and OMS "down under."

Arthur Skeels, our OMS New Zealand home director, arranged intensive schedules for me. My first trip lasted thirteen days. I had the privilege of speaking thirty-nine times, an encouraging experience for me. Our New Zealand representative had many people praying. How constantly God seemed to guide! A businessman who followed me to several places said, "God is in this trip."

John Allison, our OMS Australia home director, introduced me to Sydney for a five-week itinerant ministry. I was privileged to speak in a number of Bible colleges and Bible schools in Sydney,

Melbourne, Tahlee, and Perth, as well as in Launceston, Tasmania, and ministry over local radio stations as well as the Australian Broadcasting Company. God opened many doors in Baptist and Church of Christ churches, Wesleyan and Anglican services, and Campaigners for Christ rallies. Ministry was also scheduled in Canberra, as well as in smaller cities.

Spiritual Warfare

One of the most memorable experiences was on the West Coast in Perth. One day of prayer and fasting led to the strongest prayer warfare I had ever experienced—and some of the greatest spiritual victories of my life. It was marked by God's presence, Satan's opposition, and God's glorious triumph. And it led to God's deliverance of a woman and a man from demon possession during meetings in the Scarborough Baptist Church.

God specially honored his Word there, where I spoke on communion in prayer. God was so graciously present, and I began to feel he wanted me to spend Saturday as a day of prayer. On Friday night, I told my host, the secretary of the board of deacons, not to expect me for meals on Saturday, as I had an appointment, but I would be back in time for the evening service.

On Saturday, I arose about daylight and, with my Bible, hymnbook, and notepad, I walked to the beach and found a quiet section among the trees, with no one in sight. I began with a time of intimate devotion with Jesus. I read fifty to sixty psalms, just feasting on the Word, so conscious of Jesus's presence. I began to pray for India, for God to push back and rebuke the darkness of Satan and to give us much more of a breakthrough and harvest of souls. As I prayed on and on, I began to enter into real spiritual warfare with Satan.

Then, I felt led to change my speaking topic for that night. I felt I should speak on "The Power of Satan and the Power of God." As I prepared new notes for that message, fasting and praying all day, I felt the Lord's enabling and empowering. In the late afternoon, I went back to my host's home, changed clothes, and then we left for the Saturday evening service.

As we drove along, my host asked a question. When I opened my mouth to answer, I was surprised. Not a sound came out. I was instantly puzzled that I could not speak. I was not sick, nor did I have a sore throat. I had not prayed a word aloud all day, as my prayer wrestling was in silence, and I was alone.

When we got to the church, a deacon stepped up and opened the car door for me. He spoke to me, and I moved my lips but could not make a sound. "What's the matter?" he asked. "Can't you speak?" He read my lips as I tried to explain. Then he said, "What are you going to do?" I tried to emphatically say, "I'm going to preach!" But nothing came out.

"Amen," he replied, as he read my lips.

I went straight to the pastor's office and got on my knees. When the pastor started the service, I knew I had the message God wanted me to give that night. He had put it so clearly and definitely on my heart. So, when it came time for me to preach, I stepped to the pulpit and opened my Bible to Ephesians 6:10–18.

I tried and tried, but I could not make a sound. I grasped both sides of the pulpit with my hands and strained, but I still could not make a sound! How could Satan do that to me? I did not belong to him. I was filled with the Spirit. I had spent the day fasting and praying in answer to God's definite guidance. He had given me a new message for this service. I was walking in the light and trying to obey God!

As I stood there trying with all my might to make a sound, it probably seemed longer to me than it actually was. All over the audience the people stared at me! What was going on? I didn't know. Finally, I got the first word out of my mouth. I paused, gathering my strength, and got the second word out. Slowly and with extreme difficulty, I got the words out one at a time. "For... we... wrestle... not... against... flesh... and... blood...."

I felt no sense of God's presence—all seemed dark before me. But bit by bit speaking became easier. It still required determination and physical straining to say each word, though, and I could not understand what was happening. I had been obeying God all day. I knew I had his message. There was no explanation other than God was using me to defeat Satan's strong opposition—in a very real spiritual battle.

Throughout the message, I contrasted God's strong and infinite power to defeat Satan with Satan's strong, but limited opposition. I felt no anointing, no liberty of the Spirit, no sense of the Spirit's presence. I was only trying to obey God. When I finished my message, the pastor just dismissed the service without a closing song and went to the exit to shake hands. I simply stood at the pulpit bewildered, with my head down as I prayed, "Lord, I don't understand, I don't understand!" I had tried to obey him in absolutely everything.

Suddenly, I heard a female voice call, "Brother Duewel, Brother Duewel." As I opened my eyes, I saw a small woman standing in front of the pulpit. "Yes?" I said, as I went down and stood beside her.

She said, "Six months ago I was born again, and I know I was born again. But I engaged in black magic before my conversion. Now the demons won't leave me alone! Each night when I go to bed, they gather around visibly and hoot at me!"

Never before had I experienced such spiritual resentment. Instantly, I was filled with righteous indignation. "Sister," I said, "we are going to pray right now. The devil has no right to torment you like that!" We got down on our knees, and I began to pray. Almost unconsciously I turned to Satan and rebuked him. "Satan, you have no right to this woman. She does not belong to you any longer. She belongs to Jesus now. Take your hands off her and leave her alone. In the name of Jesus, Amen."

My prayer had essentially been, "Satan leave her alone from her demon oppression" (not demon possession; Christians can be demon-oppressed, but not demon-possessed). I was so spiritually incensed at Satan that I attacked him, and him alone, forgetting that the pastor was at the front door of the church, shaking hands with the people. When I arose from my knees, I was certain Satan had his marching orders, which he would have to obey. He did, and he never bothered her again! No doubt that was why he tried to hinder my speaking.

We returned to my host's home, and I went directly to my room with some questions. Would I have a problem speaking in the morning, my final service? Would Satan bother me again the next day? How could he have an effect on my body when I was victorious in the Lord? No one chooses such encounters, but we must not run when we confront them. Rather, in the name of Jesus, we must resist Satan (James 4:7).

Sunday morning, I was still perplexed about the service the night before, and as I prayed, I was determined to save my voice for the final message God had given me. I went straight to the pastor's office when I reached the church, so no one could stop me to talk. I got on my knees and started praying silently. I thought, anyone who opens the door will not interrupt me when they see me on my knees.

After a few minutes, a young voice called, "Brother Duewel, the young people would like you to answer questions about India." I paused, asking in my heart, "Lord, what should I do?" Slowly, I responded, "All right." During the whole Sunday school hour, I gave myself to these young people, answering their questions. I knew then the victory was ours!

Behind the pulpit, I was still praying, "Please, Lord, help me! Don't let me have a problem with my voice." God gave more victory. The atmosphere of the morning service was almost heavenly! Just before the pastor introduced me, he said, "We're going to learn a new song this morning. Turn to the back page of your church bulletin." There on the bulletin was my poem, "At Jesus' Feet," which I had read when I spoke the first night! I didn't know he played an instrument, and I didn't realize he was a composer! He had composed music for my poem and began to play the organ—simple, yet beautiful music.

I had never heard one of my poems sung as a hymn! Tears filled my eyes, and I was so blessed as we sang. What a change! As I began to speak, the hand of the Lord was on me, and I felt his sweet presence (2 Kings 3:15; Ezek 3:22; 33:22). The Lord anointed me as I poured out my soul in the message. When I sat down, the pastor gave an invitation. About fifty people came forward—some to be born again, some to be filled with the Spirit, and some answering the call to the mission field. *What a blessed time!*

After the closing prayer, the pastor instructed me to go to the door, and he exhorted his people, "If you're going to pray for Brother Duewel as he goes back to India, tell him so as you shake hands." About three hundred people left through that door, and as I shook hands with them, I quickly said to each, "Pray for me."

As I reached for the hand of one man, God gave me the gift of discernment (1 Cor 12:10). I suddenly said, "Brother, God can meet your need!" Suddenly, his whole body began to vibrate. I seized his arm to steady him, and a deacon of the church took him by the other arm. I said, "Go to the pastor's office, and as soon as I finish greeting the people, I'll come to you."

Later, I knelt beside him and said, "Give the Lord your voice and tell him what you want him to do for you." He opened his mouth, and his whole body began to vibrate again. When he closed his mouth and stopped trying to pray, his body quieted down. He started to pray again, and again his whole body vibrated.

Finally, he got the words out of his mouth. "God... be... merciful to... me... a... sinner!" Instantly, he was delivered and could pray without hindrance. He was soon rejoicing in the assurance of the forgiveness of sins.

Flying back to Singapore, Calcutta, and Allahabad, I tried to catch up on mail, classwork, and various other duties. About two weeks later, a letter came from Perth, from my host, the secretary of the board of deacons of the Scarborough Baptist Church:

> Brother Duewel, the deacons want me to tell you about the man you brought to the pastor's room after the Sunday morning service. That was the husband of the woman who was delivered from demon oppression the night before. We as a board of deacons had a covenant of prayer for his salvation for six months.

Praise the Lord! No doubt the day of prayer and fasting and the struggle to speak Saturday night were all part of the price for his wife's deliverance from demon oppression and his new birth and deliverance from demon possession. I had no background on this couple whatever. I didn't need any. All I needed was the Holy Spirit's presence and power. The Holy Spirit is all we ever need. When he has us, he can take care of all the details we don't know. He is the all-sufficient One. *To God be all the glory!*

During our twenty-five years in difficult, resistant North India, we were driven to our knees again and again in spiritual warfare. We tried to establish and train our ministerial students in lives of holiness and prayer. The overwhelming spiritual darkness and comparatively fruitless ministry drove us to prayer repeatedly (and often to fasting). Again and again, we pushed back the spiritual darkness through prayer.

When I was deeply involved in prayer warfare, the battle came at God's choosing, often when I was in a series of meetings. Frequently, I felt led to set apart hours or a day for prayer and fasting. Again and again, when I felt this drawing to prayer, there was some conflict with demonic power. But out of the crucible of wrestling in prayer, God brought tremendous victories, and, on various occasions, deliverance from demonic power for others.

It happened in various countries in situations of which I knew nothing in advance, but God in his faithfulness prepared me for the spiritual battle. Although the Evil One confronted me directly and in several parts of the world, nevertheless, I hungered to know more of God's power in my personal life and his guidance in prayer. There was always so much more that needed to be learned in intercession in the whole area of guided deliverance prayer.

Evangelical Church of India

God answers prayer! What makes the difference? Massive prayer. There is no substitute for prayer, and probably no missionary work in India has all the prayer that God would like to see. But he used "mighty prevailing prayer" as a spiritual "jump-start," and he increased the momentum.

One of my early students, Ezra Sargunam, went on to become bishop and to lead the Evangelical Church in India (ECI) in visionary church planting. There's no doubt in my mind that the ECI grew rapidly as an answer to prayer, with the aid of more than seventy evangelistic church planting teams, each with four to six young Indian men evangelizing in an area. In the beginning, it was often slow work, and it could take six months, a year, or even longer before a small church was raised up. But prayer is the spearhead of the initial thrust that opens hearts and minds. In my later years, when I've heard reports

Ezra Sargunam, church director, with ECI Church Growth Graph

about the ECI, I've been thrilled to learn that in many of those cities for which the great host of prayer warriors originally prayed every day, the Lord raised up local ECI churches.[26] *To God be all the glory!*

Today, the ECI as a denomination ministers in multiple language areas in India and operates ten regional Bible schools in addition to three degree-granting seminaries. The three seminaries use English for instructional purposes and, therefore, can train people from other sections of India.[27] The regional Bible schools teach in the regional language and train primarily for their own area, with a shorter course of two or three years. The ECI has even launched their own Indian Missionary Movement (IMM) with over eight hundred indigenous

---

26 Denominational statistics report that the ECI has 8,330 permanent local churches and 14,410 house churches. As such, it is the largest national church ever established by OMS! ECI trains church planters both in formal and informal theological education through our thirteen Bible schools in different parts of India (*The Church Planter*, December 2019).

27 ABS teaches in two linguistic tracks, English and Hindi.

missionaries supported from their own established congregations, serving primarily unreached (northern) tribal groups.

3
The Vice Presidency Years

When our family returned to the USA on furlough in 1964, we expected a normal year. However, I did not sleep a wink between New Delhi and Los Angeles. My heart was crying before the Lord, as I prayed over and over, "Where are the souls? Where is the harvest?" We had poured out our lives and tried to ground our students in holiness of heart and lives of prayer. We had scheduled holiness emphasis events and days of prayer. We had fasted and prayed. Over and over, I cried, "Oh, God, where is the harvest You sent us to reap? How can we get a breakthrough? How can we reap the harvest? Surely You want us to have more fruit than this, Lord. What more can we do? How can we see the harvest?" Tears were in my heart almost all the way.

After twenty-five years, OMS India, which was a small missionary group, had started three Bible seminaries in three language areas, and national coworkers had graduated from each seminary. The result of our years invested was twenty-five churches with fifteen hundred baptized believers. Surely God was expecting much more than that!

Between Honolulu and Los Angeles, I prayed, "Oh, Lord, give us one thousand people who will commit to pray fifteen minutes a day for at least one year, specifically for our OMS India work!" I prayed that over and over until my heart was at rest. Throughout that year of travel, I shared that challenge with those who gathered, and ultimately God gave nearly fifteen hundred people in America, the British Isles, and South Africa to take on that commitment. That was just a portion of what the Lord had in store for us that furlough period. *Praise his name!*

SURPRISE REASSIGNMENT (1964)

We arrived in Los Angeles and attended worship on Sunday, and then the OMS board executive committee meetings began Monday. First Vice President Dr. Bill Gillam had experienced a sudden period of illness, and at the executive committee meetings, we were urged to intercede for him. As we got up from our knees, someone said, "While we were praying, I felt impressed that Wesley should stay home at headquarters and help lift the load."

It seemed everyone in the meeting had received the same impression, although to my knowledge, nothing had been suggested earlier—nor had I sensed anything unusual or unique before, during, or following that prayer time. But I was glad to help in any way possible. I had already booked a number of weeks of public speaking engagements in the British Isles, but I offered to cancel the rest of my scheduled furlough appointments in the States following my appointments in the British Isles, if that would help lift the headquarters burden.

Initial Deputation Commitments

After several camp meetings in the USA, I was off to the British Isles for a busy two months of wonderful conventions and various meetings. The meetings ranged from small ones in godly homes of Spirit-filled intercessors to the World-Wide Missionary Conference, the International Revival Convention, and meetings at the office of World Evangelical Fellowship (WEF). God's presence, guidance, and blessings attended those meetings, and we realized how much we depended upon all our partners' prayers. Never had we been more conscious of the Spirit's guidance, anointing, and yearnings!

Those were precious days of watching the Spirit work! The crowd filled the aisles in one church, and the Spirit came in holy awe. Young children and older folks alike vowed to pray in a new way. In a little home group of hardly two dozen loyal, loving, attentive people, nearly half of them pledged to pray fifteen minutes daily for souls and revival across India and for our OMS ministry. Almost all the members of another church came forward to give themselves to God for souls. Thirty or more people stood before the pulpit—many weeping, each taking some new step of commitment for missions. The hand of God came so mightily that altars were lined with people taking definite new steps of obedience and surrender for God and his missionary cause. Many wept or had hours of counseling, with questions about the Spirit-filled life, the challenge of missions, or opposing demonic powers. It felt like we were standing on holy ground. A businessman spent much of the night weeping. He called from his firm, weeping over the phone, while customers and staff stood around him. God had broken his heart for the needs of the world.

Divine inspiration came for many verses and poems as I lingered on my knees in evangelist John Wesley's tiny prayer room. While kneeling in the home of John Knox, who prayed, "Give me Scotland or I die," God's anointing seemed so real. I preached and prayed in the chapel begun by the converts of the Welsh revival. In the home of the famous Welsh evangelist, Evan Roberts, a portion of his Bible was given to me. Bowing in an old Moriah Chapel beside two of the original converts from that great 1904 Wales revival, we pleaded for new revival around the world and on the OMS fields around the world. What hallowed prayer times![1]

Darlene's Life-Threatening Accident and Miraculous Healing

In October, I was in the British Isles when Satan attacked in the midst of all this—plunging our seven-year-old Darlene to within minutes of death. I was awakened early one morning by a long-distance call from Dr. Bradford Steiner, a close friend and former family doctor in India, now in the States, who reported that Darlene had been in an accident at home. Her left arm was seriously cut.

Darlene's playmate accidentally banged the window, and the old glass shattered (not safety glass as is common today). Shards struck

---

1   Evan Roberts was a famous Welsh evangelist in the early 1900s involved in many revivals around the world.

Darlene's arm above and below the elbow, severing the main artery and severely cutting the muscles in her arm. Blood began spurting profusely. Panic-stricken, her playmate ran down the street to tell her mother. Darlene ran into the front yard and collapsed, and the pastor next door summoned an ambulance.

Dr. Steiner was on duty in the emergency room. Darlene was in shock, near death from the loss of blood. His love for her, and her grave condition, intensified his emergency actions of repeated blood and plasma transfusions. A vascular surgeon performed the delicate surgery Darlene needed. He repaired the muscles but was unable to repair the artery, and the danger of infection was imminent. Darlene's hand was cold from lack of circulation. It seemed impossible to save her arm.

Immediately, I placed long-distance calls to our Belfast, Manchester, and Glasgow offices and sent letters to our four India areas, pleading for prayer. I longed to be at my daughter's bedside, yet it was impossible to leave immediately. I poured out my heart. Within hours, as word of the accident spread, worldwide prayer support was rallied for Darlene. The OMS Los Angeles office alerted all Prayer Circles, and God answered.

Like a ray of light in the dark, Darlene's life had been spared by a chain of divine providences. The doctor judged that, otherwise, she would have died in three more minutes from loss of blood. A train held up traffic for fifteen minutes, delaying Betty on her way to the hospital, but the ambulance had already crossed the train tracks. The vascular surgeon was in the emergency room only occasionally, but that was his day to be there. His skill was of utmost importance.

Family portrait, Cincinnati, OH, circa 1961

After many transfusions, Darlene's arm grew warm and was saved. Five days later, she was dismissed from the hospital with no infection, but there was also no prognosis as to the future use of her arm. The non-believing surgeon said, "I'd say ten percent of the result is from medical care and ninety percent from prayer." Use of her fingers and circulation in her arm all improved, but the main concern was her index finger, which the specialist said was "defunct." It was unclear whether that meant she might lose its use or lose it through amputation.

When I received further word about Darlene's condition on October 26, the cast was off. She could move her arm some, and she was beginning to pick up things a bit with her hand. She couldn't go back to school for a couple of months, but she made steady progress, and indications were that the use of all her fingers would be restored, as God's healing continued. Therapy treatments strengthened her muscles.

Tearful neighbors referred to Darlene as the "miracle girl." All who prayed knew they were not hampered by distance, and God graciously answered the many, many prayers lifted on her behalf. *To God be all the glory*!

The Importance of Faithful Intercessors

God placed a special prayer burden on the heart of one of our praying friends in Southport, England. She knew nothing of the reason but felt so burdened to pray that she got out of bed and prayed specially for my family. I have no doubt that lady's faithful intercession helped make the life-and-death difference for Darlene.

While on my trip in the British Isles, a woman who was a stranger to me said, "For the past eighteen years, I have been praying every day for you and your wife, Betty. I recognize you from your picture in *The Missionary Standard*." Here I was, a missionary from India—riding on a bus in Northern Ireland—and a complete stranger was telling me this!

A similar incident occurred while I was shopping in a Woolworth store. A lady stepped up and told of her prayers for us. On another occasion, after a service in Australia, a lady said, "I want to tell you that for years God has been waking me at 4:00 a.m. every morning to pray for you." From friends in New Zealand, America, and Canada came many assurances that our lives and labors were being supported by prayer. Think of coming from a pulpit to be greeted with, "Oh brother, how wonderful to see in the flesh the one for whom I have been praying for so long!"

Later, an elderly lady with tear-filled eyes took my hand and said, "You are my missionary! You are my missionary! I've been praying for you for years!" We yearned for those prayers. Yet, we often felt we didn't merit such gracious intercession when so many national workers who desperately needed constant intercession had so few to pray for them. It was a humbling experience to meet those choice saints.

THE LAUNCH OF WORLD INTERCESSORS (1965)

At the request of the OMS board, our family moved to Los Angeles so I could assist in headquarters administration during the remainder of our furlough. I settled in at the Los Angeles office and I began my duties. The board meetings in Los Angeles and Winona Lake that summer were memorable times. I felt inadequate for the responsibility thrust upon me, but I did my best during that furlough period.

As 1965 was about to begin, I praised the Lord for all his goodness during the past year. I praised him for letting us see another new year. I prayed that the upcoming year might be the time of his miraculous answers to my deepest prayers. My heart ascended to God for my beloved ones and, as the new year dawned, John and I sat in the living room talking and watching TV till 1:30 a.m.

That first week of the new year, I felt the Lord's nearness in a very precious way. I thanked him for the dark places he brought into my life—the darkness of loneliness, the darkness of battle, the darkness of unanswered prayer. He meant more and more to me, and I knew that someday I would rejoice in the light of communion, in the light of major victories, and in the light of glorious answers to my deepest prayers. *Praise his name!*

His love seemed so wonderful, so precious, and so unspeakable! I thanked God for my office, where undisturbed, I could be alone and commune with Him—my Beloved, the One so altogether lovely to me. I was confident that when he saw fit, he would bring me forth into the light of answered prayers. I praised his wonderful name! The Lord also gave me three more poems: "Let All the People See," which was my prayer for more of his glory and power and seal upon us; "Oh, Love of God," reveling in his wonderful love; and "Perfect that Which Concerneth Us," my prayer for God to bring his guidance and workings into our lives and into the place of his plan. I believed the Lord would complete that which he had begun—he would perfect that which concerned us. I knew he could not fail. *Praise him! Praise him! Praise HIM!*

My heart seemed to leap for joy whenever I could slip alone with the Lord into the living room of our home. He inspired me to write the poems, "Let Naught Else Defeat Thy Will" and "Intervene by Pow'r Divine," my prayer for God to do that on our behalf. When I moved to the living room alone, almost as if to meet a lover, the Lord's love seemed so precious, real, and joy-giving. Another poem flowed forth, "Alone with Jesus." How good God was! He was flooding my heart to overflowing. I yearned for his answers to soon dawn upon us. I knew he does all things well. *Praise his wonderful name!*

Starting a week of USA deputation meetings, I felt almost desperate as there was so little time for preparation on messages. Administrative responsibilities kept filling my time, and I had only two preparation days. But again, God helped me. One evening, I felt so surrounded with loving prayer and such a precious nearness that the plan for my messages came easier, and I felt so much more of the Lord's help. Thank God for the reality of loving prayer! I knew the difference it makes; I felt it. I wanted to share it more and more deeply in his will.

I experienced many times of deep longing and hunger for God to work. And wherever he opened the door and arranged my time, he was at work. In all my life, that week stood out as one of the most outstanding spiritually. How I loved massive, extensive reading in God's Word! It built a reserve for the hours and ministries God would incorporate into our lives. There was such close and precious fellowship throughout that time in his Word, regardless of the venue.

Prayer Circle Convention

In March, I flew to Wichita, Kansas, to attend an OMS Prayer Circle convention. Mrs. Yvonne King would be sharing there. When her part in the program came, she told of her and her husband's trip to India. First, she told about how, as we climbed the steps to the Nepali temple, a Hindu priest saw me and nearly shouted, "Your God answers prayer. Look at me. I was dying. You prayed for me, and now I am a well man!" I had indeed prayed for him a month earlier, while showing a visiting minister the aspects of Hindu worship. That priest had been lying on his deathbed, but I prayed for God's mercy on him, and our good and gracious God heard and spared his life—and that priest knew it!

Then Mrs. King told a story I shared with you earlier. Of course, she told it from her perspective. "I want to tell you about the time I felt more of God's presence than I ever had before in my life," she said. "It was not at a camp meeting. It was not in a Communion service. It was not in a prayer meeting or a church service. It was in Benares, India, in a mud hut on the bank of the Ganges. Dr. Duewel was talking and praying with a Hindu holy man who did not have on a stitch of clothing, and who usually didn't say a word out loud, but was being told the gospel. When Dr. Duewel prayed, I felt the whole hut was filled with the glory of God!" When I testified and prayed for that Hindu holy man in the Hindi language, though Yvonne understood nothing, she felt surrounded by the presence of God. *To God be all the glory!*

Back at Headquarters

I was asked to organize and chair the administrative committee meetings during Dr. Eugene Erny's absence. First Vice President Bill Gillam and Treasurer Les Ike were very positive and supportive about God using me in chairing this committee. Unexpectedly, as we came out of one of the meetings, I was asked to speak in chapel. There, God helped in a special way, and there were tears in the eyes of several coworkers and staff members, followed by a tremendous prayer time.

In mid-March, after speaking at Rees Memorial Church in Pasadena, I flew to Canada for the Hillcrest Bible College Missions Convention. While there, I received a telephone call from John regarding his desire to travel to Selma, Alabama, to support the civil rights protesters. After a considerable time of prayer, I talked to Brother Redpath of Greenville College and gave my permission for John to go.[2]

In April, Darlene had further surgery on her fingers and arm to repair the damage from the accident. By June, she had recovered enough to have her cast removed. Today, Darlene is the mother of two adult sons, and anyone who meets her never knows her life was saved through timely intercessory prayer lifted heavenward by people who had no idea their call to prayer made all the difference! They were linked to God's power, and through their prayers the impossible was achieved in Darlene's life. Prayer is always the path to miracles! *Thank the Lord, there is nothing too hard for Jesus. God is the same yesterday, today, and forever!*

Expanding the Circle of Fellowship

That same month, I represented OMS at the annual Christian Holiness Association (CHA) meetings, with wonderful and enriching experiences. We heard many great messages, and God orchestrated my days and scheduled my time with CHA leaders and others. He refreshed me so, and I hungered and hungered for more of his anointing. God seemed so near. I attended a meeting at the Bethany Fellowship in Minneapolis, Minnesota, where there was also a strong anointing.

---

2   From diary entry, March 18, 1965. Editor's Note (Mrs. Hilda Duewel, 2020): "John was at Greenville College in Illinois and requested parental permission to go with a group of students to Alabama for a civil rights march. A Greenville College administrator/professor called Wesley, and he gave his consent for John to participate. Over the years, the family greatly respected Wesley for giving this consent." It obviously meant a lot, since John Wesley recounted this incident on the occasion of his father's funeral service on March 15, 2016, found in *All for Jesus: A Celebration of the Life and Ministry of Dr. Wesley L. Duewel*, 30–32.

Then came the Evangelical Fellowship of Mission Agencies (EFMA) meetings, and we enjoyed great spiritual fellowship with mission leaders. I was amazed at what automatic fellowship I enjoyed with leaders of various groups, almost unaware of denominational distinctives, for in Christ, we were one! We shared his vision, bound together by his fellowship, and life seemed so full of hope and meaning. It was as though we had known of one another long before we actually met. We were brothers in Christ.

A former friend from India, Dr. Henry Starmers, took me to Northwestern School, where we enjoyed fellowship together, just as we had in India. Fellowship was also renewed with my former GBS roommate and best man at our wedding, Dick Appel, who twenty-five years later was now Secretary of Church Extension for the Pilgrim Holiness Church. *Praise the Lord!*

Prayer Warriors

One day at headquarters, coworkers Bill Gillam and Alice Huff asked for my opinion about the Prayer Circle department of OMS— whether I liked the name and so on. I had never liked the name, because I thought the word *circle* implied something primarily for women, and we needed a broader, more inclusive name. Their follow-up question was raised: "Well, what would be a good name?" Almost instantly, the name "World Intercessors" was decided upon. Ultimately, the administrative committee assigned me as international director for the World Intercessors department.

"Prayer warriors" were encouraged to make a commitment to pray once a day, pausing at noon for this special prayer time for the following four items: world harvest, revival, missions, and particularly OMS. Many people around the world made that prayer covenant. More than a thousand were raised up in South Africa, and others were raised across the USA, Britain, Canada, and the OMS fields—Japan, Korea, and elsewhere—through the cooperation of various OMS leaders.

Balancing Responsibilities

Every weekday morning was busy with many office duties: signing letters, revising copy for a new prayer tool called the *Intercesso-gram*, dictating various memos and letters, and double-checking committee meeting minutes. In the evenings, I was working on a "Prayer Army" list, doing more office work, and praying for God's guidance and anointing on the development of World Intercessors.

During administrative committee meetings, Bill Gillam urged the executive committee to make a decision about my permanent assignment no later than the coming December. The committee agreed that he and I were both needed and that I must remain at headquarters preparing for whatever our roles would be when Dr. Erny retired the next year. Bill recommended I pack up and dispose of our personal belongings in India. OMS treasurer, Les Ike, agreed and said succession planning must begin—regardless of what roles anyone would fill.

The Week of Decision

I longed for no appointments other than what God wanted me to have, for no special prominence, only for God to use me as he desired and to give me the fellowship I desperately needed. I asked him to let me hide out of sight, if that would please him, but oh, I longed to be more used by him, to be more pleasing to him, to have more of his power and more sacred fellowship. That was what mattered above all. I pleaded for God to hear my cry!

Elected as Second Vice President

Because I had continually expressed our desire to go back to India, there was some slight disagreement within the executive committee. Dr. Erny was of a split opinion, feeling that I was needed both at headquarters and in India. Others felt I should not plan to go back to India.

The morning of the board meeting where the decision would be made, I made a simple statement. It was a summary of what I had initially written to the board, of my call and love for India. I said that if they left the decision to me, I would go back to India, but I would accept any decision they made. The board invited me to leave the room while they discussed my appointment. It was the hour for God to act! I needed him to put his seal on whatever decision they made. I longed for him to speak to them and through them. I had no desire of my own, except longing to be more used by God. I paced the floor calling out to him. He knew the context of my hunger, and he knew the aspects of my need and plea. My heart cried out, "Father, the hour is come. Glorify Yourself."

After some time, I was called back into the room. They told me that although they felt I was much needed in India, I was even more needed at headquarters and that God's anointing had been on my work there. Despite my pleas with God and my protests before the committee, they elected me as second vice president. Bill Gillam continued as first vice president and Dr. Erny was reelected OMS president for at least one more year. So in addition to serving as the nonresident field director for India and as the international director of World Intercessors, I was to assume the unknown responsibilities of second vice president. The board said the World Intercessors prayer movement might mean a thousand times as much to India as my returning personally! And so, I was reassigned to live and work out of our mission headquarters in Los Angeles.

They had special prayer for my coworker, Dale McClain, and me, and Bill Gillam was moved to tears as he prayed. Many participants said there was an unusual sense of God's presence.

After that, any of my spare time was given to the promotion of World Intercessors, but I was constantly so loaded with administrative duties that my productivity was severely hampered.

A New Anointing

About this same time, I met an evangelist who told me how he and his wife met together and prayed hours for me. He recounted that, one time when they were together in prayer for me, my life, and my work, it suddenly seemed like a disk of light settled down on them. They believed the glory of God had come on them as they prayed for me, and subsequently, they spent the entire night in prayer.

As we prayed together, I felt God must make us opportunity-conscious, responsibility-conscious, world-conscious (that is, for the whole world), Holy Spirit power–conscious, and prayer-conscious. Within my spirit, I prayed, "Oh may God come upon OMS, and may we rise to the full stature to which he calls us."

I felt God's anointing all day long; he kept me surprisingly fresh. And perhaps as a result of that couple's prayers, God gave me eight new articles in a series of Bible studies on holy warfare, which could be used in *Revival Magazine* or elsewhere.

The Burden to Write

The previous year, the board had given me an assignment to prepare an OMS theological statement. I'd felt impressed by the Spirit to devote all my spare time working on the booklet about the Doctrine of Holiness and felt God had especially helped me. However, as I progressed on the project, I felt clearly that I should present it to a wider public to help people have the definite experience of grace. It might be published by an evangelical publisher other than the OMS and have an outreach among non-holiness people. That would make it more effective, particularly in Australia and New Zealand, where they were begging for a clear theological statement. Eventually, the Lord helped me finish a small pamphlet, "Be Ye Filled with the Spirit," which became a mimeographed forty-three-page booklet, "Be Filled with the Spirit." I prayed that the Lord would use it for his glory, and we produced 150 copies.[3] Dr. Erny strongly approved of it, saying it was the right approach, without a lot of *shibboleths* and without compromise. He suggested it should have a chapter on gifts of the Spirit, especially tongues, and a chapter on the Holy Spirit and missions.

---

3   Dr. Duewel's book, *More God, More Power*, published by Zondervan in 2000, was based on the original mimeographed copy, "Be Filled with the Spirit."

HEADQUARTERS MOVE FROM LOS ANGELES (1965)

For ten or fifteen years, there had been an increasing concern that OMS should move from its Los Angeles location in Hollywood to a place more centrally located to our constituents. Our focus centered on three possible locations: Atlanta, Indianapolis, and Kansas City. At the Winona Lake convention in 1963, information was received about a possible location near Indianapolis, owned by Mary Gillam's brother and family—the Thompsons. A committee of five laymen—Enloe Wallar, J. Byron Crouse Sr., Ray King, W. L. Smith, and Lee Jeffries—drove to Greenwood, and then returned to the Winona Lake convention to report their recommendations.

When the men had visited the property, they had a prayer meeting on their knees in the pasture near an old farmhouse. They sensed such a witness in their hearts that this was God's place and time that they went straight to the National Bank of Greenwood. They had not been authorized to negotiate on behalf of OMS, but they pooled money from their own pockets to make a down-payment on the property of ten thousand dollars.

Relocation to Greenwood, Indiana

We left Los Angeles in 1965, traveling with Joyce Toombs Wall (wife of Evan Wall), who was Eleanor Burr's secretary and who helped as my part-time secretary. With Joyce and me both driving, we decided to travel nonstop.

When I wasn't at the wheel, I prayed. I longed so for God to give me a new anointing as I entered this new phase of my ministry. For the first time in my life, my goal was not life and service in India. It was difficult to adjust to that thought, and I would need God's provision if I was to fulfill his purpose. I determined to put prayer first, with India still a strong focal point. I asked God to give me a secretary[4] of like spirit to share understanding and prayer burdens, or I would feel

---

4   Miss Patti Nofziger arrived in Los Angeles, from Oregon, shortly before our move to Greenwood, and came across country with us. She served as Wesley's secretary until April 1968, when she returned to Oregon for her

alone in that new ministry. I would need to put a deep emphasis on constant prayer, intercession, and revival, to live for and in them in a new way. *What a tremendous responsibility!*

Betty, Darlene, and I arrived in Greenwood in December, several weeks before the rest of OMS moved from Los Angeles. John was still in college in Greenville, Illinois, but by this time Chris had switched to the university in Madison, Wisconsin. We reached Ormiso[5] Heights, the new OMS headquarters campus, two days after leaving Los Angeles. How good God was to give us such a safe, speedy trip with no trouble whatever. Chris arrived at noon from Wisconsin, and she was happy to be with us in Greenwood. The next day, John arrived, and we enjoyed a meal together. We talked and talked till about 3:00 a.m.

The campus was still under construction, with two or three houses almost completed. We used one of them over Christmas, sleeping on the floor until we acquired furniture. Cindy Williamson lived in the original farmhouse for weeks until a house trailer was placed on the grounds. One end was used for our OMS office, and she lived in the other end. We slept on mattresses on the floor, stuffed rags and newspapers in the garage doors to make them more airtight, and wore winter clothing—sometimes coats or overcoats. For some weeks, I worked in the garage, which doubled as the office until our house on campus was ready for us.

Temporary Offices at Winona Lake

OMS held its annual convention at Winona Lake each year from 1944 through 1969, and a property for a regional office was secured there. During our 1958–1959 furlough, we lived at Winona Lake, renting rooms from the Free Methodist Youth Department leader and staying in the basement when not representing OMS on weekends.

---

marriage to Keith Wonderly. Later, they together served in the Audio-Video Department in Greenwood.

5 *Ormiso* came from the first two letters of each word in the full name Oriental Missionary Society given to the Greenwood campus headquarters and was used in the era of telegram communication.

One Sunday morning was free, however, so we attended the Free Methodist Church just a few blocks from their World Ministries Center. They were having revival services. One of their leaders was the evangelist, and the song leader was Robert Andrews. After the service, the song leader came to me and said, "Brother Duewel, you will never know what that night meant to me." I could not remember what he was talking about.

Free Methodist Church Connection

On our previous furlough, I had represented OMS at a camp meeting in Illinois, where I was assigned to room with a young man named Robert Andrews. That cottage had an adjoining room, and when we explored, we found an inexpensive, empty coffin. We talked and prayed together that night around the coffin. I forgot about it, but he said that night became a turning point in his life. *Praise the Lord!*

While enrolled in Greenville College, Robert was the student representative in the summertime. He asked, "Where do you plan to send your children to college?" I told him I had no plans and explained that OMS had no college in the States, nor did the small denomination of which I was a member.

"Why don't you send them to Greenville College, the Free Methodist School in Illinois?" he said. When I replied that I didn't know how much money I would have available, he said, "Oh, Greenville College gives a discount to the children of missionaries, regardless of denomination."

That early contact, years ago, had eventually led to first John, and then Chris (initially) enrolling there. Over the years, Robert Andrews became the radio voice each week for the Free Methodist Church and was much used of the Lord. Eventually, he was even elected bishop of the church—Bishop Robert Andrews. Our connection with the Free Methodist Church started while OMS was using Winona Lake as our regional headquarters.

THE NEW HEADQUARTERS LOCATION (1966)

Praise God from whom all blessings flow! How good God had been that past year; how near he seemed as I entered the new year. How faithful he was to us. My heart just overflowed with praise to him. I don't know when a New Year's Day made me feel so full of praise to the Lord. Oh, that it would mean his answers were very, very near! Praise his name! Praise him for such a precious nearness! I praised him for what he would bring to pass. The new year was in some respects a new stage in my life. I was now permanently assigned to the homeland. Nothing mattered as much as pleasing God, giving joy to him, and fulfilling his purpose for my life. I prayed that he would bring about the conditions that would help bring his purpose in my life to the fullest extent possible.

Challenges in the Move

The headquarters staff in Los Angeles started the new year working, loading office equipment on a plane headed for Indianapolis and, for the staff, driving across country. Soon they were able to start receipting donations again. Since the administration building was not quite ready, a building at the corner of Main and Madison in Greenwood was rented for the office cashiers. We were so short of funds that we needed every dollar to support construction operations. The new headquarters building construction planning, for instance, had to be wisely conducted.

Rev. and Mrs. Louis Duewel Memorial Prayer Chapel

As a society, OMS exists by prayer, and we depend utterly on God through prayer! So, we wanted a prayer chapel, and we felt it should be central, on the main floor, and just inside the entrance, to indicate prayer was foremost and central to OMS.

Various people funded memorials in honor of someone, and as second vice president, I longed to fund that prayer room in honor of my godly, praying parents. I ventured to trust God to enable me to do it. God provided, and the prayer chapel was constructed and dedicated in memory of Rev. Louis and Mrs. Ida Duewel, documented with a small plaque inside the room.

First Overseas Trip

In mid-February, the board was called into session, and executive committee meetings were held all morning long, adopting many motions. In the absence of Les Ike, I served as secretary. A trip to Korea for me was approved, and Dr. Erny suggested I should be gone no longer than five weeks. He wanted me to spend three days in Hong Kong, two weeks in Korea, and about a week each in Taiwan and Japan. Executive Vice President Dick Capin did not want me gone too many months, but as a former missionary to Korea, he heartily approved of the Korea trip. I wished also to visit India, especially to sort through and pack our belongings still there, but I thought that visit impossible until later.

Dick said I was the only one on the committee who used a businessman's approach to administration. Often when he felt he was not getting his ideas across, my restatements seemed to help the committee understand and accept them. He said he thought I had a moderating influence.

We developed a fruitful reciprocal working relationship, and he shared with me his testimony of how the Lord helped him get his CPA certification through the many difficult experiences and exams. As he shared, he was moved to tears and several times could not speak for several minutes. He said I was the first OMS missionary to whom he had given this testimony. I assured him that he was God's gift to OMS and that I felt God gave us to one another to complement each other in the ways the Society needed. He was very, very appreciative.

Still wishing I could go to India on this first overseas trip as second vice president, I prayed much about including a visit there, but I left it in God's hands. Treasurer Les Ike mentioned it would be only two hundred dollars more and favored the idea. While I was away in mid-March, traveling through the South, the administrative committee approved a stopover in India.

This change would cause me to reach the great subcontinent around mid-May, at earliest, placing my visit during the very hot season. But I wanted to spend a day in Calcutta and perhaps a day or two in Varanasi. I would need at least a week or ten days in Allahabad. I also wanted to spend a day in Delhi and perhaps make a trip up to Landour for a day of fellowship, prayer, and committee time. I planned to be back in Greenwood for the executive committee meeting scheduled for early June, if possible.

My first stop was Japan. Upon arriving, I felt God gave unusual anointing, and I felt that anointing throughout the visit. The long-time Japan Holiness Church (JHC) general superintendent, Rev. Akiji Kurumada,[6] said he had read my articles in *Revival Magazine* for years, but this was the first time he heard me preach. God's tremendous anointing moved me and others to tears at times. Several missionaries said they believed my time was planned by God. Many Japanese leaders were moved by the challenge of World Intercessors.

By the end of my visit, Miss Hirjoku (aka Hiroko Ito), Brother Washio Yamazaki, and several other Japanese coworkers had made commitments to launch World Intercessors throughout northern, central, and southern Japan among the JHC membership.

From there, the Lord carried me on to Seoul, where all the OMS missionaries greeted me, as well as several church leaders, including General Secretary Rev. M. C. Li, and President Li Jin-Woo. The Korean church hosted a very nice reception. They asked many questions about India, Hinduism, and demonic power. That evening, we enjoyed an informal gathering at Ed and Nanoo Kilbourne's home on the OMS

---

6   Kurumada Sensai was a sixteen-year-old telegraph operator when he was converted in an English evangelism class led by E. A. Kilbourne. He later became a professor at the Bible Training Institute. He was a leader of those who stood against Nakada in the 1930s when Nakada got into Japanese Israelism. He was imprisoned by the government during World War II. After the war, he led a group of pastors who withdrew from the Kyodan (United Church) that had been formed under government pressure before the war. He was general superintendent for many years and continued to pastor until he was nearly one hundred years old. He died in 1987. [David Meek, former OMS Japan field director, June 12, 2020].

campus, answering several hours of questions about the new head-quarters property in Greenwood.

I was briefed by the OMS Korea field committee on developments in Korea over the past two years. "Uncle Bud" Kilbourne led us to a seminary chapel service with about two hundred students. A real, *tremendous* volume of prayer arose among the attendees; one could almost feel the vocal reverberation. My prayer was that it would be the beginning of all God accomplished in those days.

We drove to the Han River tent church, which was then a central group, after the river washed away their former church area. Four churches grew out of that tent church, with about 150 people in regular attendance.

Another church was packed, with some standing and over a thousand people in attendance. The evening worship service was jammed with benches squeezed in beyond capacity, a packed balcony, and full aisles, with many standing outside. What a thunderous, lengthy prayer was offered at the conclusion! Then we sang, "Fill Me Now." Never had I heard it sung with such gusto and volume. Many were exclaiming, "Amen! Hallelujah!"

A nice letter of encouragement arrived from Bill Gillam, which informed me I had been elected to the executive committee of the Evangelical Fellowship of Mission Agencies to represent the Holiness block of missions. Bill added, "Wesley, your life is such a blessing to me and to all of your colleagues in OMS. I praise God he has put you in the place of leadership at this time, for such a strategic moment."

At the conclusion of the general conference in Korea, a mighty volume of prayer erupted like thunder. The Lord was very near and real, melting hearts. People were weeping and praying in the seats. Some said they were so stirred that they had not been able to sleep for hours the previous night. Some came with faces aglow but could not express how deeply they were stirred. I praised the Lord for putting the burden for organized, concentrated prayer on the people's hearts. I was convinced the Lord truly blessed my trip to Korea.

From Korea, I returned to Japan, thrilled to hear the report about how God had been using Miss Ito, who expressed such a burden for World Intercessors. She had returned to her church and organized a World Intercessors group there, and she was writing letters to Christians in different parts of Japan to put World Intercessors on their hearts.

We flew to Taichung, Taiwan, then went as far as Hsin Chu by train, to a local church, where Jonathan Cheng was pastor and Paul Hsiao (pronounced *Shaow*) from the seminary served as the interpreter. We continued to the Taiwan Holiness Church campus for the midweek prayer meeting, where again the idea of our responsibility and the role of World Intercessors was introduced.

Before leaving Taiwan, my coworker and good friend Ed Erny encouraged me to set aside three months a year for writing. I never forgot his counsel, although I did not realize at the time how prophetic it would turn out to be in my life and ministry.

During my brief layover in Hong Kong, I again presented World Intercessors. I flew to Rangoon, Myanmar, and then on to Calcutta. It was great to be back in India. It felt like home. While in Tipperary with other missionaries, I shared the story of Darlene's accident and her miraculous healing, our move to Indianapolis, the development of World Intercessors, the special India prayer fellowship, and the Lord's working recently in Korea and Japan.

God let me celebrate my fiftieth birthday while in India. I prayed he would begin to use my life more fully than ever before. I hungered for him to crowd much more into my life in my remaining years than he had been able to do thus far—more of blessing, anointing, guidance, usefulness, and joy to him. How I wish I could have spent much of the day in prayer!

In Allahabad, I spent significant time sorting and packing my family's personal belongings to be sent back to the States. I departed from Delhi the end of the first week of June, flying through Karachi, Pakistan; Beirut, Lebanon; and then Jerusalem by morning.

The next day, in England, we began the first meeting of our British board of trustees. Norman Dudgeon invited me to lead in devotions and chair the meeting, and we discussed the World Intercessors program. We also had a wonderful prayer fellowship, with nearly fifty people in attendance that evening. Ethel Dudgeon had tears in her eyes when we said goodbye on the morning of my departure. Norman was thankful I had come and said how much it meant to them. They wanted me to come back to Britain the next year, if at all possible.

Back at Headquarters

After I'd had an overnight rest at home, Dick Amos and I started out at noon for our annual OMS retreat in Mishawaka, Indiana, which preceded our convention at Winona Lake. Soon after arriving, I discovered that I was not only to share in the speaking responsibilities but also to bring the main message Sunday afternoon at the closing service. That service was called the "World Intercessors Convocation." It was thrilling to report how God had moved in people's hearts and developed momentum for World Intercessors during my first trip overseas in my new position.

In mid-September, we had our first men's early-morning prayer meeting in the new headquarters prayer chapel. There was a real sense of liberty, and my heart was moved to tears as I prayed for OMS, my family, and my heart's cry before God. In our noon chapel service that day, which was also the first service in the downstairs fellowship hall, God was so present during a playing of a recorded tape prepared by the evangelism committee. It was almost like the beginning of revival. I prayed that God would use it wherever the recording was distributed.

The following day, five Men for Missions International (MFM) members came, and several OMS staff worked with them as they set out 108 trees and shrubs. God was so good. The greenery made the office building look much nicer. We planted various kinds of trees—yew, juniper, and spruce—and shrubbery. The mission signs were on the property, two entrance gates were hung, floodlights had been installed on all three sides of the building, and the huge, raised letters spelling out CHRIST THE HOPE OF THE WORLD were fastened in place over the foyer on the outside face of the building. The landscaping, lighting, and signage certainly improved the looks of the property.

In early October, Norm Cummings, an Evangelical Fellowship of Mission Agencies (EFMA) executive committee member, and I drove to Winona Lake for an EFMA executive committee meeting. I found everyone so friendly, calling me "Wes," as if I had been on their committee for years. I was really amazed at their close brotherliness.

When they decided to appoint a three-man program committee for EFMA portions of the National Association of Evangelicals (NAE) convention, I was surprised they immediately put me on with Wade Coggins of EFMA headquarters, and Norm Wilson, past president. When they said "Wes" twice, it did not immediately dawn that they meant me. Suddenly, I looked up, and the convener said, "You." I protested, saying I was so new to the committee and needed more orientation before such an assignment. But Clyde Taylor and others immediately laughed, and Clyde said my objection was overruled.

Returning to headquarters after such a spiritual high, such a longing, such a deep, deep hunger for India came over me. For several hours I could not get away from it. Time and again I was almost at the point of bursting into tears. I don't know why God let that burden, hunger, and longing sweep over me so. My heart was in India. I wished I could spend three months there and just pour out my life and my heart in loving prayer and messages among our India churches. I didn't know how much I could do, but if enough people were praying, maybe God would send some touches of revival. I was not chafed at being at the headquarters office, but why did God keep India so deeply on my heart? Perhaps he wanted to say some new things about our work in India.

Praying in the Prayer Chapel

Just before Thanksgiving, Father and my stepmother, Viola, arrived in the late afternoon. They were so thrilled with everything they found at headquarters. On Thanksgiving Day, we had a precious prayer time in the prayer chapel. Father and Viola seemed so happy together. She took such good care of him and seemed to love him so. It was such a joy to see them interact. He was surprisingly active for eighty-two years of age. He held meeting after meeting up to six weeks in duration, emphasizing Bible study and often speaking several times on Sundays.

Later, returning to OMS headquarters, we viewed a film, "The Religions of the World." Father asked that we go into the prayer chapel again. He really poured out his heart in prayer for our family and OMS. He thanked God for Mother and was so over-joyed that the prayer chapel was in her memory. He also thanked God for me. He was deeply moved. Viola poured out her heart in prayer as well, praying in the Spirit. The Lord anointed as I prayed for OMS, our family, and Father and Viola.

Viola and Father both spoke of what a blessed day it was, how much they enjoyed being with us, and how much better they would be able to pray for OMS now. They left early the next morning, returning to Missouri.

Free Methodist Church Wabash Conference

As OMS was scheduling my deputation ministry in South Africa, we received a cablegram from our South Africa secretary, Miss A. M. Buitendag, asking, in relation to me, for a "reply by return cablegram if ordained, and what denomination." We were very happy worshiping in the West Morris Street Free Methodist Church in Indianapolis, so I picked up the phone and called Pastor Don Riggs. "What do I have to do to become a Free Methodist minister?" I asked.

"Why, the bishop is in town today! I'll ask him!" In a few minutes, he called back. "Can you come over right away?"

Wesley with Don and Iris Riggs, Birthday at OMS

I jumped into the car and drove across town to the Wabash Conference of Free Methodist Church office and met with the Free Methodist Conference board. There were about ten laymen and ministers, in addition to the conference superintendent, Rev. Bateman.

Pastor Riggs introduced me to him and Bishop Paul Ellis, and they invited me into their session. I already knew the bishop and three other men of the committee. I explained that I wanted to transfer my ministerial credentials, and the bishop said, "We're the accepting committee for the conference, and we accept you right now. Technically, the conference has to accept you, but they'll do what we recommend. If you insist, I will call a special session of the conference to finalize this, but as far as we're concerned, you are now an ordained elder of our Wabash conference."

They planned to formally present my membership application, and then I would appear before the conference board ministerial committee. A few hours later, I informed South Africa that I was an ordained Free Methodist minister. I didn't know what that announcement did until I reached South Africa later that year.[7]

THE WORLD IS MY PARISH (1967–1968)

As I was reading the Word, I felt the Lord giving his refreshing promise for the new year from John 11:40: "Jesus saith unto her, Said I not unto thee, that, if thou wouldest believe, thou shouldest see the glory of God?" (KJV). In the NIV it reads, "Then Jesus said, 'Did I not tell you that if you believed, you would see the glory of God?'" At the staff meeting, I was asked to speak on prayer. Praise the Lord for a spirit of prayer that settled on the whole group!

Mid-month, I felt spiritually dry, so I spent several hours reading the Word, and I began to feel the Lord's nearness. The day after Christmas, I finished reading the Old Testament for the sixtieth

---

7   On June 12, 2015, during the 131st Annual Conference of the Free Methodist Church, Dr. Duewel was given special recognition for forty-eight years as an ordained elder of the Wabash Conference.

time, this time in the Lamsa edition.[8] Then I began reading the New Testament again, in "Today's English Version," published by the American Bible Society. I was surprised how fresh it was—almost like the Phillips translation.

As the OMS India nonresident field director, I was seeking God's will about when to visit India again. I only wanted his will and longed for his plan in everything with all my being. I had such a precious experience with the Word, taking most of the evening just to listen to it in my heart. Oh, how I love God's Word! It was always so refreshing to my spirit.

Second Overseas Trip

On January 26, I departed on a Trans World Airlines flight for my second overseas trip as second vice president, this time to Athens, Greece, and eventually on to Johannesburg, South Africa. Our flight stopped over in Rome for forty-five minutes, where I stretched my legs. My, how beautiful the sunrise was that morning, with beautiful hues in the sky below and no sun visible until later. The Alps were beautiful, and we also saw Corsica. I enjoyed a precious time with the Word and in silent conversational prayer. Eventually, Mount Stromboli and Mount Etna in Sicily came into view as we crossed over the boot of Italy.

Flying South African Airlines from Greece through Rome, Lisbon, and Cape Verde Islands, eventually we arrived at Johannesburg. The circuitous air route was due to the apartheid policy of South Africa—only Portuguese territories permitted South African Airlines to fly over

---

8   *The Holy Bible from Ancient Eastern Manuscripts* (commonly called the *Lamsa Bible*), published by George M. Lamsa in 1933, was derived from the Syriac Peshitta, the Bible used by the Assyrian Church of the East and other Syriac Christian traditions. Lamsa, following the tradition of his church, claimed that the Aramaic New Testament was written before the Greek version, a view known as Aramaic primacy. Lamsa thus claimed his translation was superior to versions based on later Greek manuscripts. While Lamsa's claims are rejected by the academic community, his translation remains the best known of Aramaic to English translations of the New Testament. https://en.wikipedia.org/wiki/Lamsa_Bible. Accessed August 14, 2021.

their countries. I was met at the Johannesburg International Airport by our faithful home secretary for South Africa, Miss Anna Magdalena (aka A. M.) Buitendag, who had been with OMS since 1938, and her assistant secretary, Miss J. P. du Plessis. Those two dear ladies had quite a testimony of how God led them to join OMS.[9]

As it turned out, my Free Methodist credentials really opened the door in South Africa. When I arrived at Roodepoort, the assistant pastor there greeted me with "When the devil becomes a Duewel, then the Duewel becomes a jewel," and I knew immediately he caught the meaning of my last name in German. *Praise God for all his open doors!*

At each Dutch Reformed service, I was welcomed in both Afrikaans and English by the pastor. After the service I was given thanks by the pastor and then usually given an address of gratitude in English by someone chosen beforehand. Although it was their custom for someone to give a brief official appreciation, I praised the Lord that a number of times the person who extended appreciation was visibly moved. The Lord had spoken through his humble servant!

Welcomed in South Africa

On only two occasions before had anyone from OMS visited South Africa: Dr. C. P. "Uncle Putts" Culver and Dr. Roy Adams. Because their previous ministry had made them *foretrekkers*, meaning they were highly regarded, there was a favorable openness to our visit. Many times, the ministry of these two dedicated OMS coworkers was mentioned, and on each occasion, their presence left people with a pleasant fragrance of memories. On this occasion, no doubt due in part to their loving labors, the Lord took me through the nine provinces of South Africa, primarily in and around the Gauteng province in which Roodeport, Johannesburg, and Pretoria are located, but also down through the Free State to Welkom and KwaZulu Natal to Durban, as well as to Port Elizabeth in the Eastern Cape provinces and Cape Town in the Western Cape provinces.

---

9   In the unabridged version of *All for Jesus*, Dr. Duewel provides a more complete history on how Miss A. M. Buitendag and Miss J. P. du Plessis were called by God to launch the OMS South Africa ministry.

I challenged people in almost all my services to commit to fifteen minutes of daily prayer for our OMS India ministry for one year. At no other place in the world had I enjoyed such a consistently warm response to my messages as in South Africa. However, Northern Ireland was a close second.

We were grateful to God that well over a thousand new World Intercessors were raised up during our weeks in Africa. Ministers assured me their churches would be praying from that time onward, laypeople rose to their feet to state their prayer life would never be the same, and young people came weeping to pledge daily prayer and to enlist in World Intercessors.

How could I ever forget the ninety-four-year-old aunt of the prime minister of South Africa, who held my hand lovingly in hers, assuring me she would pray for me, OMS, and world harvest every day as long as she lived? Those were choice prayer warriors! And what faithful workers for South Africa God gave us in Home Secretary Miss Buitendag and Miss du Plessis, who had loved, prayed, and given their time, strength, and means for thirty-seven years.[10]

Return to Great Britain

It was my privilege to visit Great Britain again, with World Intercessors prayer the main emphasis of my ministry. God raised up several hundred new prayer warriors. It was a real joy to share in the ministry of the International Revival Convention, where Dr. Paul Rees gave daily Bible readings, and in a revival rally, where Rev. Duncan Campbell was the speaker. God was uniting his people in hunger for a real revival! That year we sensed it in a new way, and God was also uniting us in faith and expectancy for his revival.

At the Liverpool annual conference, we had the best attendance ever, with about one-third of the congregation consisting of young people. At the International Convention in Southport, OMS had the largest house party, with half the crowd composed of young people,

---

10 Dr. Duewel did return for subsequent ministry in South Africa on at least two other occasions, including October 24–November 5, 1974, and September 8–16, 1997.

many of whom had been saved in the recent Billy Graham evangelistic campaign. In Wellington Hall in Belfast, at the Worldwide Missionary

UK, International Revival Convention at Southport, 1967

Conference, I had never seen the building so full. God was giving many new candidates and an increase in missionary giving month by month.

As I left Great Britain, each day's mail brought in more registration slips from those desiring to become a part of this international prayer movement. I was confident we would reap the blessings from this increased volume of prayer for years to come. God was doing such wonderful things for OMS in the British Isles. He gave us the most solid base we ever had there.

Back in the States

In early October, the NAE and EFMA executive committee appointed me to the program committee for the next NAE missionary event. The next day, a number of us dined separately as a group. Three of us—representing OMS, WGM, and OC International—were interested in the possibility of entering Indonesia. The others were already working there. Much helpful information was shared, and God's blessings were phenomenal, but ours was a cautious optimism, since the government, using a visa quota system, could clamp down on the entrance of an unlimited number of missionaries.

While opening mail the first week of October, I found my credential certificate as an ordained elder of the Free Methodist Church. It was dated August 9, 1967, and signed by Bishop Paul Ellis. The following Sunday, we went to worship at West Morris Street, with over five hundred people in attendance. The Ernys went with us, and

God was present in the service. The restoration and rebuilding of the church from a devastating May fire was making good progress, and it seemed the Lord was bringing "beauty from ashes."

In late October, the Lord led me to Minneapolis, then to Aberdeen, South Dakota. Then I drove to Eureka, South Dakota, staying in a lovely German farming community. God gave such a warm response among these Evangelical United Brethren and United Methodist Church German farmers. He was preciously present throughout our ministry, and many were deeply moved. Showing slides of the Indian mela festivals and Varanasi seemed to be an eye-opener to both the pastor and his people. God's Spirit seemed to be heavy upon us.

In early November, Betty, Darlene, and I left for Nashville, Illinois. We stopped at Vandalia, Illinois, to see the old state house where Abraham Lincoln served. We stayed at the Bernreuters' home, and we had a lovely meal at the home of Raymond Brink. I had not been in Nashville for forty-five years. We drove past where our first parsonage was when I was called to India, but sadly, it had been torn down, and a new Methodist church and educational building occupied the whole area.

Late that evening, God wonderfully helped and gave a great missionary service, resulting in folk who later went to Grenada for a three-month, short-term ministry. They took up a generous offering, and ten people joined World Intercessors. Father and Viola were also there, and after the service we enjoyed a long talk with them, which both seemed to appreciate. They, too, were going back to Grenada for several weeks at Christmas, perhaps up to three months. Father presented Bible studies and held special meetings for two weeks each, in six churches.

Following Thanksgiving Day, I flew to Washington, D.C. and spent several days with John. While there, I visited Richard Halverson's church, Fourth Presbyterian, and spent time with Cliff and Betty Robinson, Barney, and others, while I stayed with John until the morning of November 27. Then I flew to New York for the joint EFMA/IFMA executive committee sessions and a WEF meeting, where there was a real heavy prayer burden for China, reminding me of my mother's burden, which I shared.

We received other very happy news that week. Chris and Ed Zahniser announced they were engaged to be married. Just before Christmas, we spent a lot of time shopping with the family. Then on Christmas Eve, Father and Viola left for Grenada, for a camp meeting, and stayed through Easter, teaching two to three classes a day in the Fire Baptized Holiness Church's junior college of 220 students. My father was almost eighty-four years old and still writing Sunday school lessons for a missionary page in *The Flaming Sword* every two weeks, a monthly missionary exhortation, and a ministry report letter to all Fire Baptized Holiness Churches. Also, he prepared a monthly radio message, which was broadcast over stations in Independence, Kansas, and Warrenton, Missouri, as well as preparing for occasional preaching and teaching in churches.

The week after Christmas, John and I headed to the Urbana Youth Conference. He stopped off at the Walters' home. I went on to the conference, where Dr. John Stott presented the daily Bible studies to about seven thousand young people, representing more than thirty nations and more than a hundred mission societies.

As was my habit at the end of each year, I prayed as we were about to enter 1968. I read a long time in the Word and was conscious of the Lord's presence as I prayed. God seemed to quicken me with Psalm 86:17, and I prayed, *Give a sign of favor to me.* That night God was so near that I ended the old year on my knees. My first prayer was not a selfish prayer, but about the fact that I knew not what the new year would hold, but I knew God held it in his hands. My deepest cry was for God to work out his purposes for others, and that one day I, too, would rejoice in his answers.

Visiting Latin America

In early January 1968, I flew to Medellin, Colombia, sitting five thousand feet high in the mountains. The airplane made tight circles to land in the mountainous valley. What a blessing to spend six weeks on our Colombia and Ecuador fields! I was privileged to minister the Word of God over seventy times during those days.

What a joy to share in the biennial conference of our national church, the Association of Evangelical Churches of Colombia, and to be present for the election of our first OMS national president! I had the privilege of sharing in an ordination and licensing service, where nine leaders of the church were set apart in a new way for ministry, and in baptismal services, with reports of many turning to Christ. God was so graciously present, though I admit, I was very weary.

Gene Wittig, who served as field director for both OMS Colombia and Ecuador, was an amazing interpreter. His command of Spanish was almost like that of a national. God gave us opportunities to speak at multiple worship services and a retreat for pastors and teachers, with hundreds present. I attended their annual field councils and business sessions, where their heartbeat was evident, as they faced the challenges, opportunities, and problems of those days.

With the Lord's help the next morning, I spoke at our second church, Manrique, a lovely new church with a semi-open design. The pastor seemed to lack push, or motivation, but God gave a tremendous anointing. A lay leader was so overcome he could not pray for some time, then prayed with tears, and upon finishing, he knelt right where he'd been standing. The pastor gave a few words of exhortation, and soon the altar was filled with nine adults and five children praying. An earnest prayer session followed, which included the pastor-elect. We got home late, but God's hand was on the service.

At the field council with our OMS folks, there were also four Wesleyan Methodists, two Plymouth Brethren, and two Canadian Baptist missionaries. We had a good visit and a season of prayer afterward. Several mentioned that God had spoken through the message, especially one of the Canadians. It was a thrill to visit churches that had once been closed by the Roman Catholic opposition but were then opened to the gospel. They were constantly growing, with daily radio broadcasts and a tremendous outreach for Christ. My heart was broken as we passed along the streets and saw dozens of prostitutes, slaves to men's passions. I could not but weep as I bowed in prayer for them.

Thank God for the trophies he was giving each year from among those needy souls. Many of their conversions proved to be permanent, and those people were reclaimed to useful lives in society and membership in our churches. Finally, our visit to Colombia yielded dozens of people who enlisted in World Intercessors. *It was God's day!*

Flying on to Quito, Ecuador, I was met by our missionaries there, and we held a fellowship meeting. Then we visited an area where the houses were built on stilts, and then garbage was filled in around them until it became firm ground. The Guayaquil missionary group flew to Cuenca and then traveled by bus to Gualaceo, a small town with a resort-type motel. The Saraguro missionary group came by bus. God gave new encouragements about ministry to the Saraguro people. We looked forward to a solid breakthrough for God among them because they had thus far resisted any Christian advance or witness. Their present openness and receptivity to the gospel was evidence of the Spirit of God at work.

The annual Ecuador missionary retreat began early in the morning, and God gave a precious melting time. He gave a spirit of brokenness and some confession of need. In the afternoon, Christine Cavit led in song with her accordion, and God warmed our hearts. We enjoyed more than an hour of silent and vocal prayer. That evening, the Lord led in my message, and while waiting on him, there was weeping and confession of needs. *God was so real!*

Upon returning to Quito in the early afternoon, we began the annual field council meetings. There were three services, one a very difficult service, with a negative couple present. Gene Wittig gave such wisdom and guidance. The Lord sweetly, quietly hallowed the service with his tender hush. Again, we saw many tears of gratitude as different ones were counseled. The combination of the Spirit's working and my personal interest in people was how God worked. When we finished, and prayer was just ready to begin, Christine Cavit humbly asked to speak. She did not want her doubt of what God could do to hinder others. For nearly four hours there was humble, sacred testimonies, the asking for forgiveness, prayer for self or others, and occasionally softly sung choruses. Almost everyone was involved before the Lord was through with us. He just seemed to work out all the complications. When it was time for departure, some who were asked to lead in prayer lacked composure enough to do so.

Throughout my visit, there were times of a holy hush and often a definite moving of God's Spirit, as witnessed by the tears streaming down faces, the surrendering of lives to Christ, and the giving of testimonies. How many, many times we were conscious of the precious movement of his Spirit in our midst! Those times of blessing prepared our groups for the guidance God gave them and for planning new advances for Christ's cause throughout these countries.

God's Spirit came in quiet, sacred power. Business meetings were pushed aside, and one service lasted four hours, as hearts were melted together. We shared in times of prayer, confession, apology, and testimony. We sensed that God, not man, was in control!

Back at Headquarters

Meeting with Dick Capin back in Greenwood, we talked for a long time about the society's needs. We felt OMS needed a new image reflected in planning, publications, and public relations, with a new and exciting cutting edge for supporters.

In mid-April, I flew to the NHA annual convention in Washington, D.C., and stayed with John. I spent two days with him, and he introduced me to his friends. While there, I had a wonderful time with the Lord in the Word. Those were precious times of nearness and prayer, where again God renewed my spiritual faith and hunger.

Then I flew to Philadelphia for the NAE's annual convention and participated in the EFMA executive committee meeting, where I was elected vice president. I wasn't sure that was what the Lord would have me do, since serving as OMS vice president was one thing, and committing to serving as the EFMA vice president was quite another. But the contacts God gave me at the NAE convention were certainly worthwhile during those days. I sensed his guidance at each luncheon conversation and also in informal meetings between sessions.

Filling in for Dr. Eugene Erny

On the third week of April, Dr. Erny was suddenly taken ill. He returned unexpectedly from Korea, and upon receiving word of his trip being cut short, I returned to Indianapolis from my trip. I went to the Erny home, and Eugene looked very tired. He was forced to cancel two-thirds of his engagements in Korea. The next day, he was taken to St. Francis Hospital, where he underwent two days of x-ray examinations. Due to his hospitalization, I was asked to attend an Asbury Manor board meeting as his proxy. Upon Eugene's release from the hospital, Dale McClain advised him to pace himself and take a lighter load.

At the beginning of May, I went to Wilmore, Kentucky, with Dr. George Warner (WGM president), Dick Capin, and Bill Gillam to an Asbury Theological Seminary all-day board meeting. Many items were covered in prayer, and then we returned safely home to Greenwood late that night. One does not immediately know what kind of long-term impact those prayer meetings can have, but we were confident God was at work.

Succession Plan for the Presidency

Also in June, I had five busy weeks of committee meetings, board sessions, and our international convention at Winona Lake, when our directors gathered from around the world. How conscious we were of God's presence as he guided us in careful evaluations of our ministry fields. Most surprisingly, my fellow directors chose me to succeed Dr. Eugene Erny as president of OMS upon his retirement the following year.

I felt so unequipped and unworthy of such responsibility, and I would need much more prayer support. God seemed to be leading us to enter new fields, and we desired a Society-wide analysis of our organizational methods and work, to be ever more effective for his glory. An outside consulting firm, Christian Service Fellowship (CSF), was hired to review our headquarters operations and conduct staff interviews.

Third Overseas Trip—Japan and Hong Kong

The highlight of mid-July was the wedding of our daughter Ruth Christine Hope Duewel to Edward DeFrance Zahniser on Saturday afternoon, July 13. Immediately after the wedding, again I flew to Japan for a brief visit. On the way, God permitted me to have a few hours with John, in Honolulu. Our paths were coordinated perfectly. John would spend the next two years in Kuala Lumpur, capital of Malaysia, setting up an agricultural bank to serve that nation. As I walked with him to the plane, we met the two Malaysian officials with whom he would be working. They were very cordial.

Dale McClain joined me upon my arrival in Japan, and we went on to Korea for a week of prayer, planning, and counseling with our staff there. Then, we had five full days in Hong Kong, sharing the last part of the annual prayer conference of our nationals and missionaries.

OMS Votes to Enter Indonesia

In mid-May 1967, the OMS executive committee had requested that Dr. Edwin W. Kilbourne, in connection with a forthcoming trip to Australia and New Zealand, visit Indonesia and conduct an initial survey, evaluating the possibilities of opening new outreach ministry there.[11]

By June 1968, Ed had presented his report to the executive committee, and the board voted to open outreach in Indonesia. At the same session, Dale McClain and I were requested to make a secondary, month-long, in-depth survey in Indonesia.[12] That survey took place

---

11   Then it was an official policy and procedure of OMS to conduct two surveys before formally opening a field for new outreach ministry. This incident was the initial, or preliminary, survey and the least comprehensive survey of the two.

12   This was the second and more comprehensive of the two surveys. The results of both surveys were synthesized, or consolidated, and submitted to the board for official action. The OMS board in those days consisted primarily of peer group missionaries.

from early August to early September 1968. Our primary hosts, the Christian and Missionary Alliance, sponsored Inter-Mission Business Office offices in Jakarta, and based on their suggestions, wherever possible we spent time interviewing their missionaries.

Afterward, Dale and I moved beyond Jakarta and surveyed Java as a whole. What a burden God placed upon our hearts for Indonesia as we met missionary and national Christian leaders of many organizations, walked the streets of major cities in Java, gathered information and impressions, and sought God's clear directions! In Bali, hour after hour was crowded with God-planned activities.

During that month, God helped us get a grasp that would ordinarily have taken many weeks. We constantly sensed that we were being upheld by prayer. We conducted survey work in the cities of Jakarta, Bandung, Jogjakarta, Semarang, Surabaya, Malang, Java, and Den Pasar, Bali.

We tried to contact every evangelical agency with missionaries in those centers. We asked many questions and sought to learn everything possible. We visited Campus Crusade for Christ in Jakarta, and Rev. Ais Pormes, head of CCC, immediately offered that Campus Crusade-Indonesia could be our sponsor, which we gladly accepted. Every group was very cordial with us and encouraged us to actively seek entrance into Indonesia as a Society.

Returning to the States, Dale and I reported to the board of directors in its December 1968 meeting. At that time, they officially voted to open work in Indonesia as soon as possible, preferably by early September 1969. Our first missionaries to Indonesia departed on October 10, 1969. They went as far as Singapore, where they remained until it was possible to obtain visas. Dale McClain, who shuttled back and forth from Singapore and visiting in Indonesia, was authorized to arrange the formation of our own foundation (legal juridical person) as soon as possible.

During those years when I was a newly elected vice president, God gave me wonderful, repeated opportunities to visit, listen, and learn about the worldwide outreach of OMS and to love the missionaries with whom we served. I realized anew that God was continuing to answer my prayers, but in the process, he was also increasing my burden for the lost world and my love for Jesus. I realized that only through Jesus would I ever be capable of leading the mission into the unknown future. I pleaded with him to infill and enable as only he could.

4
The Presidency Years

The period from June 1969 through July 1982 was one of the most challenging, rewarding, and fulfilling periods of my life. After receiving my call to India as a child, I had worked to prepare as best I knew how to serve the Lord Jesus as a missionary there. After seeing how God opened the door to fulfill that calling in India with OMS, the specific mission organization for which I had prayed, it was almost inconceivable that God would entrust me with the executive leadership of that same organization. Nonetheless, that was how the Lord Jesus worked in my life. He also worked in my family's lives.

FAMILY NEWS
Father's Triumphant Homegoing

During the last years of his life, Father had moved back to Troy, Missouri, where he had weekly Bible radio broadcasts over stations in that area. His last recorded message was broadcast after his death, the day before his funeral. I cannot remember hearing a critical or strongly negative remark from his lips. He was always sweet-spirited. And in the words of both the apostle Paul and evangelist John Wesley, he was sanctified "through and through" (1 Thess 4:3).

He was scheduled to preach in the local church the next day and had planned to attend our OMS annual convention at Winona Lake at the end of the month, but on Saturday, June 21, 1969, he entered heaven at eighty-five years of age. God blessed me with wonderful, godly, sanctified parents, for whom I will always be grateful.

John Wesley

In June 1974, Cupid's latest capers cheered us as a family, when we read a cable from John announcing his wedding on May 20 to Miss Retno Jakti in Indonesia. She was on the staff of the United Nations in Jakarta. She had lived for several years in New York while employed by a business firm, then was on the staff of the United Nations in Jakarta. She was awarded a United Nations trip and visited her sister and husband, who were on the staff of the United Nations in New York. She visited us in Greenwood as well.

In January 1975, once again I left for Jakarta, Indonesia, and I had the pleasure of resting overnight at John and Retno's home. It was a joy to spend several quality hours with them, especially because we didn't see them again until they returned home at Christmas 1977.

John and Retno Duewel

The next day I traveled to our OMS ministry center in Malang. My ministry time in Indonesia was such a challenge and thrill to me.

On July 23, 1978, I added Grandfather to my titular prefixes, courtesy of John and Retno. Kamela Santi Duewel (*Kamela* means lotus flower and *Santi* means peace) was born in Ithaca, New York, where John had just completed exams for his doctorate. Betty had the joy of spending ten days with

Santi on Grandpa Wesley's shoulders

them, and I was with them for a few days as well. Santi was such a beautiful little girl.

By 1983, John was thirty-nine and taught part-time at Cornell University in Ithaca, New York, as he completed his doctorate. During this time, he suffered a ruptured appendix with peritonitis and was critically ill in the hospital for thirteen days. We immediately went to prayer for him. On June 6–14, we left for Ithaca to be with John and his family, and we were able to sit by his bedside for about a week of his hospital stay. We watched and prayed, and God snatched him from death's door and spared his life.

Ruth Christine Hope

Similarly, God answered many prayers for our elder daughter, Chris. In 1970, she had become Mrs. Ed Zahniser, but she stayed with us while Ed completed his military service in Korea, editing the U.S. army's *Stars and Stripes* newspaper. She helped in our OMS office, working in the auto-typist department, where she continually received compliments from her coworkers for her conscientious work ethic. When Ed returned on March 1, they left for the East Coast, where they planned to settle.

Ed and Christine Zahniser, 2006

Esther Darlene

On June 1, 1975, Darlene graduated from high school and was accepted to Asbury College (now University) in Wilmore, Kentucky. She trusted God for his help and seriously prayed about missionary service after her college days. She also served as a counselor in the youth ministry of our annual convention. Those were very busy but happy months. Darlene was enjoying her classes at Asbury, and she knew she was in the center of God's will for her life.

The next year, 1977, was a great time for Darlene at Asbury, and she really enjoyed studying New Testament Greek. Pending God providing her funds, she planned to go to Indonesia for ten weeks during the summer under the NOW Corps program. Our gracious God did provide! In 1978, Darlene shared an exciting report of her summer ministry in Indonesia. Many of the sounds, smells, and sights reminded her of India, where she was born and lived the first seven years of her life. She was given some time to see a bit of Indonesia—rice fields, oxcarts, marketplaces, a wedding—and get acquainted with the missionaries there.

On February 28, 1978, after giving a trip report at headquarters chapel, I drove to Wilmore and attended a missionary conference at Asbury Theological Seminary. My colleague, Dr. Helmut Schultz, spoke at the World Outreach dinner. While at Asbury, I challenged the student body, including my daughter, Darlene, and my future son-in-law, Terry Rueger, with the call to serve in Indonesia. Having seen Terry and Darlene spending time together at Asbury, I wasn't surprised when I had the privilege of announcing her engagement to this young ministerial student on April 25. Terry graduated with honors from Asbury Theological Seminary on May 21, and they set their wedding date for December 9. Terry also began his first pastorate at the United Methodist Church in Oak Hill, Ohio.

Terry and Darlene Rueger

Betty and I were thrilled to be part of officiating Darlene and Terry's beautiful wedding. After their honeymoon, they spent weekends at his pastorate in Oak Hill and midweek days at Asbury College, where Darlene had a few more months before she graduated. In 1979, Darlene and Terry were happily adjusting in their pastorate in Oak Hill, but after two years, their plan was to apply to OMS as missionaries. Terry planned to earn a second master's degree, and then they were going to start funding for the mission field.

Since Darlene and Terry were living with us while they fulfilled their deputation ministry, Betty had a special opportunity to be grandmother to our newest grandson, Jonathan Paul Rueger, born on November 24, 1981. We praised God both for Jonathan and for providing eighty percent of Terry and Darlene's share support for India.

We continued to pray for their visas, however, which were not forthcoming. When it became evident that the door to India was not going to open, OMS prayerfully asked them to consider joining our first team of missionaries headed for France. They joyfully accepted and started redirecting their communications and prayer requests toward France.

By April 1983, Darlene and Terry were partially packed and hoped to go to France soon—if their visas arrived in time. Little Jonathan was growing and was such a great joy to us. One day, as I showed him the picture of Jesus on the wall again, he spoke the name of Jesus for the first time. I was delighted. In answer to our prayers, Darlene and Terry and little Jonathan arrived in France on April 16.

Betty

In 1970, God answered many prayers for my dear wife, Betty. While I was traveling the world, she not only kept in contact and cared for the family but helped maintain *The Missionary Standard* subscription list, a huge challenge at headquarters. In May 1972, in addition to her home responsibilities, Betty also helped in the prayer letter department, which was another huge assignment involving sending up to twenty thousand letters each month. Over two hundred thousand pieces of mail were sent each year from that office to supporting and praying friends of our missionaries.

On March 5, we received word that Betty's father, William Raisch, had unexpectedly succumbed to pneumonia and heart failure. His funeral service a few days later was a time of victory and witness of God's precious grace. We were saddened once again on December 3, when her mother, Margaret, went to her eternal reward. With both of her parents

Wesley & Betty Duewel at OMS Headquarters

Wesley and Betty Duewel, circa 1982

entering heaven that year, we became ever more aware of our parental responsibility and mortality.

Home and Away

In 1970, God answered many prayers for our family. In August, Betty, Darlene, and I took a well-deserved vacation trip to Colorado. We enjoyed that family vacation trip so much that we did the same thing again in September the next year, camping for two weeks to California and back! Of course, we combined mission business and family vacation, making over two hundred contacts for the Society. I always felt it was my duty and was compelled to contact and cultivate constituency during our vacation travels.

On January 5, 1973, we hosted an open house for OMS headquarters staff and close friends. The choice fellowship and Betty's array of homemade goodies made for a delightful evening. In March, almost a dozen of OMS's best speakers gathered for a two-day retreat in the mountains of Gatlinburg, Tennessee, for what we called a "Careers' Weekend," to share with Asbury seminarians. Betty and I attended as well, trusting the Lord to call new candidates.

The next year was a busy time for Betty, with hospitality and the office work, and for me, with international ministry in Colombia, Ecuador, Korea, Japan, Spain, Britain, Brazil, and South Africa, as well as in the States. God acted graciously on our behalf throughout the year and continued to answer our prayers.

By July 19, 1975, it was time for our annual family vacation and to enjoy some time together. On August 6, on the way home, we attended the Roxbury Holiness Camp in Orrstown, Pennsylvania. Near year-end, Betty started counting the days. I was invited to participate in the EFI twenty-fifth anniversary celebration in India, January 5–9, 1976, and we were both thrilled to return to India.

By December 1976, Betty and I longed to see our many donor friends and thank them in person for their loving prayers and faithful financial support. They were so faithful in supporting our ministry. But oh my, what a winter we had in Greenwood at the end of 1977 merging into early 1978, including that blizzard! Many records were broken by the cold weather, snow on the ground, and chill factors, which went down to fifty-six degrees below zero. However, God warmed our hearts by our constituents' constant love and encouraging letters, and their faithful support of our ministry sustained us in the midst of demanding schedules.

THE HOLY LAND (1978)

In 1978, we received a most unusual surprise gift! Provident Travel agent Jack Harrington, the agent through whom our Society was working, presented Betty and me with free round-trip tickets to the Holy Land. The only request he had was that we befriend his parents, to whom he was also giving a free trip.

On March 5, Betty and I traveled by car to Cincinnati, starting a treasured visit to Israel. We were part of a group of twenty-eight people from the College Hill Presbyterian Church in Cincinnati, making it a challenge to be very attentive to Jack's parents, but we tried to show interest any way we could.

We met the larger group and flew by plane to La Guardia Airport, and then by helicopter to Kennedy Airport, where we transferred to India Air for our flight to Geneva, Switzerland. The next day, we had a guided bus tour of Geneva. We saw the Reformation monument and the university started by the reformer, John Calvin.

From Switzerland, we boarded *EL AL*, the national airline of Israel. It was a very unusual experience to see the extraordinary security for traveling with *EL AL*. I had never seen such air security anywhere else in the world. This was my third visit to Israel, but because it was my first with Betty, it was most memorable and treasured.

We went on to Jericho, which we enjoyed so much. Our group stayed five nights in a hotel on the Mount of Olives. At the Garden Tomb in Jerusalem, small groups of Christians were singing, praying, or having Communion. Many Jews were praying at the Wailing Wall. Many wrote prayers on bits of paper and stuck them in the cracks in the wall.

But just before the Sabbath, security police stopped all photography and even all note taking. We watched about a hundred Jewish divinity students come singing and skipping, and then, row after row, greeting the Sabbath like a bride. Gathering in a large circle, they made short, abrupt bows toward the wall.

What a contrast between the rocky, dry desert of Judea and the beautiful oasis area of Jericho! I wish you could have heard the men and women weeping and praying at Rachel's tomb. Shepherds led their sheep as they did in David's time—even in the streets of Bethlehem.

As we walked along the ancient cobbled streets and the "Way of Sorrows" (the Via Dolorosa) in Old Jerusalem, we were reminded how Jesus was forced to carry his cross there. We saw or passed through many of the villages mentioned in Scripture, and it seemed as though we were back in Bible times.

We visited one of the many *kibbutzim* (Israeli settlements), but we were sad to learn that many of the Jews living there were atheists.

The trip to Galilee was beautiful. We drank from Jacob's well and saw the vineyards and olive groves. We stayed two nights in Tiberias. While we were crossing the Sea of Galilee on a motor launch, a sudden storm came up, just as described during Jesus's time, after which we saw a double rainbow in the distance.

We had a Sunday communion service in the city of Tiberias overlooking the Sea of Galilee, and I was invited to help serve the elements. I gave a message on Jesus's searching question to Peter, which he repeated in different forms three times: "Do you love Me?" I spoke on "Christ's First Message at Tiberias." The Lord especially helped, and some of our group could hardly speak. One lady said she was never so moved by a message in her life. What a thrill to know I was speaking at the same place and undoubtedly near the spot where Jesus asked Peter that question! *To God be the glory!*

We also visited Nazareth, Meggiddo, Haifa, and Caesarea, and then we spent the last night on the edge of the Mediterranean, listening to the wind and waves. We brought home such memories, feelings, and deeper Bible understandings, which blessed our lives.

ACCEPTING LEADERSHIP (1969)

Within a week of my father's passing in 1969, the OMS board of trustees conducted an installation service for my presidency on June 29. Board chairman, Dr. Paul P. Petticord, kindly and graciously introduced me, and God helped me deliver my inauguration address, when I expressed appreciation for those who had gone before me. This was my first message as OMS president, "A New Vision for OMS Today:"

> I would like to pay tribute to a wonderful team. I believed in OMS before I applied to it. I believed in it from the age of seven years! I believe in the great team of national coworkers and that wonderful family of Christians in the churches raised up by God through the Society—some 185,000 of them by now.

> I, above all, believe in God. And our motto must be *FORWARD TOGETHER*. I believe in the future of OMS, because I believe in the future of God's cause 'till Jesus comes. These are the two passions of my heart—that God will keep us humble and hungry enough for him to do what he longs to do for this, our generation.

> Let no one touch God's glory. Let no one glory in man. Let no one glory in OMS. All glory goes to God alone.

> I also believe in OMS. I believe in her doctrines. I believe in her heritage. I believe in her calling. And, God being my helper, I shall seek to give total loyalty in the days to come. I am in OMS from the very core of my being. We face new millions in this world. We face a greater and more overwhelming task than when Charles Cowman headed for Japan nearly seventy years ago. Times have changed. The world has changed. The fields are changing rapidly. But I still believe the threefold priority God gave back in those early days remains as valid today as it ever was. Emphases may change. Mediums may change. Methods may change. We may find new and better ways to express it or to cooperate and work together, but those threefold priorities are valid today.

> First: Bible training for a national ministry. We pray that God will help us see more people, both ministers and laity, trained to go forth to witness for God and win souls for

God—not mere academic training, but persons with souls on fire for God.

Second: Establishment and growth of New Testament churches. We must see holy churches raised up to carry on the witness; to serve until Jesus comes; and if need be, die for their faith, so help us God! In these days when church growth again receives wonderful emphasis throughout the evangelical world, that priority is as valid as it ever was.

Third: Extensive and intensive evangelism—to keep evangelism at the heart of everything we do. I pray God that he may keep the fire of evangelism burning in the heart of every member of our fellowship around the world so long as there is life and strength—or 'till Jesus comes.

To these things we are totally committed. We shall seek to develop and strengthen these more and more in ways old and new. The world's need and God's commission do not change. Our basic calling does not change. And by God's grace, as much as there is in us, we must give ourselves to his purpose and holy will, about which we read in Isaiah 6:1–12.

We need a new vision of the God of prayer. World Intercessors must assume a greater role in OMS than before. There is only one way we can go *Forward Together*—on our knees. Why do we pray so little when God has proved his faithfulness so often?

We have world-sized tasks to complete before Jesus comes. If any generation needed a new vision of God, we need it today. We must know in living reality the dynamic day-to-day working of the power of God in our lives. The Holy Spirit must be more than a doctrine. We need more than a second definite experience of God's grace. We must experience the power of the living God surging through all our lives out to the world in need. We need a new vision of God. We need a new word from God. We need a new experience of God. God wants to take us, like Isaiah, into the temple, alone, and there be unveiled before our eyes—until in the hush of his holiness, graciousness, and nearness our hearts are melted before him.

I shall never forget my last words with Sister Cowman. We were just about to go back to India. She was in her sunset years. She rose from her chair, stepped to the middle of the room, folded her hands together, and said, "Oh, Brother Duewel, what a great day to live for God! What a great day to be alive! I am so glad God let me live to see this day!" Oh, that God would give us all that kind of faith! OMS was born with holy passion. I have read, reread, and feasted my soul on the accounts of the hunger, passion, and prayer of our early leaders; and the testing of their faith, as they reached out for unbelievable things for God. No sooner did OMS enter Japan than souls began to find God. There was mighty travailing in prayer, with nationals and missionaries on their faces before God, in fasting and prayer. Flaming evangels were raised up—some to burn out in a short time for God.

We cannot do without holy fire today. We need fire-baptized missionaries and national leadership—people whose souls are aflame with a holy passion, who have felt the touch of God and to whom have come the seraphim with fire from the altar and set their souls aflame. We need cleansing. We need empowering flame. We need the glory of God's *Shekinah* to settle upon us again. There is only one way to have it, and that is to pay the price—the price of hunger and prayer.

Without God's holy fire, we go through the mere routine, the duty, and the busy life and mechanics of modern missions. Without God's holy fire, evangelism only has decisions; it doesn't have mighty transformations. Without God's *Shekinah* glory, the world ignores us or stares at us. There is no substitute for the fire of God in our work! We must have a new touch of fire.

We cannot afford anything that dampens that fire. We cannot afford anything that will hinder that flame from burning its brightest. We cannot afford human bigness without divine depth. We cannot afford to have carnal tensions in the place of Holy Spirit unity. We cannot afford the confusion and the bustle of self-centered busyness. There is no substitute for the power of God. There is no substitute for the throne of grace. We dare not be busier than we are blessed. We dare not attempt more than we can saturate with prayer. We dare not be more active than we are anointed. We dare not substitute our training, or our brilliance for fire-touched glory. We dare not be satisfied with growth without revival. We dare not multiply our projects unless we also multiply the power.

Brothers and sisters, I want you to join with us, hand in hand and heart to heart. Join in prayer and in hunger for souls. Join in renewing your vow to God. I am not here to plead for money. I am here to plead for your prayers. God's work is suffering from the lack of prayer. As much as there is anything in us, let us give ourselves to God, to souls, and to prayer! Oh, that God would somehow renew our vision! Oh, that somehow, he would give us a new touch of fire! Oh, that somehow, he would send us out with a new commitment to the unfinished task for the sake of God and souls!

The Bible verse God gave Betty and me—even before we knew each other in college—I later found to be a verse God especially gave to William Carey, the father and founder of modern missions, and also Charles Cowman, the founder of our Society. I commend it to us as a board, which is responsible to God and to our generation around the world: "Enlarge the place of your tent, and stretch your tent curtains wide, do not hold back, lengthen your cords, strengthen your stakes. For you will spread out to the right and to the left" (Isa 54:2–3 KJV). It is on this basis that we must "Expect greater things from God and attempt greater things for God." I am counting on the personal help of each of you brethren of the board in seeing this advance for God and world harvest. I pray that God's Word and motto for us all will be *FORWARD TOGETHER* for God and the harvest. Amen.[1]

Forward Together

The responsibility of the presidency of OMS was heavy, and God's challenge was great. By the blessing of the Lord, and in fulfillment of his call, and with the God-honored leadership of Dr. Eugene Erny and coworkers, we had grown from two outreach fields to ten. We had become a stable, complex, and forward-moving organization with ten times the staff as before. Also, we had moved our world headquarters from Los Angeles to the central location God had provided in Greenwood, Indiana.

During the last year of Dr. Erny's presidency, OMS benefited greatly from the management survey team and consulting discussions with Christian Service Fellowship (CSF). After months of self-study by our OMS personnel and management, our OMS executive committee and board of trustees were guided to take new steps of reorganization, praying that God would lead us to new effectiveness and fruitfulness in his service around the world.

---

1   This message is abbreviated here, but the entire message can be found in the unabridged version of *All for Jesus*.

We immediately began detailed planning at every level, to measure our future by the greatness of God, and because of the overwhelming size of our task, we inaugurated Society-wide annual plans for each field and institution, with field leaders responsible for carrying out the plans. We determined to reemphasize spiritual priorities and asked God to make OMS a holy people, a Spirit-guided and Spirit-anointed people, and a hungry-hearted praying people as never before. Thanking God for his nearly seventy years of blessing, I sought for us to go *Forward Together*.[2]

Historically, we had grown from "leaderism" to "committeeism." Now, we were moving into a "line and staff functionalism." Clear-cut lines of responsibility and authority were drawn up and diagrammed for each field and for the Society as a whole. Symbolic of what was extended throughout the Society, we dissolved the administrative committee at headquarters. In place of consensus decisions, we inaugurated three vice presidents over (1) field ministries, (2) homeland ministries, and (3) administration-finance. Guidelines and manuals were developed for the vice presidents. For certain legal and specified organizational functions, these three vice presidents and the secretary of the board would meet with the president, as an executive body, known as the president's cabinet.[3]

My first annual plan was inaugurated for the Society that August. I sought to involve the whole Society in an emphasis on evangelism and prayer, the spiritual life of the Society, and our dependence upon the Holy Spirit. Other plans were included for the homeland offices (aka sending countries) and headquarters departments.

Total Advance NOW

We entered a five-year period of prayer and finance termed *Total Advance NOW*, praying to see coordinated evangelistic advance on every field. It was by faith that the encouraging dividends already

2   The "FORWARD TOGETHER" slogan became the title of one of the first in-house publications Dr. Duewel launched and upon which much of the content of this section is based.

3   Extracted from Dr. Duewel's first strategic plan submitted to the board.

demonstrated would be multiplied many times over in the years ahead. Whatever was necessary to get the task done, we were trusting God to provide—whether it be gospel tents, public address systems, gospel films and projection equipment, new and greatly increased quantities of evangelistic literature, or vehicles to speed evangels in their ministry. All those tools meant training the laity in soul-winning, coordinating the outreach of mission and church, trusting God to greatly increase Society income to cover the increased overhead, and trusting him for new coworkers—both national and missionary—*to advance the work in every possible way.*

We needed an inordinate volume of prayer more than ever before, and World Intercessors needed to be greatly strengthened. Despite the economic uncertainty of those days, we needed to see ever-growing Society income, to cover the spiraling inflation on every field and to underwrite *Total Advance NOW.* We needed our stewardship department to be greatly strengthened. We needed to tighten budgetary procedures, to relate OMS and Men for Missions International (MFMI or simply MFM) more closely together, and we needed a new host of laity involved in the support, ministry, and prayer saturation of the work of the Society.

The task was too great for us, but we served an almighty God. I called everyone to support OMS with prayer, faith, and love as never before. We invited everyone to share their counsel and strengthen our hands in every way possible. We had no alternative—by the grace of God we had to go *FORWARD TOGETHER.*

We sought to cultivate and maintain a Society family climate of blessing, revival, and fruitfulness, staffed by people who were personally and spiritually victorious and radiant. We reemphasized prayer as our greatest need, with a Society-wide dependence upon the Holy Spirit. We would continue annual retreats and conventions, emphasizing prayer, testimonies and reports, and ministry of the Word, with an emphasis on commitment. A special healing service would be held each convention. MFMI would be involved, and the convention would end with a commissioning service for new missionaries. That time of my life and ministry was both a culmination and a new beginning: a culmination of years of prayer and preparation, to be all that God called me to be and, at the same time, the beginning of the fulfillment of a great burden and vision God had entrusted to me from my earliest days.

REORGANIZING THE MISSION (1970)

The year 1970 marked the inauguration of Society-wide reorganization of administration, long-range planning, and increased evaluation and supervision. Many of those changes were still underway, and continued forbearance and patience were necessary on the part of all. Two important changes were made with the historical board of directors: the former executive committee was to be called the board of directors, and the former board of directors was to be called the board of trustees. Those changes were necessary for clarifying the respective functions that brought us into compliance with Illinois law, where OMS was registered.

Every effort was being made to rapidly complete the transitional stage of reorganization, to become current in all reporting, and to strengthen and consolidate funding. But we had unforeseen delays in the programming of our data processing equipment, delays in securing much

Wesley L Duewel holding open Bible, circa 1970

needed personnel, and Rev. Gene Wittig, our vice president of field ministries–elect, was unable to free himself from his dual role of field director for Colombia and Ecuador until later in the year.

We were also praying for extra miracle funds to speed up liquidation of liabilities owed on property and equipment at headquarters. Some building expansion was needed, and a long-range retirement program had to be developed and funded. But our fields had labored loyally and well, and we expected marked progress within the next couple of years as the first annual plans were implemented.

The decision to relocate our annual convention was honored when God gave an aggregate of over twelve hundred attendees at our annual convention services, held at Anderson College (now University) in Anderson, Indiana. God's blessing was upon us, and there were many thrilling moments.[4]

Most outstanding was Vice President at Large Dr. Bill Gillam's closing message, "Whatever It Takes," which reflected the Spirit characterizing all our hearts. Three national leaders were a blessing to us, with their testimonies and presence, reminding us of our primary task of investing ourselves in training the "sons and daughters" of each nation where we served.

Conferences and Conventions

God answered many prayers that first year, and the changes made in the organizational structure and administration kept me close to headquarters most of the year. Previously, Rev. Gene Wittig, vice president of field ministries–elect, and I had been invited by the Brazilian national church to their annual national conference. God gave us very busy weeks in Brazil, but he was graciously near, giving touches of revival blessing, especially at the Spiritual Life Conference with our Brazilian church leaders. There was a real spirit of faith and obedience among our Brazilian coworkers. *To God be all the glory!*

Early in February 1970, in earnest prayer, I left for Oregon and then to Australia, Indonesia, Singapore, Malaysia, India, and Hong Kong before returning to headquarters, and then on to Haiti. It was a great day to live for God. Our hearts were constantly burdened, and our faith was so stretched by the need and opportunities before us. My request was for prayer to help us trust God for ever greater victories.

In Australia, there was the founding session of the Australian Home Council, comprised of influential Australian brethren. God met with us and gave us seven fine leaders to guide the work. We expected

---

4   *Convention* was the term used for our annual constituent gatherings, but the activity evolved into using the term *conference* during Dr. Duewel's tenure and following. Therefore, these two terms are frequently used interchangeably.

new progress there.[5] Brief stops in Indonesia, Singapore, and Malaysia placed that portion of the world even more heavily on my heart. In Singapore, God brought to coworkers Dale and Polly McClain's hearts an overflow of the famous 1970 Asbury College revival blessing, and they were scattering the fire! Dale shared God's revival touch upon his own heart as well as his increasing burden not merely for Indonesia but also for the Singapore-Malaysia area.

My two weeks in India were busy, blessed deeply, and gratifying. It was a privilege to see personally the progress in Madras and in North India and to hear reports from all five areas where OMS was working. The ECI All-India Committee had a tremendous planning session, and our Indian coworkers showed mature leadership. National leaders and missionaries spent five days together in Allahabad planning for future growth. The church constitution and operational manual were revised, and the process of indigenization was greatly sped up. Our work was sinking deep roots, and God was placing it all on a sound basis.

A brief layover in Hong Kong with our OMS family was a joy. Then with less than a week back in the Greenwood office, our colleagues in Haiti, the newest field of the Society, invited me to attend their annual field council sessions. Our OMS Haiti field director, Dr. William Gillam, and the whole OMS family planned a full and wonderful exposure to the field and to their hearts.

God showed up while I was preaching in a brush arbor with monsoon-type rains pouring down, breaking a six-month drought, physically and spiritually. Rain ran off my face to the point where it would have ruined my Bible in my hand. The water spattered up from the ground until my pant legs had a mud coating halfway to my knees. But God was there!

Then came a series of meetings with real touches of revival—lasting up to four hours and longer. Perennial backsliders were restored, and new people found the Lord. We saw judgment day conviction and strong weeping. Dozens of Haitians asked for forgiveness and made

---

5   The "Home Councils" were the forerunners of what is today's respective signatory countries' individual administrative boards.

restitution or reconciliation. On one occasion, God even came on some children, and one little boy of ten stood up and preached.

There were thirty-nine baptisms of people who had been born again, proving by their lives the change the Lord had wrought. We were on the verge of a great expansion in Haiti. National leadership in the radio station and the work was well developed and encouraging. The Haiti field was setting the pace for solid growth. *To God be all the glory!*[6]

Travel Fatalities

Our hearts were saddened by the first travel fatality in the seventy-year history of OMS. Wallace and Betty Rehner, bright-souled, energetic missionaries to Colombia, and Frank and Doris Tefft, MFMI volunteers, flew from a weekend Deeper Life Retreat, in Pennsylvania, into the waiting arms of God. I had only recently spent time with them and their three children—Helen, Tim, and Steve. The children eventually found a permanent home in the welcoming arms of our own Les and Pat Ike's family.

Later that same year, our hearts again were shocked and saddened at a second tragic fatality in the sudden and unexpected death of Ray and Yvonne King in the crash of a commercial airplane. Ray had been on our board of trustees for ten years, helped with the construction of our Japan field, and visited us in India. Their absence would be extremely difficult for their seven children, and we kept Mary Lynne, just enrolling at Asbury College; Gary, still in high school; Terri, in junior high; Lori and Lisa, in elementary grades; and Juli and Dina, preschool age, in our loving prayers.

SETTING GOALS (1971)

As we entered 1971, I shared with the OMS family that God was calling us to press onward totally and strongly in redemptive outreach. He had blessed us with a wonderful heritage—founders with burning

---

6   From correspondence with Viola Duewel (stepmother) dated March 29, 1970.

hearts and holy consecration—and with a growing OMS family during these seventy years. OMS was on the move. *To God be all the glory!*

A new age is ever emerging, and the one we were entering was evolving more rapidly than any preceding period of human history. God was calling us to be total in our obedience, sensitive to ever-changing needs and moods of the hour, and as contemporary and relevant as the love of God. God is the eternal contemporary of every soul and situation. He is eternally relevant to every hunger and every need, the answer to the need of both today and tomorrow. The Holy Spirit always has a new word of guidance and a new touch of power for those sanctified to his will and filled with his fullness.

We urged everyone to expect the Holy Spirit to speak to OMS in those days. If we were to meet the greatest need the world had ever known and reach the greatest population the world had ever seen, we had to be on the move for God! We had to preach the same message and emphasize the same doctrine but speak to the needs of the hour and adopt methods best suited to reach the most people for God. To be Spirit-filled is to be open, flexible to his constant guidance.

"OMS family and teammates," I said, "we all need each other, and we all need God!" Our prayer was that we would be so bold as to humbly say, *God needs us more than ever before.* Our challenge was to keep hungry enough, holy enough, and humble enough for God to make 1971 the greatest miracle year we had ever known for *Total Advance NOW.*

Sad News

Early in April 1970, we received a phone call late in the evening, informing us that our vice president at large, Dr. William A. Gillam, was experiencing a serious medical condition. On January 8, 1971, tests indicated that Bill had a brain tumor. He was moved to St. Francis hospital in Indianapolis, and on January 11, he underwent surgery. As much of the tumor as possible was removed, but it was malignant and widespread. Returning from Japan, Bill's son-in-law, Dick Amos, joined his wife, Judy, and her mother, Mary, at Bill's bedside. Then on

June 29, at 11:23 a.m., Bill Gillam walked down heaven's streets. We mourned our loss yet rejoiced in the assurance of his eternal destiny.

Opportunities and Obstacles

Apart from the loss of our beloved Bill Gillam, the recent past six months had been a period of seeking to emphasize OMS's spiritual priorities, evangelistic fruitfulness, aggressive missionary activity, expanding ministry, and financial growth. With the world so spiritually needy, the population of our fields so rapidly increasing, opportunities so overwhelming, and God-given results so encouraging, we would fail God if we did not plan, work, pray, and believe for rapid growth in spiritual outreach and effectiveness. We needed to trust him, as one, to supply the missionaries, leadership, and support to meet our goals.

The OMS annual convention theme was taken from Bill Gillam's last message, "Whatever It Takes." On Friday, July 2, heaven seemed very close in an auditorium on the campus of Anderson College as we gathered for the memorial service of our deeply loved Bill Gillam, who free of pain, awaits the arrival of thousands whom his godly magnetism drew into the kingdom of God. Although the attendance of all annual convention sessions was almost identical to the previous year, a thousand people who attended the memorial service could be added to the 1971 counts. Many wonderful testimonies of blessings were received and life challenges accepted through Bill, and we rejoiced in how God reminded us of his life well-lived.

In the spirit of our departed brother, we bowed in humble gratitude to God, who had accomplished great things. His holy call remained upon us. We dared not fail him or the waiting world. We needed to keep our spiritual priorities clear. We needed to continue to seek to give strong leadership in every field and department of the Society. God proved over and over again that if we stepped out in faith and obedience, he would supply our needs. In the life of faith, we knew that without God's favor, any month could bring disaster, and for more than seventy years we'd proven his faithfulness.

By the grace of God, we looked to him for the greatest period of soul-winning advance we had ever known, strengthening the national church on all our fields and training reapers for the whitened harvest. We prayed and believed for revival blessings on our fields and for many new missionaries for which our fields were calling. We needed adequate finances to make it possible to take bold, new steps in reaching the nations for Christ. As long as unreached souls were still waiting, we dared not relax, for if we did, we would have the blood of lost souls on our hands. We stood in prayer and faith for miracles to the glory of God.

STRENGTHENING SPIRITUAL LIFE (1972)

In the life of faith, one can never relax. While we rejoiced, we also kept praying. But it was glorious to see our mission's unofficial theme song, "Great Is Thy Faithfulness," verified anew year after year. The last year had been a wonderful time of answered prayer in many ways. Financially, the USA undesignated income for the last seven months showed an average increase of twenty or more percent per month over the same period the previous year. That did not just happen. A lot of prayer and faithful effort—meetings, letters, and personal contacts—made it possible. We closed the year in the black with field budgets and allowances not only paid but the date of payment moved ahead. *To God be all the glory!*

Like a trinity of spiritual mountain tops, we had three important gatherings back-to-back: the board's annual business meeting, our annual missionaries retreat, and then our annual convention, where we endeavored to inform, inspire, and involve our dear faithful supporters, kindhearted donors, and generous board members. By scheduling these three annual events back-to-back, we enabled more board members and missionary families to mix and meet with key partners in the gospel.

In early July, the OMS annual missionary retreat started. The OMS body of Christ carried a huge load when conducting our annual retreats and conventions. No fewer than seven OMS missionaries and two special outside speakers were employed of the Lord to remind us of our rich spiritual heritage and possibilities for the future "in Christ."

Our past president, Dr. Eugene Erny, brought the final evening message. We were led into Ephesians, and again we went walking in love and unity. We were shown the wealth, the walk, and the warfare. God came in a special way during this last service. Numbers lined the altar to pray and to share. Teenagers and veteran missionaries mingled their tears and voices in confessions and victorious praises. Broken fellowships were mended, and discouragements were exchanged for new challenges.

Our annual convention started right on the heels of our missionary gathering. Conventions were designed to provide information, inspiration, and opportunities for personal involvement by our constituency, who came from all around North America and included national coworkers from abroad. Held in Anderson, Indiana, this was a time of inspiration and blessing.

The first evening began with the largest opening crowd I'd ever seen. God helping me, I pressed home hard on the need for prayer. More than fifty of our own personnel participated in the convention. Our goal was to ensure that every field and outreach ministry had an opportunity to be presented. We intentionally sprinkled in victories won for praise and worship as well as challenges past and present, faced and unknown but anticipated, in order to rally needed prayer, supplication, and intercession.

At the close of each day, everyone shifted into the small gym for refreshments, renewed friendships, and a look at the field displays. Those were placed against the outside wall, leaving in the center an open area for food and fellowship, both of which were of first quality.

The annual seven-day convention was shortened to four days, interspersed with significant prayer emphasis. Nevertheless, MFMI experienced a record attendance on Saturday of nearly sixteen hundred, with three hundred shares pledged. Youth camp was the largest ever with five hundred. Our Every Community for Christ (ECC) ministry produced conversions at the rate of about seven dollars per conversion (with more than nine thousand decisions reported) that year. And the early morning prayer breakfasts doubled in comparison to previous years.

On Saturday evening, Dr. Erny stepped to the pulpit, and due to time limitations, he gave a bare-bones message: "I Sent You to Reap." The Holy Spirit powered it home, and the youth poured forward to the altar upon the invitation. The tears flowed, and God drew close.

At the closing Sunday morning, I was privileged to give a distillation of what had been said throughout the convention, asking, "Can you see Ecuador? Japan? India? Colombia?" On and on, I cataloged the burdens and challenges of each place. With God's help, I poured out my heart-burden with tears.

We thanked God for the tremendous group of missionary coworkers, cooperating leaders, national believers, and home staff members. We also thanked him for the great worldwide family of prayer warriors and supporters of the Society who made it all possible. *To God be all the glory!*

At the closing of the year, we praised and thanked God for a wonderful harvest in every aspect of the ministry. It was a great year in evangelism, with over forty-five thousand professions of faith and ninety-five new churches. It was a year of planning, initiative, and progress toward the goals on many of our fields, with increased prayer support and many miraculous answers to prayer. It was also a year of the largest financial receipts in our history, with nearly 17 percent overall growth.

We prioritized evangelism and church growth on the fields and recruitment and growth in support of our home bases. Our target was 146 new missionaries over the next two years. But our concern was not merely statistical growth. We needed to experience more spiritual growth. Three concerns were suggested Society-wide: (1) that we would be watchful that spiritual power not be diminished in any way, (2) that doctrinal unity not be diminished, and (3) that we not lose any of the family closeness of spirit. It was the Holy Spirit's day of power.

God was calling us to new dimensions of obedience and to greatly accelerated conquest:

> Now to him who is able to do immeasurably more than all we ask or imagine, according to his power that is at work within us, to him be glory in the church and in Christ Jesus throughout all generations, for ever and ever! Amen (Eph 3:20–21).

Just as Christ set his face like a flint to go to Calvary, we also set our faces to take to the world the message of full and free salvation through Calvary's price and resurrection power. If the Holy Spirit was in us and upon us, we needed to be OMS—*On the Move for Souls.*

TAKING THE PULSE (1973)

In March through April 1973, along with many of our headquarters staff who traveled, I left for almost six weeks on a five-nation tour through India, Indonesia, Hong Kong, Taiwan, and Korea. After nine years' absence from residence in India, what a joy it was to spend nearly three weeks in-country again!

India

I was able to see all our missionaries and all but one national coworker while touring four of the five areas of our work. The OMS-established national church in India had officially registered as "The Evangelical Church of India" (ECI), its legal and formal name.

New Delhi had miles of new housing developments on the edge of the city without one Christian church. Dr. I. Ben Wati, executive secretary of the Evangelical Fellowship of India (EFI), and others offered to do anything they could to help us get started.

Days in Allahabad were all too brief. They reported 104 decisions for Christ during the convention that year, and the seminary was filled to capacity with thirty-five students. It was my joy to share in the dedication service for the new dining room and dormitory, which was completed at an unbelievably low cost and would make an increased enrollment that fall possible.

Outreach was opened on the Nepal border, amid great interest. Baptisms were expected, and there was hope for at least one new congregation. There was almost no gospel work there, but there was a promise of great fruitfulness. Coworkers were begging OMS to make a survey and launch new ministry in that challenging place on India's border.

Northwest India and the Punjab area reported new blessing. Thousands of Gospels and tracts were distributed. They had ten baptisms that year, and a new congregation ninety-five kilometers from our Shimla church would be organized into an officially recognized church.

The mid-India area reported tremendous blessing. Our day of prayer with the national coworkers was filled with thrilling reports. We had six churches and twenty preaching points. Several thousand Scriptures and 135,000 other pieces of gospel literature were placed into the hands of non-Christians that year, and an all-night of prayer was held once a month.

In the Gadag area, five hundred people had attended the camp meeting. Touches of revival blessing in the district followed. Four new ministers were ordained, and we prayed that four new congregations would be organized.

Also, quite a few new believers were preparing for baptism. Training in evangelism was planned, with three-day evangelism meetings for five village centers. Five central towns were also to conduct a special evangelistic campaign.

In the southern Madras area, Isaiah 54:2–3 was being fulfilled, and God was helping new growth to break forth on the right hand and the left. There were two hundred baptisms that year. Two church buildings were under construction, and four plots of land were purchased. Eighteen of the churches were making strong progress toward self-support. Eight to ten new congregations were expected to be organized, and the goal of the district was one hundred churches by 1980.

A second ECC team was launched in June! Approximately two thousand full church members were in our Madras district. Many others were being prepared for baptism. One church practiced daily prayer sessions. Another church held all-day fasting each Friday, with some people from outstations spending the whole weekend so they could learn more about Christ. There was demonic opposition, and many demons were cast out. In several places, laity were really on fire for the Lord. One pastor was severely beaten by a mob, but a week later the mob leader came and asked for forgiveness. He was saved, and three other families came to Christ.

The Madras Bible Seminary (MBS) was filled to capacity. Eight new graduates could hardly wait for school to conclude that year so they could be out in the harvest, sharing in soul-winning with the others. We desperately needed to renovate the seminary and make room for more students. The

Madras Bible Seminary

district was asking for another million tracts as soon as we could make them available. God was giving us the greatest days in India I had ever seen. A well of praise overflowed in my soul!

Indonesia

It was also great to visit Indonesia, where our missionaries were preaching their first sermons in the native language. For some years, dramatic reports about revival in Indonesia had circulated. On our survey trip, as Dale McClain and I interviewed leaders of various denominations, we had been repeatedly advised to emphasize what was happening as a tremendous harvest opportunity, with pockets of revival here and there, but not to exaggerate the picture or imply that revival was sweeping Indonesia. Some hadn't followed that advice and, as a result, several books appeared claiming miracles of turning water into wine, raising the dead, and so on. Practically all evangelical groups tried to disassociate themselves from those exaggerated stories, but some people were quick to believe anything they heard, particularly if it sounded miraculous.

Some tremendously significant new prospects were opening before us in Indonesia just as we were ready to move forward for God. Our missionaries were involved in Bible classes, student contacts, and children's work. Although we experienced delay after delay, we discerned the hand of God in the delays. We believed for a greater tomorrow as God guided our field team in developing the ministry, and I believed that trip to Indonesia was of the Lord.

Hong Kong

In Hong Kong, we had a series of six wonderful youth rallies. Much prayer was invested in plans for God's future direction in the work there, as we sought new fruitfulness and church growth.

Taiwan

In Taiwan, it was my privilege to participate in an Easter Sunday baptismal service, which included people won to Christ through our radio ministry. The radio ministry had experienced a tremendous response, with more than a thousand converts that past year. One of those was an eighty-year-old, rejoicing in the Lord. Renovations to the seminary campus were proceeding quickly. New well-trained national staff were taking their role in the seminary, and we needed to rapidly run through the wide-open door God set before us.

Korea

In Korea, I was surprised to be welcomed by seven OMS missionaries at the Seoul airport. When we arrived at the prayer conference center, Dr. Peter Kao was my roommate. I met numerous other well-known leaders, like Edwin Orr, David Bryant, Richard Loveless, and Tom Tarrant.

At the prayer conference, a thousand copies of my article "Recruiting Prayer" were distributed. It was prepared for the EFMA at the request of Mrs. Vonette Bright and Ben Jennings, and copies were distributed in Korean, Mandarin, and Japanese. Little did we know we would soon see a new day of partnership in worldwide missions with our national churches!

One rainy night, we had a city-wide, all-night of prayer in Dank Sang Park. People prayed all night long, with very few leaving, and there were still nearly seven thousand present the next morning. Then there was a second all-night of prayer. It was the largest rally ever at Dank Sang Park. Our Korean coworker Dr. John Chongnahm Cho interpreted for Dr. Harold Lindsell, one of the main speakers. God gave me an amazing experience when a man from Kenya said he had been reading my writings for twenty-five years. He prayed that he might meet me, and God answered his prayer at the conference. There was also a lady who remembered me from my time in Sri Lanka and India.

It was great to also be in Korea for the biennial session of the OMS Conference of Asian Holiness Churches, composed of Japan, Korea, and Taiwan, with a hundred delegates and observers, plus representatives of the Japanese and Korean churches in the USA as well as OMS field leaders from the Orient. The leaders of those national churches voted to begin world missionary outreach in partnership with OMS.[7] God enabled the second great reunification of our churches. Satan had tried to divide our OMS-founded Korean church, but Korea then had more than 750 organized congregations.

God was doing amazing things in the armed forces of Korea, where OMS had more than fifty seminary graduates in the chaplaincy. It was almost a mini-revival, with two to three thousand baptisms per month. I received word of more than 5,700 military men baptized in Korea by our seminary chaplains in two weeks' time.

God had shown us the reason for the long delays in the seminary relocation in Korea—He gave a far better plot of land, supplying the funds to purchase it. Construction operations began within a few weeks. The seminary had more than 250 students. My, what a joy to

---

7   This gathering was the precursor to what eventually became the Asia-Pacific Federation of Holiness Churches. That association has gone through several name changes but consisted of all the OMS-established, or OMS-related, national churches located in the Asia-Pacific region.

hear them sing. They prayed and fasted one meal a day for more than a month, and God brought wonderful answers.

Rapid Growth

We were in the most rapid period of growth we had ever known. It was a year of accelerated God-guided growth in faith, outreach, finance, and personnel. God gave us fifty-four new congregations, and 42,678 professed Christ as Savior. Isaiah 54:2–3, my life's verse, was being fulfilled in a thrillingly new way. *To God be the glory!*

With our board of trustees, I shared: No advance is fast enough when you are advancing for God. Do we believe one soul is worth more than all this world? Do we believe millions more are lost today than ever before? We are setting more goals than ever before. A quick count this week shows our fields have set at least 562 goals for next year. We must pray, work, and run to fulfill them.

Some things must never change: Our threefold call to evangelism, training national leadership, and church planting and church growth. Though our goals are more modern, more contemporary today than they were seventy years ago, God gave OMS these objectives in the very first months of OMS. Our doctrine must never change. We may try to state it more clearly. We may use contemporary terms, but our doctrine must never change. Our call, our spirit, our unity, our dependence on the Holy Spirit, our family spirit—these must never change.

We must be willing to change. Leaders will change, methods will change, and the media we use will change. If changing them will bring more souls to Christ, bring more believers into the sanctifying fullness of the Spirit, or train more hundreds to be soul-winners, then the faster we move, the better.

Not only did we as a Society seek to put evangelism first, but I asked for everyone to be a personal soul-winner. I was attracted to OMS through two nationals—a Korean and a Japanese who were constantly winning souls. I prayed soul-winning would be the mark of an OMS missionary.

We needed to double our prayer support, to find ways to multiply prayer. The most repeated promises of God are that he works when we pray. We cannot earn his blessing. Prayer prepares the way of the Lord, and then he works.

Above all, I appealed for everyone to go deeper in the Holy Spirit! OMS always stood for the deeper life of the Spirit and ministry in the power of the Spirit. So, I asked everyone if they could witness that they were definitely born of the Spirit, filled with the Spirit, led of the Spirit, praying in the Spirit, and experiencing the anointing of the Spirit. I said,

> There is no OMS International apart from the Holy Spirit. So many Christians are born of the Spirit but have never been filled with the Spirit, living defeated lives. They have a powerless prayer life and a powerless witness. Part of their life is still unsurrendered to God. They lack Spirit-given purity and Spirit-given power. OMS must live in the miraculous power of the Spirit.

FOCUSING ON EVANGELISM (1974)

Our thirtieth annual convention in early July set the pace with our largest turnout of over two thousand registered participants. At its close, eighty-seven missionaries lined the altar, the greatest number to be commissioned at one time.

In Japan, youth crusades in three major cities generated more than thirteen hundred professions of faith in Christ. Youth camps began on Oshima Island—where the church sent its first missionary family overseas since World War II—and an evangelistic luncheon in Tokyo drew three hundred women with numerous salvation decisions.

In Korea, a new witness booklet launched a desperately needed five-year literature program for our churches. A special summer extension school provided training for pastors. The sad division in our Korea national church work was largely healed, with the return of 108 churches, 118 pastors, and 25,897 believers. The new, enlarged seminary building was well underway. Earlier, I mentioned how God was doing amazing things in the armed forces of Korea, where OMS had more than fifty seminary graduates in the chaplaincy. January was when those more than 5,700 Korean military men were baptized in just two weeks. About half of them were baptized in one day at a site one and a half miles from the DMZ. The Korean air force chief of chaplains, Lee Kyung Soon, and fifty-five other chaplains—all grads of our Seoul seminary—led in these mass baptism services. Hundreds of thousands openly confessed faith in Jesus Christ as their Savior. More than fifty thousand men sealed their testimonies with water baptism.

From Taiwan came word of more than a thousand converts from a year's radio broadcast ministry, and Scriptures were sent to five thousand newspaper ad inquirers. Six new churches were under construction, and the Taichung Bible School campus reconstruction was nearing completion.

Hong Kong wrote of a new evangelistic center established in Kamtim, with evening Bible classes drawing inquirers, 150 children graduating from OMS schools, and the first basic teachers' training classes underway.

After two years' delay, approval for OMS registration in Indonesia propelled formal opening of a strategic student evangelistic center, with seventy-six students enrolled for Bible studies. Also, an evangelistic center in a newly opened area with forty thousand people without a witness, gave access to an ethnic group of five hundred thousand having tremendous spiritual need.

India reported 36 percent growth in church membership and 29 percent growth in church offerings in the last year. Our India team was thrilled with the largest attendance ever at ABS. New fruitfulness was reported in the formerly slow-bearing Northwest region, with a 47 percent increase in baptisms in the Gadag area and a 50 percent increase in church offerings by village Christians. Also, there were new congregations and church buildings in the Madras area. There were unusual cases of deliverance from demon possession, and God's healing power attracted Hindus to the claims of Christ.

When entering OMS Spain, six seasoned missionaries were ready, along with the divine provision of an office. We sought legal recognition for full-fledged outreach while conducting surveys. Already, thirty-five thousand students were enrolled in Light and Life correspondence courses.

On our Brazil field, God gave touches of revival in October. Missionaries sent word of double enrollment in our seminary, three new congregations formed in suburbs of Sao Paulo, a new church building and seven-class Sunday school in Londrina, a new congregation in Andrandina, and many decisions for Christ through an OMS-sponsored "Congress on Evangelism" attracting three thousand attendees.

A breakthrough of Ecuadorian Indian youth attending OMS youth camp encouraged our Ecuador staff, along with an upswing of interest in women's Bible study groups and house-to-house visitation. In the resistant Saraguro mountain area, regular gospel witness was reaching eighteen villages with encouraging results. Quito outreach demonstrated great strides, and a youth congress registered two hundred participants, plus many decisions for Christ.

In Colombia, a rapid increase in extension seminary students raised the total to twelve classes in five centers. OMS Bible and bookstores were supplying many Bibles and books on the Holy Spirit to priests and nuns, with hundreds of letters telling of spiritual victories received from the radio ministry. A new wing on our Christian high school in Bogotá added to this unique outreach, and over three hundred delegates from many denominations attended the first national Christian education conference held at our OMS center. Cristalina school students led nearly 850 children to Christ in child evangelism meetings during vacation months, and 91 percent growth of OMS church membership during the past five years made OMS one of the fastest growing groups in Colombia.

Haiti, as well, gave indication of thrilling growth. A typical month at the Bethesda Clinic recorded more than three thousand patients treated, 1,220 laboratory analyses completed, 6,500 pieces of gospel literature distributed, and 130 won for Christ. Church membership in the last three years had increased 41 percent with twelve new churches established, and a goal to establish fifteen to twenty more in the coming year.

World Intercessors reported more than three dozen prayer-and-share retreats held in the same six months, with over 1,300 registered in attendance; twenty-five new prayer fellowships organized; hundreds of new prayer families and over 220 new prayer partners enlisted; with over 3,300 new commitments to world intercessors; and more than 18,750 receiving the *Intercesso-Gram* monthly. Each month almost four thousand "Prayer Dime Calendars" were sent out, and almost 650 new prayer calendar commitments were received.

MFMI was busy as well, coordinating more than seventy-five cars used by furloughing missionaries who had traveled over 1,250,000 miles that year, saving the Society more than four hundred thousand dollars. Witness and work crusades continued to increase and bless our fields. New volunteer associate staff broadened the outreach, and countless thousands of dollars and human resource hours extended God's cause through these dedicated laity.

As for finances, we praised God for another year of his supply for all our needs, despite national confusion, financial fluctuation, international devaluation of currencies, and acute inflation, which hurt all our fields, as well as homeland operations. In response to our special end-of-year appeal letter, God provided more than thirty-eight thousand dollars.

We praised God for all he was doing through OMS. Those were surely his harvest days. He had given us more converts that past year than ever before—an average of one soul every ten minutes, day and night. We were overflowing with praise to the Lord. We were sowing, often with tears, but thank God, we were also reaping, singing as we brought in the sheaves. Yet our victories seemed so insignificant in the face of such overwhelming need that we felt as did Luke, "We are unworthy servants; we have only done our duty" (Luke 17:10).

We praised God that the year had been filled with extensive and fruitful evangelism on most fields and had shown strong advancements for Christ. By faith we approved new ministries and budgets to support them. God supplied unusual financial growth, and the faith steps were implemented despite great financial pressure. Some major projects, however, urgently needed funding.

Apart from the constant hunger for more and more of God's blessing and power upon us and the hunger for more and more souls to lay at his feet, my two heaviest burdens for which I solicited both prayers and suggestions were: (1) a great need to recruit more field missionaries; and (2) a great need for additional financial support to fund our homeland staff. We needed a financial miracle in offerings before the end of the year.

Based on my experiences in Korea, Japan, Brazil, and South Africa, I sensed the spiritual potential was tremendous. It reinforced to me that it was God's harvest day. We were believing him for total growth, ever increasing effectiveness, and new sources of personnel and funds. We were studying how best to restructure for ever-widening international involvement and cooperation in reaching the nations for Christ, and I pleaded for daily prayer and helpful suggestions and cooperation. God had given us a wonderful year!

PREPARING FOR OMS'S SEVENTY-FIFTH ANNIVERSARY (1975)

The most suitable form of commemoration of the seventy-five years of God's ministry through OMS—from 1901 to 1976—would be a strong advance for him. Starting in 1975, we called upon the board, every field, every department, and every missionary to join in making such an advance possible. We challenged our constituency to join in faith for the greatest year of progress and victory we had ever known. We prayed God would make it a special year of prayer and evangelism! It was a time to seek him in a new and greater way than ever before. God had given great victories in answer to our labor and prayer.

It was not a time to sit back and congratulate ourselves on the past seventy-five years of God's faithfulness. It was a time to humble ourselves, asking God's forgiveness that we had not accomplished far more. It was a time to intercede mightily for additional years of far greater miracles if Jesus were to tarry. We had to consecrate ourselves totally, more than ever before, to the unfinished task that increased with the rapidity of earth's exploding population.

The board of trustees took strong steps of faith as we declared the calendar year of 1976 as our official seventy-fifth anniversary jubilee year. It was set apart as a year of prayer, during which we hoped to double our prayer enlistment worldwide. The OMS work was advancing strongly, with constant reports of conversions, baptisms, the founding of new local churches, and fruitful evangelistic crusades and efforts. Despite worldwide inflation and financial pressure, God continued to supply our needs, and the work was growing rapidly.

The year was also set apart as a year of all-out evangelism, with a goal of seventy-five thousand souls for Christ, a greatly increased distribution of Scriptures and gospel literature, and a special one-million-dollar fund for evangelism, urban center evangelism, and many other special funds within the total one-million-dollar goal.

In the midst of continued rejoicing at the thrilling hand of God revealed in so many reports from our twelve fields, I could not forget that for every soul won, a thousand more waited for God's transforming power. God was holding us responsible for each of them. If we were a thousand times more fruitful than we had been, there would still be an overwhelming need remaining to be met. If any one of those unreached were our own son or daughter, we would strain every effort to reach them. In God's sight, each one was more precious than our entire world. We could not relax our efforts. We had to multiply them. But above all, we had to multiply our prayer coverage of all OMS witness and ministry.

As we evaluated OMS programs, we compared our reports with the great heritage of what God had already done for and through us, current potential in the present OMS team of missionaries, and the great unfinished task for which we were each personally responsible and for which OMS was collectively responsible by the call of God. We could not afford ineffective service and ministry. We could not afford spiritual defeat or mediocrity. We could not afford merely to mark time and to serve without repeated outpourings of God's Spirit upon us and frequent tokens of his special blessing and seal. God held us responsible to multiply results. We existed for results.

Among the projects approved for the coming year was a special new ministry to Mainland China, consisting of a daily fifteen-minute radio broadcast under the title "Streams in the Desert," to be broadcast from two 250,000-watt Far East Broadcasting Company stations, one in Korea and the other in North Luzon, Philippines. That broadcast began January 1, and by faith, we were committing ourselves to the heavy cost of nearly $125 a day. We were putting the devotional *Streams in the Desert* by Lettie Cowman into the new Mao script of Mainland China, and we had means to get a steady number of those into China itself, even though they would have to go in quietly and by ones, twos, and threes. We needed to focus united, believing prayer on this new ministry of blessing, which would have a twofold purpose: to comfort the hidden Christians on the Mainland, and to be God's tool for soft-sell evangelism to touch hearts in their time of need in life's crises. We were believing God to mightily use that broadcast, including the daily portion from *Streams in the Desert*.

ANNIVERSARY CELEBRATIONS (1976)

Our seventy-fifth anniversary convention was held in Greenwood with twelve hundred registered and two hundred guests from eighteen nations. We commissioned fifty-six missionaries returning to their fields, the most ever, and forty-six new missionaries, all but one for the fields. Altogether, one hundred and two missionaries, committed to the Lord, were heading to their fields of service.

That summer, the OMS board had reelected me to another term as president. What an overwhelming responsibility! I asked for prayer daily, for capable and strong leadership in that day of opportunity. I remembered the words of the apostle Paul, who said that we Christians would stand before Christ to be judged for things we do after we are saved (2 Cor 5:9–11). One reason we try to win souls, he says in verse 11, is because of this fear of Christ's judgment. We will be judged for how we use our time, funds, possessions, and opportunities.

Paul said some Christians were using their time, abilities, and funds to build a life like a house made of straw (1 Cor 3:10–17). Though Christ laid the foundation, what we place thereon can be so self-centered that judgment fire can burn it up. Saved, but with a wasted, lost life—lost time, lost money—because it was not invested for Christ. The blood of souls can be required of Christians (Ezek 3:18). Paul did not want his hands to be stained with the blood of men he had failed to warn and win (Acts 20:26). That same responsibility weighed heavily upon me in leading the mission.

Celebrating God's Great Faithfulness

As I prepared my report to the board before we entered our seventy-fifth anniversary year, I thought about January 1901, when Charles and Lettie Cowman sailed for Japan, and then how in February of that year they reached Japan and began the OMS field ministry.

On September 25, 1924, Charles Cowman's spirit left his battle-worn body and he entered heaven. His wife, Lettie, found a slip of paper in his Bible, his last written words to her and OMS: "Go on with my unfinished task," a message to us on this seventy-fifth anniversary. Cowman's challenge was reiterated to the OMS board.

We recounted how One greater than Charles Cowman, his own Lord and ours, gave a command to the apostles just before he ascended to the right hand of the Father. Acts 1:2 tells us that he ascended, "after giving instructions through the Holy Spirit." What was that command, that last all-important command of Jesus Christ on earth?

> Wait for the promise of the Father. . . you shall receive power when the Holy Spirit is come upon you; and you shall be my witnesses both in Jerusalem, and in all Judea, and Samaria, and to the end of the earth (Acts 1:4, 8 RSV).

The next moment he rose into the sky.

The past seventy-five years had been a record of God's call, OMS's obedience, and God's faithfulness. In 1976, OMS reported 509 missionaries co-laboring with 2,300 national coworkers. The words "Great Is Thy Faithfulness," our unofficial hymn from the days of the Cowmans, rang out as the testimony of the OMS missionary body and family for seventy-five years.

We praised God that the thrust for world evangelism continued. That year, nearly 113,000 people sought Christ. That was an average of approximately one soul each five minutes. We praised God that baptisms increased 144 percent over the previous year. God helped us do a better job of discipling than ever before. Yet we were hungry for much more. I prayed that by the end of the decade we would have at least 150,000 souls coming to Christ annually.

We were thrilled by the strong assurance of God at work through OMS. We were blessed but burdened, because funds were coming in slower through the summer, which delayed missionary candidates in their anticipated deployment.

We saluted the Brazil conference of our Japanese church on its fiftieth anniversary, as well as Central Taiwan Theological College in Taichung on its twenty-fifth anniversary, the Taiwan Holiness Church on its fiftieth anniversary, and the Association of Evangelical Churches of Colombia on its twenty-fifth anniversary. We had so much for which to thank God!

We called upon everyone to stand united in a new dedication to Christ, to his last and Great Commission, and to the fulfilling of his unfinished task. With seventy-five years of history behind us, the call of Christ upon us, and both a lost world and eternity before us, we needed to dedicate ourselves anew to reaching our world for Christ. My prayer was for God to keep OMS—*On the Move for Souls.*

Concluding our seventy-fifth anniversary year, unofficial OMS historian, Rev. Robert Wood, quoted the nineteenth-century English poet Robert Southy, from his poem "The Battle of Blenheim"—"But what good came of it at last?" A casual reader might ask that same question. At last. Was that the end of glorious victories and celebrations? The answer was simple: it was not "at last"—yet. There are no "at lasts" to that which continues.

Looking Back: The Work Must Go On

The Cowman Memorial Bible Institute compound in Shanghai was reduced to rubble during the Sino-Japanese conflict in the late 1930s. Japanese authorities occasionally permitted Brother E. L. Kilbourne to visit the ruins. On one spring day in 1939, he and Mrs. Hazel Kilbourne shuffled through the charred debris, and he made these observations:

> As we . . . were about to enter our precious home, I looked in the weeds, now growing over the sidewalks, and spied a sheet out of a hymn book . . . Picking it up I showed it to Mrs. Kilbourne, and we rejoiced together, for the song was "The Work Must Go On!" Is it not an article of faith with those of whose God it is said, "He overthrows the mighty"?

How do you go about foiling the plans of the One who arranges things so that man's wrath only adds to his glory? Was the phrase "the work must go on" unconsciously ringing in Brother Kilbourne's mind when the board of directors met in the summer of 1939 and unanimously approved opening the new field of India? Once again, the Society planned a move when it was illogical to do so. OMS had no financial resources to expand outreach, and within days, Hitler stormed into Poland and ignited the war.

Two future presidents of OMS were used by God in that decision. Rev. Eugene Erny had been with the mission since the early part of the decade and assumed the helm in 1949. Rev. Kilbourne, informing the constituents of the board's decision to enter India, reported that God had put a definite challenge upon Rev. Erny's heart regarding India, especially about training and sending forth nationals for the establishment of a native church along aggressive evangelistic lines. That last phrase contained the genius of OMS and expressed my own concern while enrolled at GBS.

Though God's leading to India preceded World War II, one can see his hand in the timing from this distance. Had the Society not been called, or had the leadership been insensitive to that call, would OMS have been forced to close up shop when ministry became impossible in its three Orient fields?

OMS's entry into South America was directly related to the exigencies of war. Charles Culver and Roy Adams, the latter recently from Asia, had flown off to look things over in South America. By October, the board announced that "after months of prayer and personal observation of the needs and opportunities" to the south, they felt "led of the Lord to begin work in one or two of those countries."

"We are not unconscious of the obstacles," one wrote. Regarding personnel, Mrs. Cowman explained, "We have not felt led to send our China missionaries to our new field. . . but are praying for workers with a definite call to that field." She wrote in March 1943:

> A very clear and definite call from God. . . came to us a
> few months ago. A burden and travail were laid upon us
> that lasted for weeks. We saw South America reaching out
> her hands of need. We heard her cry for help. With this
> call which was as definite as that of 41 years ago when we
> followed him into the lands of the Far East, the prayer was
> made almost hourly. Lord, show us who will go with us into
> the land of the Southern Cross.

Then, at last, came the command, "Up, for this is the day!" Mrs. Cowman announced the coming to the Society of Dr. Ben H. Pearson, who was not only to lay the foundations of our work in Colombia but also to chronicle those years. Disclosure of the acceptance of John and Beatrice Palmer, veteran English missionaries with another agency in Argentina, was made a month earlier. Before many years, the Colombia missionaries experienced grievous trouble equal to any faced by others in the East. Their courageous, unflinching response would be the same: regardless, "the work must go on." It was the same passion that gripped OMS as we faced the "at last," when the work is finally finished.

Moving Forward

We were moving forward, perhaps faster than ever before. It had been thirty-six years since Betty and I sailed from Los Angeles with five other OMS missionaries to launch our work in India. But now our responsibilities carried us from field to field, from conference to conference, from committee session to committee session. Our role was to help and coordinate, plan for new advances, answer several thousand letters a year, encourage, strengthen, guide, and challenge to new faith and sacrifice at home and to new faith and advance on the fields. That year's responsibilities had taken me to Asia-Pacific areas four times, and all the actual travel time going and coming was less than two weeks! Many other weeks that year were spent in conventions, conferences, and one-night meetings in many cities.

The speed with which God was answering prayer seemed to be quickening in many places. The growth of the work kept us almost breathless as we sought his constant blessing and the constant prayer and support of his people. We were pouring out our lives for God in every way we knew how. Repeatedly, I feared we would not keep pace with all God was depending upon us to do in those wonderful days.

CELEBRATING AND SEEKING (1977)

The year 1977 was a period of continued OMS growth, a year of joy and blessing. We praised God for an ever-expanding ministry around the world. The rapid growth God was giving OMS was a constant cause of rejoicing, yet growth was also a factor in many pressures and some problems. Growth cannot always be predicted, and it is never even. Rapid growth in one department can put pressure on other aspects of the ministry or work. Rapid growth in new congregations may bring real pressure in follow-up and finding pastors. Lay leaders may need to be trained. It cannot be done overnight.

Great growth causes overcrowded churches, seminary dormitories, and classrooms—and heavy pressure on overloaded faculty members. Rapid growth of new believers calls for increased programs of discipleship and special campaigns in the churches for deepening the spiritual life. That is especially true where many are unable to read and write.

Field growth, for which we longed and prayed, always brought greater pressures on our homeland offices. We praised God for a growing constituency. Without them the fields could not advance. But accounting procedures for the growing ministry, with provision for personalized and designated giving for missionaries, students, evangelists, and projects, were exceedingly complex. Over seventeen thousand accounts were in our computer, plus over 110,000 individual donor accounts. The work to receipt, account for, and report on funds, maintain mailing lists, keep up with the multitude of prayer letters, and produce field and promotional brochures all imposed many pressures.

When we had a shortage of personnel, we couldn't just immediately go out and employ someone. First, we had to recruit people who felt God's call to OMS. Then they were screened and had to raise their personal support. We needed to find housing for them. Thus, the gap between the moment when need was experienced and when a person began service required an extensive length of time that brought pressure both in the department where the need existed as well as related departments.

We thanked God for the growth, but we asked our brethren to pray for the multifaceted, interrelated elements of outreach around the world. On all our fields, there was the constant pressure of financial inflation and the constant pressure of funding for the rapidly expanding ministries. Again and again, we were driven to our knees as we sought God's answers.

Last, there were the constant pressures Satan brought upon the work, which were discouraging and caused tension between brethren, raising questions in people's minds. Those on the field often wondered why we could not get personnel and funds to them more adequately and more quickly as they faced the overwhelming opportunities before them. It seemed almost criminal when people of vision, with hearts longing to reach their countries for Christ, sensed the whiteness of the harvest, the wide-open doors, and yet were unable to enter them adequately for God. Those were the kinds of matters that drove us to prayer. We depended on intercessory prayer and sensitive, caring, generous hearts.

Korea Evangelical Holiness Church Seventieth Anniversary

However, "return on investment" was extremely gratifying. How I wish you could have been along for the seventieth anniversary of the Korea Evangelical Holiness Church! It was my privilege to address one of the night rallies as about eight thousand met in a large stadium.

But what moved me far more was seeing more than 236 plaques awarded to our Korean brothers and sisters. These were distributed to twenty-six small groups, such as the widows or children of the Korean pastors martyred for Christ, those imprisoned for three months or more, those who founded orphanages, those who gave beyond their tithes and offerings to the church building fund for three consecutive years, and those who had won a minimum of a hundred souls to Christ for a minimum of three consecutive years. One member had already won more than three hundred to Christ that year. Again and again, our eyes were filled with tears as people came forward and stood with bowed heads as the citations were read.

What a praying people! One of our churches had held nonstop prayer for the past three years. All our churches conducted early morning prayer meetings each day of the year. Many had all-nights of prayer each Friday night. Many youth groups prayed all night each Thursday night. What tremendous praying—like the sound of many waters referred to in the book of Revelation! May God teach us all to pray more!

As we closed calendar year 1977, fewer than two dozen years remained in the greatest century missions had ever known. Yet the earth's population was to grow from less than two billion to nearly six billion in the twenty-first century. While great numbers had been won to Christ through all evangelical agencies, the twentieth century was to be the century of the greatest unfinished task the church had ever faced.

OMS had come three quarters of the way through the twentieth century, and God had been accelerating the pace of our ministries in recent years. What did he expect us to accomplish in the coming years? Whatever he was planning, it would be possible only as the Holy Spirit came upon us with a mighty renewal and revival throughout our ranks and fields. If we were to adequately fulfill our mandate in our present fields and be led by the Holy Spirit into new fields, we would require a God-given insight, vision, and guidance; a God-inspired holy daring; a creative innovativeness; and an unwavering and ever-enlarging faith through the ministry of the Holy Spirit. As God gave growth on our fields and our national churches matured, developed new leadership, and increased their ministries, they, too, would need repeated visitations of God. Apart from these, they would be in danger of disunity, doctrinal weakening or diversion, political methods of the world infiltrating the churches, and a decline in holy living, vigorous evangelism, and church growth.

Our only answer was repeated outpourings of the Holy Spirit upon our worldwide family. The Holy Spirit is given as we prepare our hearts by new obedience and as we seek God's face in all-out intercession. Would we maintain the vision, the holy passion, and the clear-cut doctrinal commitments of our founders? Would we lose the momentum of the Spirit? Would we become large, but spiritually weak and flabby? In time, would we divide, decline, and die?

On each leader of OMS weighed the heavy responsibility of whatever eventuates in the tomorrows. If we grew so carelessly, we'd lose our character and fire, and that last quarter of the century could see the demise of OMS International. *It need not happen. It must not happen.* But it would happen unless we kept our spiritual priorities clear and guarded them with our very lives. Our prayer was that God would help us do so.

We searched our hearts before God, as we did each new year, asking him to show each of us the steps we personally could take to make the next year a time of grace and power in OMS worldwide. It had been a busy year of ministry, growth, problems, and blessing.

We needed more of God's presence and power, more staff, and more funds. We had so much for which to praise the Lord and so much for which to keep believing. We really wanted to make the next year count for God. I wrote that, as we planned for fulfilling God's mandate to us, "the only answer is repeated outpourings of the Holy Spirit upon our worldwide family. The Holy Spirit is given as we prepare our hearts by new obedience and as we seek God's face in all-out intercession."

THE GREATEST NEED (1978)

In the early months of 1978, there were pastors' conferences, field council sessions, committee discussions, planning sessions, personal counseling, and ministry of the Word in Brazil, Greece, Indonesia, Hong Kong, and Haiti. Then there was nearly a week of survey work in Bangladesh and Indonesia. God was at work in retreats, meetings, worship services, and many hungry hearts.

For nearly two months straight, I traveled from city to city and from one nation to another visiting many fields. At least forty-seven times I had the privilege of sharing God's Word. Even more thrilling, however, was what I observed. God was at work!

In Brazil, while I was speaking to a group of pastors, a young boy walked in off the street. After listening a short while, he came right up to the pulpit and asked to be led to Christ. "I have never been in a place so filled with faith," he said. God met his need that night!

Also in Brazil, pastors and workers humbled themselves and publicly asked one another's forgiveness. I saw many people moved to tears as God spoke. My interpreter was so broken that he could hardly speak, and the man called to lead in prayer wept so convulsively that he had to stop several times. Our wonderful coworkers gave exciting reports: dozens were preparing for baptism, new converts were standing firm despite persecution, and a pastor planned to conduct double morning services in a few months because his church building was already crowded out. God spoke to hearts in precious ways, moving deeply and wanting to give a special harvest.

I sat beside one of our new village lay leaders in Indonesia and marveled at his faith. "My people have no religion," he explained, "but they want one." They had been deceived by Communism, and it had failed them. In home after home, family members were slain in the bloodbath that came as Christians were sought out and slaughtered. Naturally, the people rejected the religion of soldiers who killed their loved ones.

They had also lost faith in their indigenous religion, but their government said they must choose a religion to be good citizens. So, they were waiting and ready to make a choice. Dozens of new churches could be founded, I was assured, if only we had workers to send.

We desperately needed more missionaries—couples who knew how to win souls and were willing to pioneer new locations so that thousands could be reached. We needed more mission partners, who would pray, give, and yes, even sacrifice. We desperately needed more finances to build our seminary so national "sons and daughters" could be trained.

That was God's hour. I had seen the harvest. But who would hear his call and obey? Challenging, I asked, who would. I explained everyone could be part of God's answer if only they would say yes to his voice. I pleaded with everyone to please, get on their knees and tell God they would obey. In my tenth year as president, my one desire, above all others, was for Society-wide visitations of God the Holy Spirit among us. I longed for OMS to be visited with real, lasting, widespread revival. There was much evangelism in OMS then, but revival is always more than evangelism. Revival includes the awesome, overwhelming presence of God convicting sin, melding his people together in new baptisms of holy love, cleansing them of carnal manifestations that cause friction and interpersonal problems, and empowering them for anointed, God-guided, God-saturated service.

Of the threefold call God gave to OMS through Charles Cowman, the planting and growth of the church was central. Evangelism was to lead to church growth. Leadership training was to provide the Spirit-filled manpower for both the evangelism and the church.

I asked each field in OMS if they were succeeding in secondary things but failing in their primary purpose. I told them nothing else must usurp this primacy; all else must be subservient to it. The main thrust of OMS as a whole—the main planning, effort, and fruit—had to be evangelism, which yields the growth of the church. Above all else, that was God's call for OMS.

We had the privilege of electing a larger than usual group of new members to serve on the board of trustees over the next couple of years. It was highly important that we elected capable people of God, totally committed to OMS doctrine, heritage, and priorities. They would become stewards of the future of OMS. We needed men and women who would be active on the board and use their influence, expertise, and resources to strengthen OMS. We also needed balance between clergy and laity.

While it was a thrilling record that our new churches had grown 395 percent in baptized church membership in the past ten years, several of our fields and many of our local churches were comparatively static. We needed evangelism–church growth specialists to help all our work to reach its potential and Christ's objectives for us. The church offerings of our local national churches had increased 800 percent in the past ten years. If our numerical and spiritual growth were that vigorous, we could anticipate revival, and our constant prayer was for God to bring us genuine revival.

My deep hunger for this new year of OMS endeavor was Society-wide Holy Spirit revival, Holy Spirit anointing, and Holy Spirit–blessed church growth. How many years would Christ give OMS to complete his task? Could this be the greatest decade, or even the last decade, of Christian missions? Would communists close more nations to the gospel? Or would China open once more to the gospel?

CHINA: THE SLEEPING GIANT (1979)

History verified that OMS advances were continually born in intercession. Prevailing (conquering) prayer was always our greatest asset and most dire need. Thus, OMS Founders' Day on March 13, 1979, was set aside as a worldwide day of prayer for the Society. Addressing the OMS missionary body, we reminded ourselves,

> Prayer warfare takes time, for there are few "spiritual quickies." Character is formed with the succession of many experiences. Consider the period of training involved for an athlete or musician. We learn to pray by praying. Often spiritual wrestling is involved. When the Holy Spirit creates a prayer desire, we share in divine, agonizing love.

After some years of prayer by OMS founder Charles Cowman and E. A. Kilbourne, OMS entered China in 1925. When finally expelled by the communists in 1946, OMS had a North China district, a Central China district, and a South China district. In addition to churches and evangelists in these areas, we had a Bible seminary in each. It had been thirty-three years since we were forcibly separated from our Chinese loved ones. What was God's call in regard to China for OMS today?

At that time, our "Streams in the Desert" radio program was broadcast twice daily by Trans World Radio's (TWR) 100,000-watt shortwave transmitter to Mainland China. During that year, we increased our daily transmissions to ten per day, depending on the day of the week. We continued to use the facilities of TWR on Guam. Our signals were heard clearly to the border of Tibet, and we received encouraging letter responses. Printed English lessons were provided to students who followed our elementary and advanced-level English-teaching broadcasts. A Chinese visitor to various parts of eastern China wrote how almost every Christian he contacted was a regular listener and deeply grateful for the "Streams in the Desert" broadcasts.

We had gone to considerable expense to send seven members of our board into one or another section of China during the past year. Others of our missionary and national staff entered China for a weekend and made some personal contacts. We indirectly contacted several of our former Chinese workers there. Some had been without a Bible for twenty years. The "barefoot doctor," daughter of Mrs. Anna Hsiao, who spent a number of years in Chinese prisons for the sake of Christ, was able to join her mother and brother in the USA. An OMS-sponsored tour group visited China for nearly two weeks in November. As a member of the Evangelical China Committee, jointly sponsored by the EFMA/IFMA and a group of North American Chinese evangelicals, we tried to keep abreast of the China scene.

At that time, China entered into one of the greatest and most dramatic periods of change facing a major nation in modern history. Each month brought further evidence that the country was relaxing restrictions and turning away from the convulsive revolution, seemingly engineered or encouraged by Chairman Mao. Where was his "Little Red Book" now?

Was that the beginning of a wide ranging "about-face" that would bring a new day for nearly one-fourth of mankind? Already newspapers in China referred to a "second liberation." The first was from "colonialism." The second would be liberation from the excesses of Maoism.

Was the sovereign Lord of the universe about to give at least some beginning liberty for Christians? Would this be an answer to our daily burdened prayer for a wider door for the gospel in China? The heart of Christ longed for the then nearly one billion Chinese. He died for every one of them. The Holy Spirit was moving thousands of Christians to earnest prayer and fasting for China. We asked if our donors were among those praying and fasting for the people there.

In June, three of us departed on a survey trip to Japan, Hong Kong, and Mainland China. We finally departed after some lost luggage holdups. It turned out to be a strategic trip. We were able to take in over a hundred Scriptures. One of my great burdens was to recruit five thousand people who would remember China in prayer each day. We sent quarterly news and prayer items for China to those who signed up to pray. Already, tremendous changes for the better were happening there. Suddenly, it was legal to own a Bible, sing hymns aloud, and listen to foreign broadcasts. It was truly a new day.

China was changing rapidly. It seemed to be moving away from Mao and his philosophy by demystifying the founder, re-evaluating his philosophy and policies, diverting from his daily published quotes, and demonstrating a new willingness to experiment by borrowing aspects of capitalism to advance China's national interests. There was a new realization that the nation must have a sound economic foundation for the future. The new government called for industry led by professionals, not peasants. There was emerging new government leadership, cultural liberty, liberalizing education, new moderation in the penal system, and new latitudes for mobility, travel, and the exchange of ideas, both in print and via media.

Most importantly for OMS, China was becoming more open to religion. In 1949, conservative estimates said approximately one million Protestants were in China. In 1977, those estimates grew to somewhere over three million. Of course, the situation for Christians and the degree to which local government chose to enforce the old order or move toward the new order varied. Visitors to China reported an uneven and discordant perspective. Severe restrictions hampered the growth and development of Christianity for years. In some places, persecution was so oppressive that prison sentences for Christians and martyrdom were routine.

However, there were increasing reports of revival, mass baptisms, divine healings, and ground-breaking public religious events, including speeches, congresses, institutes, seminars, and ecumenical gatherings. These various meetings could be placed in one of four categories: (1) private, restricted, or contained prayer meetings, (2) Bible studies, (3) testimonial meetings, and (4) somewhat open, or cautiously public, preaching and exhortation meetings.

China's doors were not closed to God! China was open to love, prayer, giving, radio, literature, and short-term visitors. Only God knew how long and how wide this door would remain open. OMS had the responsibility and the opportunity to re-engage and re-activate its commitment to one of our longest standing fields. We owed it to those coworkers who gave their lives for Christ and his kingdom. We could help those offspring of former colleagues who had worked side by side with us in the early years! OMS had the opportunity to touch the lives of millions born since the doors had closed nearly seventy years ago, the opportunity to sow the precious seeds of the gospel in the hearts and lives of nearly one-fourth of the world's people, who for all practical purposes had never heard the name of Jesus.

Wesley with Mainland Chinese Students

Having just returned from visiting five of her great cities, I was more convinced than before that God was at work in China. Other nations have risen and fallen, but China lives on. He was at work there, and I believed he was preparing a great tomorrow for his church in that ancient land.

There was increasing evidence that true believers suffered and even died, but thousands remained true to Jesus. Most could not meet together for worship in any open sense, but they learned to meet secretly in small numbers in homes. We had reports that many young people had recently come to Christ, and they were often bolder in witness than the older people. Carefully, and at great risk, they were beginning to share Christ with those they hoped would not betray them. The emptiness of heart and life under Communism prepared people to listen. From more and more sections of China came word of new believers, new baptisms, hidden work, hand-copied Bibles and of *Streams in the Desert*—the most loved Christian book in China, next to the Bible.

Hour after hour, powerful Christian stations were beaming the gospel into China, in their own language. For years, almost no Chinese listener dared write to those stations outside their country. But then restrictions were relaxed. Instead of two to thirty letters per year, as was customary, more than ten thousand listeners responded. China had huge factories building radios, one employing 3,800 people. We saw radios freely available in many stores for the people who had enough money to purchase them.

For years, Christians with whom OMS cooperated were preparing a new translation of the Chinese Bible, in the simplified Mandarin script. In recent months, thousands of tourists had been welcomed back into China—mainly Chinese, but also Westerners. Thousands of New Testaments, Scripture portions, and books were taken into the country.

As we entered the decade of the eighties, my challenge was to trust God for a period of unity and blessing. We asked him for effectiveness in ministry, great harvest results in evangelism, and constant church planting and church growth. We depended on his grace and supernatural power more than ever before. Missionary work is spiritual warfare. The only way to claim great victories is by prayer, faith, and obedience. My prayer was that God would make that decade the greatest OMS had ever known. *Praise the Lord!*

GROWTH AND CHALLENGES (1980)

How can I recount this tremendous time in God's whitened harvest field? I'll try to share the vision of what he did. The Hong Kong Evangelical Church celebrated their twenty-fifth anniversary in 1979. It was good to touch base there and be updated on our Hong Kong and China ministry. Bit by bit, God was opening the door wider to reach China with literature and radio. We had just placed an order for a new Chinese edition of *Streams in the Desert* for Mainland China, five times more than before. A total of five thousand copies reached the Christians there in December alone! OMS had eight to ten radio broadcasts a day going into China. A constant flow of letters came out of China, proving how God was using the radio ministry. I praised God that in spite of accelerated opposition and problems governmentally, religiously, and socially under the motivation and coordination of Satan, the Holy Spirit was triumphing.

God gave a touch of revival to our Indonesia field. Many missionaries said it was the best year they had experienced. God had given beautiful unity. Many had been burdened and were praying. Many spent the entire night in prayer. One night, four pastors came and asked to be taken into town. They believed God was going to send revival, and they wanted to have a communion set ready. The next morning, many melted to tears and asked forgiveness of one another. Bitterness, resentments, and personal conflicts that had hindered for years were healed.

God gave a new beginning. As in Bible days, Satan contested every advance. But God was raising up new congregations of believers. We desperately needed additional funds for church land and buildings.

God's Day in India

It was a tremendous joy to return to India in January and February 1980. It was almost like New Testament times to see the tremendous growth God was giving OMS. In my month in India, I saw greater evidence of God at work in our OMS ministry than I had ever seen there. India was our second largest field, and it was experiencing constant and fairly rapid advance throughout the whole country.

Our South India churches celebrated their twenty-fifth anniversary in January. Our national church rented the large Nehru Stadium for the occasion. Believers from our churches and many Hindus with Hindu markings still on their faces, plus friends from other denominations, swelled our crowds to between fifteen thousand and thirty thousand in attendance. Even the Hindu state governor came to congratulate our people.

Among some of the joys I shared were ordaining twenty-eight pastors in one service, dedicating the one-hundredth new church building in recent years, seeing over four hundred baptized in one service at the ocean, and preaching to a crowd at our twenty-fifth anniversary service—as large as twenty-five thousand to forty thousand, according to estimates. We were now at work in thirteen districts in India, and each week our coworkers were ministering in eight different languages.

How well I remember the faith battles and the slow beginnings, but also the tremendously loyal ministry of so many of our Indian and missionary coworkers during the early years! It seemed that God had seen our prayer and fasting, heard our tearful heart-cries, seen our labor and sweat, and was now multiplying the harvest.

Not long before this writing, I received word that a new city for which I had been praying for many years had started an OMS-related church with many new converts. The work seemed to be spreading, and they hoped that within a few years, we would have a whole new district of churches there. New districts were developing on the border of Pakistan in West India and on the border of Tibet (China) in North India. A new district in a new language area was on the southern coast of India. All three of these areas were opened by the direct initiative of the Holy Spirit more than by our planning.

We needed to build more than forty new church buildings for new congregations in India in the coming months. Let me repeat: God was at work! Advance was reported in the whole of the country! We asked people to stand with us in believing prayer, and we believed it was God's day for India.

The Japan Holiness Church's Eightieth Anniversary

In March 1980, our Japan church observed its eightieth anniversary of OMS ministry. What a privilege to be invited and to share in a period of fellowship and ministry, culminating in the anniversary meetings commemorating the founding of OMS church ministry in Japan! I wish you could have joined in the services in Hibiya Public Hall in central Tokyo, near the Imperial Palace. It was a joy to see the main hall and balcony crowded with at least two thousand of our Japanese believers. On the platform, in addition to our Japanese leaders, were honored guests, fraternal delegates, and representatives from Korea, Taiwan, and Hong Kong.

Dr. Paul Rees, who first ministered in OMS work in Japan in 1925, was the specially invited speaker. For years, he was a member of our OMS council of reference. He alternated with me in bringing the messages. His father and half-brother were two of the five men who ordained Charles Cowman, OMS founder, in December 1900. Rev. E. L. Kilbourne, who first went to Japan with his parents in 1902 at the age of twelve, was the guest of honor.[8] He and I were asked to join Japanese leaders in ordaining five Japanese pastors and commissioning the new church leader. Uncle Bud raised his arms and shouted "Hallelujah" in an emotion-filled, quivery voice.

A highlight of the weekend's activities was the music. Whether it was Kemp Edwards singing "My Tribute" in Japanese, instrumental solos, the youth orchestra, or various choirs, all blended in praise to God and provided a warmth and fragrance that enhanced the services immeasurably.

At the last service, hundreds of laymen and youth made clear-cut new commitments to soul-winning or to Christian service. About 250 responded to the altar call, with 133 dedicating their lives to full-time service. Fifty-eight young people signified their desire to enter Tokyo Bible Seminary for training. We felt we could hear the echo from an angelic choir, "Hallelujah, Hallelujah!" Uncle Bud commented, "This is one of two of the greatest experiences of my Christian life."

The church set a new goal of establishing a total of two hundred churches, at least one in every prefecture. We left blessed, challenged, and filled with new faith for a great tomorrow for Christ in Japan. I was thrilled with the anointed and united leadership. We in OMS always want to be a strong part of the team seeing that vision realized. It was really living history.

At our annual OMS retreat and convention, the Bible studies were led by Dr. Dennis F. Kinlaw, Asbury College president and OMS board chairman. At the close of the service, a shudder of apprehension and concern went through the departing crowd when it was discovered that Dr. Erny, down in front surrounded by his family, could not leave

---

8   "Uncle Bud" Kilbourne was ninety years of age at that time.

his seat. Dr. John Mitchell and Dr. David Brabon were on hand, and they quickly had an ambulance called, and our president emeritus was taken to the hospital. Within a few hours, he was conscious and had suffered no paralysis or discernible disability, but he remained in the hospital for tests and observation. Hundreds of prayers were focused on the man whom God used to lead and stir so many of us into missionary service. We praised God that our patriarch was protected from serious physical problems.

As we moved toward the climax of human history and the return of our Savior, we expected two somewhat parallel movements: (1) accelerated harvest endeavors and results, under the sovereign, triumphant direction and enabling of the Holy Spirit, and (2) continued accelerated opposition and problems, governmentally, religiously, and socially, under the motivation and coordination of Satan. That intensified spiritual warfare would challenge all spiritual missionary endeavor.

Along with the evidence of growth opportunities was also evidence of opposition. Strong Muslim opposition hindered us in some localities in Indonesia, and strong Hindu opposition hindered us in some mountain sections of North India. Visa delays and problems continued to concern us in some nations. But despite these delays and discouragements, our teams were pressing on and seeing gracious results. My prayer was that God would deepen and spread the work from field to field.

A NEW VISION (1981)

At the Stanita Foundation board meeting, and with other OMS leaders, I shared the thrill of witnessing the Stanley and Juanita Tam family disburse $1,225,000 for evangelism across the world on OMS fields. Every day we praised the Lord for this dedicated family and asked for his continued anointing on their business enterprises and our careful stewardship of those funds.[9]

---

9   The Stanita Foundation is a legally incorporated private business operating for the sole purpose of world evangelism and was named by combining the two major owners' first names, Stanley and Juanita Tam, into the new acronym, "Stanita."

Those funds helped in Indonesia, where there were reports of dramatic deliverances during their camping ministry at the seminary. Also, news from Allahabad reported a splendid group of new students in our seminary there. Our annual Spiritual Life Convention had hundreds attending, many seeking new victories for Christ. In Northwest India our Indian coworkers were facing strong opposition, but news from China was very encouraging.

Our then vice president of field ministries, Dr. Everett Hunt Jr., and I surveyed the Philippines as a possible new field. We traveled to India in between, and, subsequently, the Hunts also surveyed France (where our daughter Darlene and her husband, Terry, eventually served). We also visited our work in Hong Kong, and God renewed the burden for that crowded area. He was blessing the ministry and had opened a new door for us in another strategic location. In light of all that was happening, what did God expect of OMS in the eighties? What was our responsibility as a board of trustees? What was the responsibility of our field leaders and committees to God, to our OMS heritage, and to our constituency?

I felt deeply convinced that we needed to issue a new call and challenge to fruitfulness for God. Some of our fields seemed riper than ever before; there was much evidence of the Holy Spirit's presence and working. But the doors of some fields could swing closed to our missionary service. Not only was Communism advancing in many places, but ancient religions were also reviving. Surely Christ would soon return. What we would do for God, we must do immediately.

With a new burden and vision on my heart, in 1981, I prepared a resolution calling on the board to designate the ten-year period of 1982–1992 a "Decade of Harvest," beginning and launching full-scale with our next plenary session in July 1982.[10]

We needed a small action committee to assist in planning, guiding, and implementing this program for all-out endeavor in evangelism, church planting, and church growth. It would involve each field leader

10   This report was the first published reference to a Decade of Harvest, which eventually became a ten-year, Society-wide strategic thrust.

and field committee giving careful and prayerful consideration, in consultation with our national church leaders, for steps they could take in implementing this vision and call. The Lord kept open the doors of our fields and continued to open new doors before us. The potential response in those last two decades of the twentieth century was tremendous. The Holy Spirit was sealing that day as a time of harvest. We had to buy up the opportunities while it was day. We recognized that pressures impinged upon us—the international financial crisis of inflation and shortage of income, the occasional militant opposition of other religions, occasional and ever-latent, mission-church tensions, and the constant opposition of Satan. But by God's power and grace, we were determined to press on, and by faith we called for a decade of rapid but solid advance, a decade of harvest. Our Lord is coming again, so I called for us to prepare his way.

God seemed to honor our retreat and convention events because his presence was unusually present during our annual board meeting. Our board chairman, Dr. Dennis F. Knlaw, gave us a tremendous challenge related to the sacrifice of following God in faith, a sacrifice absolutely essential if God is to bless the world. His dealings with our souls are necessary so the world may be blessed through us.

God came upon us with a tremendous spirit of intercession, which lasted well over an hour before we began our business session. For months, the Holy Spirit had been burdening my heart with our tremendous responsibilities as a missionary society to fulfill our call and be all God wanted us to be. I did not feel satisfied with the evangelistic efforts in some areas of OMS work, nor with the rate of church planting and church growth in many places. On some of our fields, we could be facing an uncertain future in ten years. Could we be sure that the door for our missionary cooperation would remain as open as it was then?

Once the business agenda got underway, God led in a unanimous resolution to declare the decade July 1982 to July 1992 as a "Decade of Harvest." The coming year would be spent in careful exploration of our fields, institutions, personnel, and cooperating national churches.

We explored steps to form united partnership, both within our present fields and moving out into new fields in a comprehensive, intensive thrust for evangelism, church planting, and church growth. I called for prayer asking that God's vision, anointing, and supply would be our daily and increasing portion.

"Decade of Harvest" was one comprehensive term that would include evangelism, church planting, church growth, and discipleship. We wanted a title that would encompass our joining together with all our cooperating national churches, all our training institutions, and all our staff worldwide. Why did we announce it then, but not begin until the plenary session in 1982? We wanted all our field committees and field councils to share in prayer and brainstorming discussions. And we wanted every OMS missionary to feel involved from the early stages. We wanted to invite our national churches and their leaders to share from the outset, in prayer and planning. We wanted God to guide us together into his strategy for the greatest advance for him any of us had ever known. We needed all our regional and home directors and home boards to plan for constituency enlargement, to provide the prayer and support base we would need.

We wanted to keep in continual contact with everyone during the coming months as we prayed and planned. Then, when the field leaders came together in November, they could share their preliminary thoughts and vision of each field. Those would be further refined, prayed over, jointly discussed, and planned. By the plenary session in July 1982, we could launch into the first stages of a full-scale, Society-wide plan continually adapted field by field to our opportunities, resources, and God's guidance.

Each time I completed a three-year term as president, before the new election by the board of directors, I made a statement to the OMS worldwide family, asking them to feel perfectly free to elect anyone of their choice. Each previous end of term, I had been reelected. I had marked my sixty-fifth birthday on June 3, 1980, and I would be sixty-six just before the completion of my fourth three-year term. Dr. Erny was reelected year by year from his sixty-fifth to his seventieth birthday, but I did not want the board to feel compelled to reelect me even with that precedent.

According to the OMS bylaws at that time, the president was to be elected by secret ballot, and I personally, strongly endorsed this procedure. The intent was to avoid mission "politics." I did not believe it was glorifying to God, or conducive to Society unity, for anyone to "candidate" or lobby for executive offices or for anyone to campaign for someone else to be elected to those positions. I felt there should be much prayer and free mutual discussion, but no campaigning or politicking.[11]

Therefore, I felt I should make a statement at the special board of directors meeting convened in November, before they had to decide the following summer. I did not believe such a decision should be made on the spur of the moment but that there should be adequate time available for prayer and consideration. I wanted them to discuss the issue freely with the members of the missionary council, and then meet prayerfully before making their decision.[12] When the time came, Dr. Dennis F. Knlaw, chairman of our board of trustees, reported to me that a free and full discussion was held and a straw vote had been taken by secret ballot. A majority consensus recommended a new election in June at the special meeting of the board of directors. I was given the privilege to announce this and to guide its implementation.

There was discussion about another possible future ministry for me. It was suggested that OMS needed doctrinal and related books, which some felt I should write. But some felt I might not get to this important task unless I was freed for it. Other suggestions involved conference, seminar, and special speaking ministries on fields and in the homelands, strengthening our World Intercessors emphasis, and assisting in the Decade of Harvest. For me, it was not a time for

---

11 Editor's note (David Dick): Dr. Duewel once said that he felt anyone who intentionally lobbied for executive leadership was *de facto* disqualified for the office.

12 The missionary council was composed of all the duly elected, or appointed, field directors, and it served as the highest administrative body of the mission, working in concert with, and under the direction of, the mission officers to launch, oversee, and evaluate ministries.

questioning, fear, or undue concern. It was a time of praise to God for his faithfulness over OMS's past eighty-one years, faith for all the advances and harvest God was planning for and through OMS in the tomorrows, and more earnest intercession on the part of every one of us than we had ever known. God's tomorrows are always greater than his yesterdays as we continue to obey him and put his priorities first.

I pleaded with everyone—let each one do everything personally within their power to keep OMS free from personal ambitions, political-type maneuverings to get one's own way or one's choice of persons into office. Rather, I exhorted everyone, "Let us each pray and trust the Holy Spirit for his perfect guidance." I asked God to bind us all closer to him, to each other, and to our unfinished task more than ever before.

A TRANSITION YEAR (1982)

Dr. Everett N. Hunt Jr., our then beloved vice president of field ministries, was elected my successor. And at the close of my presidential tenure, our gracious God lifted and encouraged, as I assumed leadership of the "Decade of Harvest," to challenge our staff to make new commitments of prayer and obedience.

We challenged national churches to "the greatest harvest partnership we have ever known." We called upon field leaders to become "models of power in prayer and evangelistic passion before their missionaries and national churches" and said, "Oh, for God to transform this Decade of Harvest into God's Day of Power." During the opening session of the annual OMS board meeting, my remarks to the board closed with, "God will, if we will." Each of us made new personal commitments and asked ourselves, "How far will I go to reach our unreached generation for Christ before he returns?" I asked, especially, for prayer for God's anointing as we launched our Decade of Harvest.

A Year of Preparation and Faithfulness

In my thirteenth annual report, I gave tribute to God's continual guidance and supply of all our needs. The OMS team had seen his sustaining through busy days, pressure, uncertainties, and recurring opposition from Satan. In many respects 1982 was one of our best ever.

But change was on the way. Surveys, forecasting, choosing initial members of the team, and even some initial funding were actively prepared for launching the two new fields of France and the Philippines that coming September. All the fields and most of the national churches were sharing in planning for the Decade of Harvest. And a special committee was working on the organizational restructuring of the OMS administration.

The organizational development of the Society was shifting from a smaller "family" organization to a larger "corporate culture," which demanded more definition, guidelines, and rules and regulations to preserve integrity and leverage organizational resources. The growth and development were cultivated and encouraged through a philosophy of interdependence and mutuality consistent with the nature of the triune Godhead, reflected in the original Society family spirit.[13]

We celebrated God's faithfulness in many ways. In all our staff members' extensive travel, God continued to give such faithful protection. Some of our leaders and staff had been through a fiery furnace experience, but God was by their side. The new financial fiscal year was ahead of the last year in total receipts. While it was not sufficient to cover inflation, it was a wonderful testimony to God's faithfulness in light of our economy and was far better than the trend in diminishing receipts in many other missionary and charitable organizations.

It was also a year of intense spiritual warfare. Church-mission tension in Colombia decreased some, and tension within the seminary in Korea decreased greatly, but it was a sad year of tension in India—both between national church leaders in the north and south and between church leaders in the south and missionaries in the north. On the other hand, church-mission unity was strengthened in Haiti and Brazil.

---

13   The Wesleyan Doctrine of the Godhead characterizes the Trinity with attributes of interdependence, mutuality, and reciprocity.

In Indonesia, unity within the church and between church and mission was also strengthened. When God plans great things and the Holy Spirit works in power, Satan does all he can to block, discourage, weaken, divide, or defeat. And indeed, we were confronting the principalities and powers of darkness throughout our work. But we also prayed and fasted till God gave our national churches the most spiritually powerful and effective leadership they had ever enjoyed. Neither our churches, nor we, dared to merely mark time or remain static. We had to model not political leadership but Spirit-filled, prayer-empowered leadership.

Yet I believed we were on the verge of some of the greatest days we had ever known. We were not discouraged by Satan's attacks. We were determined to marshal our spiritual resources and believe God for miracles of salvation, church growth, recruitment, and new spiritual revival in our work. We were encouraged to pray, plan, and work for a tremendous Decade of Harvest beginning the next month, July.

Slogans are useless, but if the Decade of Harvest was our passion, we could see great spiritual and numerical advance in the coming years. God did not want either without the other. He desired both great spiritual growth and great numerical growth. It was not unspiritual to press for statistical numbers; it was biblical. The Acts of the Apostles repeatedly emphasizes the "numbers," "many," and "a great number," as coming to the Lord and into the fellowship of the church.

Organized churches increased 10 percent, church buildings 14 percent, church membership 17 percent, Bible and theological students in training 17 percent, decisions 24 percent, church offerings 31 percent, and Scripture and literature distributed 108 percent. Our national churches reported that they had thirty foreign missionaries serving under their own or other auspices.

God had guided and directed throughout Dr. Erny's tenure as president, and in some circles, OMS was known as the "gold standard" among faith mission agencies. By the end of my tenure as president,

God had provided, protected, and blessed with the result that OMS was reaching out and operating in its "zenith."[14]

Dr. Everett N. Hunt Jr., elected as my successor, and his wife, Carroll, served twenty-two years in Korea before their appointment to our home office. They were well qualified and competent to assume leadership of the mission. And so, Betty and I were to enter a new phase of our ministry.

One of the board members said to me, "Wesley, maybe the Lord wants you to write some books." But at the time, I was so busy with speaking engagements that I didn't really have time to write. Then two other people came to me and said, in almost identical words, "Wesley, you're going to have to decide whether you are going to speak to a few hundred people or write for a few thousand people." The second time this was said to me, I took it seriously, and the Lord used it to prompt me to think in earnest about focusing on a writing ministry. As you'll recall, Dr. Erny had also encouraged me to set aside time to write.

It was a great privilege and awesome responsibility to serve as the OMS president for those thirteen years. It was a role I neither sought nor to which was I equal. I praised God for a strong team, for loyal coworkers, and for their consecrated ministries. Any success was due to them and their untiring efforts. Increasingly, the stories of God's Spirit working through our worldwide efforts would be the account of his blessings on our national churches and coworkers. *To God be all the glory!*

Inauguration of the New President

On September 25, we celebrated the inauguration of Dr. Everett N. Hunt Jr. as the sixth OMS president. The ceremony was held in the First Baptist Church in Greenwood. Afterward, a reception was held in honor of both Ev and Carroll Hunt and Betty and me.

---

14   Throughout the late 1970s and the early 1980s, there was a consensus among Asbury students in the Wilmore community, among whom the editor was one, that OMS was one of the premier agencies through which someone could fulfill their call to the Great Commission.

I couldn't help but reflect on my presidency. I started with great trepidation in myself but with great faith in what God had in store. As I looked back over those years, I saw God's great faithfulness over and over in my life, in my family's lives, and throughout the Society as a whole. Now, as I was about to launch into a new chapter in my life, I was just as excited as ever to see where and how God would lead me. Whatever we faced, I knew he was going to be there and that whatever we accomplished would be for his glory. Dr. Hunt graciously appointed me as assistant to the president for evangelism and intercession. My office was moved to a lower level in the Gillam wing, and Miss Hilda Johnecheck, who remained my secretary, continued to contribute her invaluable assistance. Betty traveled with me at times to speaking engagements in the USA and overseas, at which time we enlisted a host of new prayer warriors. We also turned more attention to my writing books on such topics as prayer, revival, and the Holy Spirit.

God's Wonderful Family

From the time I was reassigned from India to headquarters, the Lord was pleased to bless me with many new friends. OMS also assigned me to be the official representative to the Evangelical Fellowship of Mission Agencies (EFMA) and to the Christian Holiness Partnership (CHP).[15] I felt like such a junior to these men of God, who all had my respect. Therefore, I asked God to help me, and I tried to share in any way I could through prayer, loyalty, and faithful attendance and participation. I felt how urgent it was for God to use all these organizations and committees, as well as how privileged I was to fellowship intimately with those God had raised up to lead the various societies in the evangelical movement.

I also had the honor and privilege of representing OMS within a number of other fraternal evangelical organizations. As a result, the Lord also graciously gave me the opportunity to serve as an officer of

15   The EFMA was originally known as the "Evangelical Foreign Missions Association," but is now known as "Missio Nexus," and the CHA was originally known as the "Christian Holiness Association," but was subsequently known as the "Christian Holiness Partnership" (CHP).

these various organizations. My membership afforded me an opportunity to not only represent the mission but also to gain access to leaders and their reports of what God was doing in the world through the organizational networking and interagency fellowship that naturally occurs in these gatherings. I saw these opportunities to represent OMS also as a prospect to keep pace with what God was doing in the world and help the Society to capitalize on the information, inspiration, and involvement of God in the worldwide *missio Dei*.

The following is a partial list of the fraternal organizations with which I had the privilege of associating and, at various times, actively serving and/or leading:

- American Society of Missiology (ASM)
- Asbury Theological Seminary (ATS) Board of Trustees
- Evangelical Council for Financial Accountability (ECFA)
- Evangelical Fellowship of Mission Agencies (EFMA)
- Evangelical Press Association (EPA)
- Evangelical Theological Society (ETS)
- Francis Asbury (Bicentennial Celebration)
- Interdenominational Foreign Missions Association (IFMA)
- National Association of Evangelicals (NAE)
- National Holiness Association (NHA)
- Christian Holiness Association (CHA), originally NHA
- Christian Holiness Partnership (CHP), originally CHA
- National Religious Broadcasters (NRB)
- Good News Movement (GNM), United Methodist Church
- Wesleyan Theological Society (WTS)
- World Evangelical Fellowship (WEF)

The psalmist writes to all those wonderful evangelical leaders with whom I had the privilege of serving, "May those who fear you turn to me, those who understand your statutes" (Ps 119:79). So many evangelical leaders of organizations knew me on a first-name basis, and we rejoiced together when we met. We had many similar interests, concerns, and holy desires, and we shared many joys. We just seemed to have a built-in understanding of one another. Those days were a wonderful period of my life.

I was strengthened and encouraged by the people I met in those fraternal and interdenominational contexts. I was so spiritually enriched. Through my personal relationships, I reaped the spiritual blessings of so many of God's evangelical leaders, both while serving in India and in the USA. When I began to write my first book on prayer, *Touch the World through Prayer*, I asked my EFMA brethren to pray for the Lord's anointing in this task. I felt I was doing it not merely for OMS but for all the evangelical missionary organizations.

I was not worthy to live such a privileged life, but that is how the family of God works. Because we shared similar responsibilities and hungered in such similar ways to see God bless his people and work among them, we enjoyed a supernaturally given kinship and fellow understanding.

5
The Decade of Harvest

The Bible clearly teaches there will be a mighty harvest time for God the Holy Spirit, at the end of the age. There will also be a massive harvest of sin and evil, but God will bring to consummation the unanswered prayers of his people, and the gospel efforts of the past decades and centuries. The faithful work of the Holy Spirit will reach a climax in one great harvest period before Jesus returns. It will be the final building of the church, the final recruitment of Christ's bride— that multinational bride from every tongue, tribe, nation, and people.

A NEW, DYNAMIC ADVANCE (1982)

In the years before the Decade of Harvest, God had been guiding many church and missionary organizations to prepare for a new, dynamic advance for God and souls. The Holy Spirit is in a hurry to complete the unfinished task of the church, the fulfilling of the Great Commission! He was using radio, audio-visual, multi-media, television, and literature in dimensions never before dreamed possible. God was stirring older missionary societies to dream new dreams and to set new priorities. He was raising up new organizations for specialized ministries, as the Holy Spirit wanted to quickly complete the building of Christ's church.

It was in that context that we envisioned the Decade of Harvest. We dared to believe the vision was born in the heart of Jesus Christ, the Lord of the harvest. He placed the burden upon my heart in 1981, when I challenged the OMS board of trustees to issue a clear call for a society-wide Decade of Harvest, an all-out evangelistic, church planting emphasis from July 1982 to July 1992. Our board, moved by the Holy Spirit, unanimously adopted the program.

The OMS worldwide partnership with national churches was raised up by the guidance of the Holy Spirit. Each national church was an autonomous body, and we were thrilled to have them as our partners. We didn't want to be paternalistic, nor squelch, nor limit their initiative. It was our prayer that the Decade of Harvest would be a united vision, incorporating the goals, objectives, and plans God gave to each of the national churches. Some of them were already being moved by the Holy Spirit before our challenge reached them.

We wanted the Decade of Harvest to be a grassroots movement rising from all our field committees, all our national church executive committees and leaders, and the hearts, prayers, and vision of multitudes of believers in our related churches around the world. We needed to listen to what the Holy Spirit was saying to them, to see with God's eyes and their eyes and then state a composite, unified vision and goal of the total God was giving to us all. It would unite us to pray, plan, and work for the greatest harvest any of us had ever seen.

Harvest Goals

Were some of the faith goals of our national churches too visionary? Were they beyond what we could reasonably trust God to do? Only God knew his plans for the coming decade. When we combined and synthesized our goals, we came up with the following six major goals for the Decade of Harvest:

1. 100,000 new believers
2. 500,000 new baptized members
3. 100 ECC teams (Every Community for Christ)
4. 2,000 new local churches
5. 2,000 additional national workers in training
6. 100,000 people praying daily

It was not enough for us to plan carefully, recruit funds, work faithfully, and be as busy as possible for God and souls. Unless God the Holy Spirit came upon us in mighty anointing and enabling, we would never be able to reach those goals. But if he enabled us, they could all be reached and exceeded. The question remained: How fully would God's Spirit be able to work in and through us?

We felt the secret to success for the Decade of Harvest ministry would be recruiting one hundred thousand people to pray daily for God to enable us to reach those Decade of Harvest goals. And we expected them to be raised up among present and new friends across our home-base countries of Australia, Canada, New Zealand, South Africa, the United States, and in the British Isles. We expected them to be joined by multiplied thousands of believers on OMS fields around the world.

Sharing the Vision

Due to previously scheduled conventions, committees, seminars, and meetings, and a full month spent in India and three weeks in Great Britain, I spent only four weeks in the office after the 1982 summer board meetings. In each ministry area, there were thrilling evidences of the miracles God was performing in salvation, church planting, and answers to prayer.

My first trip was to North, West, and South India, encompassing four pastors' conferences, many local churches, seminary students, a large baptism, and a church dedication. What a challenge for harvest! My heart was broken anew by the lost multitudes and awesome need. After a day of crisscrossing Bombay (today Mumbai), wading through mud and water in the slums, seeing the poverty, and six new churches God raised up, my burden was so heavy that I turned to two of the pastors and cried out, "We ought to ask God for two hundred churches in Bombay alone."

Onward, the Lord led to the British Isles during much of November and into December, ministering in Britain, enlisting the one hundred thousand prayer partners we needed for our Decade of Harvest ministries. We prayed daily for a million souls and two thousand new churches to be established around the world.

EXCITING NEWS (1983)

When the initial reports from around the world started rolling in, we were very excited. We heard some amazing stories and read about where and how God was working in our various fields, and we compiled praise notes and new prayer requests for circulation and distribution.

We praised God for the over 1,850 organized churches on our fields, the nearly six hundred unorganized churches and preaching points, plus the several thousand home groups that met weekly for Bible study, prayer, and fellowship. We asked for more prayer for God to send revival to all, and we praised him that each group was a lighthouse in the world's darkness, a center for harvest outreach.

We asked God for the more than five hundred thousand members of our local churches on fourteen fields. We asked for prayer, that each one would be Spirit-filled and involved in the harvest by personal prayer, personal witness, and personal soul-winning. We praised God for a 21 percent growth in baptized members above the previous year. We also praised him that not only were believers in our national churches contributing almost thirty-two million dollars to support their own church ministries but that a missionary vision was evidenced in a number of places.

We praised God for seventy-nine evangelistic teams involved full-time in the harvest. Each year they held thousands of evangelistic services, made multiplied thousands of evangelistic home visits with their witness and literature, and seized opportunities for God. We asked prayer for God to bless and anoint them and give them souls right away.

We praised God for more than 146,000 Bibles, New Testaments, and portions of Scripture sold and distributed the past year, and more than 2,600,000 pieces of gospel literature. Far more was accomplished than was reported. We asked prayer for the Holy Spirit to bless all literature used in the harvest and for his follow-up on all those reached.

We praised God for hours of radio evangelism through OMS ministry. Using the super-powerful radio stations of FEBC and TWR, we broadcast the gospel into almost every part of China. Our own station, Radio 4VEH in Haiti, broadcast in Creole and French to Haiti, in Spanish to Cuba and the Dominican Republic, and in English to the West Indies, Bahamas, Turks, and Caicos Islands. We were using thirty-four other radio stations in Brazil, Colombia, Ecuador, Japan, and Taiwan, with a number of local church broadcasts.

We praised God for nearly a half-million one-minute gospel messages given by phone to those who called our telephone ministry and for thousands of counseling follow-up calls. We asked for prayer for more and more eternal results.

We praised God for more than ten thousand people in our camps on eight fields, where nearly two thousand decisions for Christ were recorded. We asked prayer for those to become firmly established in the Lord and for many to become Christian workers in God's time.

We praised God for thousands being reached by medical evangelism; for more than a thousand who sat each week in our English classes, which were taught evangelistically; and for the thousands being reached by our gospel film ministry. We asked him for many, many new believers.

We praised God for more than thirteen thousand children, many from non-Christian homes, enrolled in seventy-nine church-related primary schools and for more than three thousand enrolled in our secondary schools. We asked God to make each teacher a soul-winner, to give spiritual victory to each child and youth, and to reach their homes with Christ's transforming power.

We praised God for twelve Bible seminaries and training institutions, and for the more than two thousand students and potential leaders in training for God's ministry in the whitened harvest fields. We asked prayer for him to call and prepare many more and to make each one Spirit-filled, solidly grounded in the Word, and effective in ministry for the Lord.

God was already answering prayer, and we continued focusing attention on the worldwide harvest team of 3,685 OMS staff and national coworkers serving our churches and institutions and busy in outreach and ministry on fourteen fields. We asked prayer for daily guidance, anointing, and fruit. And we asked prayer for reaching our Decade of Harvest goals, through the mighty work of the Holy Spirit. We reminded new prayer warriors that both OMS and Earth's millions depended upon their prayers.

RECRUITING AND COORDINATING (1984)

Starting in mid-January of 1984, I had a month of assignments in Colombia and Ecuador. Within an hour of arriving at Guayaquil, Ecuador, we went to the OMS Camp Pallatanga, located at an altitude of about four thousand feet. Our missionary retreat was held there, and the Spirit of God met with us wonderfully. At each stop, I shared the vision for the Decade of Harvest and tried to enlist as many new prayer warriors as possible.

From there, we drove to Cuenca, a mountain city of two hundred thousand people, at an altitude of 8,400 feet. It was a five-hour trip, much of the time on mountain roads. On the Lord's Day, we enjoyed wonderful fellowship in our churches. Monday brought another three hours of travel through much fog over winding, mountain roads to our vocational Bible school at Carboncillo, higher in the Andes. There, we met with our students, and then we squeezed in a visit to Saraguro, where God was doing new things among the native people. We drove the long trip back to Cuenca, and much of Friday was spent driving to Guayaquil, on the coast, where a Canadian OMS work team of twenty-nine arrived. Saturday we all went by bus to Camp Pallatanga and back. What a joy it was to have the Canadians with us for the dedication of the camp, where we looked to the Lord together. Sunday that week was Election Day, only the second free election in the history of Ecuador. We watched the military with their machine guns patrolling the voting places and streets. We were not allowed to cross the town, so we remained sequestered with the work team in our hotel.

The next morning, we caught a flight to Quito, capital of Ecuador, at an altitude of ten thousand feet. I struggled with a nosebleed at the airport, but I was able to lie down awhile at the OMS dorm before taking another flight to Bogotá, Colombia.

The next morning, we left Roy and Carolyn McCook's home, crossed the city, and began the pastors' conference. During my second message, my legs began to tremble, and I nearly collapsed. The son of one of our colleagues, Dr. David Brabon, flew from Medellin to Bogotá and found me critically ill with pneumonia. My ministry for the next two weeks was canceled, and I was ordered to rest. After about two weeks, I returned to Greenwood, but I had to take it easy for a time.

From mid-April through early May, I went back to India for another busy time of ministry. We arrived in Allahabad on Palm Sunday. It was our ABS fortieth anniversary year, and the next day was graduation for another group of newly trained soul-winners.

Early the next morning, we started on a several-day trip to minister in new centers and churches I had never seen. It was a hot all-day journey of nearly six hundred kilometers the first day. The temperature was 113 degrees in the shade, and the metal roof of our small car radiated heat as if we were baking in an oven. The Lord, however, gave strength and blessing. The last night, we had the joy of dedicating our new church in the city of Varanasi, the famed holy center of Hinduism. I had prayed for this strategic center for more than forty years. What a joy God gave for us to share in the victory procession as new believers were led by our coworkers!

Easter Sunday brought various services: a sunrise service with 250 present, a morning worship service at the church on our seminary campus, and a night rally for all the Christians of Allahabad, with more than a thousand in attendance. Then, in my old familiar Hindi language, I taught multiple daily classes for more than a week, including a special refresher doctrine course and one on the "prayer life of the pastor." Later, we shared in ministry in Delhi among four districts of churches. We rejoiced in the Lord's presence, which seemed especially close throughout the rest of my ministry in the Orient.

May found me in Japan, speaking in special services at Tokyo Bible Seminary, plus church ministry. I was tremendously impressed with the caliber of our Japanese seminary students, who were truly reaching after the deep things of God. There was a planning session to double the capacity of the seminary, for which we praised God. What a thrill!

In early June, flying from Japan, through Hong Kong, to Korea, we participated in the International Prayer Assembly in Seoul, then circled back to Hong Kong for more ministry.

In the autumn, we had multiple opportunities to meet with faculty, staff, and students at the Central Taiwan Theological College in Taichung, always sharing the Decade of Harvest vision and enlisting more prayer warriors. God was raising more prayer warriors for the harvest.

REACHING THE WORLD (1985)

One of my most exciting assignments continued to be recruiting and coordinating prayer for our Decade of Harvest. Our records showed that during those first three years, on average, God gave us one new believer every nine minutes around the clock, month after month! We continued to seek prayer support for God to greatly increase our fruitfulness in the next few years. Wherever God was working in power, Satan was also trying to resist and hinder; therefore, we prayed daily for the physical and spiritual protection of all our wonderful coworkers, and for God to give a tremendous harvest.

For several months, I worked nonstop writing my first major book, *Touch the World through Prayer*. I felt the Lord's special call to put priority on this literature ministry, and I repeatedly felt his anointing. The manuscript was complete, and Zondervan was negotiating to publish the book. One mission board had already placed a tentative order for two thousand copies, and another for six thousand. Later, representatives from another group visited my office, and I felt sure their organization would want several thousand copies as well.

It was a joy to continue in a writing ministry. With each new book, I first prepared my heart. Then, I spent many hours reading, underlining, and studying Scripture through the aid of commentaries, Bible dictionaries, encyclopedias, and surveying the writings of other Christians in the areas relative to my writing. I prayed continually for God's help in expressing his thoughts faithfully and in ways that would grip readers and hold their attention. I so longed for the Holy Spirit to be able to use my writing to accomplish his purpose. And my thanks were extended to those who partnered in prayer. Later, 13,500 copies of *Touch the World through Prayer* had been ordered in advance.

By December 1985, God helped me start my next book, which was on the Spirit-filled life. Then one night, during prayer, he gave me the outline for a brief book on missions. I was not sure of the exact title, but it was so exciting to be involved in Christ's world harvest, even when Betty and I could not go ourselves but were involved through prayer and support. I tried to convey that excitement to those who didn't travel. I didn't want anyone to miss the privilege, joy, and rewards in heaven from intercessory prayer, just because they were unable to be regularly involved in face-to-face missionary work to the unreached.

ENCOURAGING DEVELOPMENTS (1986)

In early July, God was wonderfully present during our OMS annual mission retreat, followed by our annual convention and the summer board meetings. The board elected Dr. Edward Erny, Eugene's son, as our seventh OMS president.

Dr. Edward Erny's Inauguration

It was a joy and privilege to be part of his inauguration, since I had known the family for my entire OMS career, and now Ed was following in his father's footsteps as leader of the mission.

At the opening of the service, one of the platform leaders came hurrying to where I was sitting and said, "Come at once to the platform. Ed wants his Uncle Wesley on the platform. We didn't realize what you meant to him." What a brother-in-the-Lord Dr. Eugene Erny had been to me! We were more than friends. We had gone through happy times together, confronted demonism together, cared for each other, and prayed together.

Our families had also visited the cooler mountains together, where our children attended Woodstock School. We suffered from carbuncles together—I bandaged his neck, and he bandaged my arms. We were together when the doctor put our son, John Wesley, in the hospital, because the doctor didn't want Betty to see him die. *But, praise God, he did not*! We were together when little Ed Erny came down with polio, and we were together another time, when young Bob Erny accidentally poked his eye with scissors, and Mrs. Erny walked the floor praying, "Oh God! Am I going to have a blind boy?" Then during Eugene's final weakness and illness, I visited him every day. As I came to the door of his room one day, the nurse said to him, "Here comes your friend!" He instantly replied, "That's not my friend; that's my buddy!" *To God be the glory!*

Harvest Fruitfulness

Month by month, our Every Community for Christ (ECC) team members requested prayer for people by name. Some were ill, and others were slaves to drink, or looking for work. Some families were disappointed they had no children and asked that their home would be so blessed. Wherever our teams went, constant needs confronted them. As they fasted and prayed, witnessed from house to house, and held open-air and home meetings, they saw the power of God demonstrated. As Jesus answered prayer, more and more people came to him, convinced he was the living God. Many prayers each day for the Decade of Harvest helped win those victories. What was harvest, but harvest through prayer and fasting? There's no other way. Prayer and fasting are the answer.

More than one hundred church planting evangelistic teams were active on OMS fields around the world. Each day, the teams consisting of about 350 evangelists relied upon our prayer. Dozens of new congregations were organized, and new worship places were dedicated every year.

To date, 244 new congregations had been fully organized. That was far less than our goal, yet what a triumph of the gospel already! Think of the several hundred coworkers involved. Think of the wearying spiritual labor, day after day. Think of the prayer and fasting, tears, sweat, and lifeblood expended! No congregation was established without paying a real price in labor, love, and prayer. As a result, several hundred new, beginning congregations were formed but not yet fully organized. But many would be, that year. Many donors were a part, and we continually thanked them for their prayer and support!

After three years, the number of our trained national coworkers had increased by more than eight hundred. But we still had so many gaps in our missionary ranks! Where were the missionary candidates we needed? We asked for prayer to find them and pray them in.

Yet, thank God, trained brothers and sisters in our national churches were taking their places in seminaries, schools, and churches. OMS has always emphasized the role of the trained national. Don't measure the strength of OMS by its several hundred missionaries alone. Also count the more than three thousand trained pastors, evangelists, seminary teachers, and other trained coworkers and the hundreds in our evangelistic teams.

During those three years, 1,215 splendid, God-called young people graduated from our Bible seminaries to begin their ministry in God's harvest. Most of those were working in the outreach of the OMS-related national churches. Some were trained for other churches and groups.

Add to those the additional hundreds of laypeople who took shorter courses of Bible instruction at local centers and churches. Most of those courses were taught at night by our seminary staff or key pastors. Those laypeople would be more effective in their local churches and in local witness as a result.

We encouraged our prayer warriors to rejoice with us that in just three years' time, the membership of our national churches had significantly increased. The actual figures were usually larger than we publicized.

Already in the Decade of Harvest, God had given us more than 175,000 people who confessed to receiving Jesus Christ as their Savior. Now, all those had to be taught, established in their faith, baptized, and incorporated into new churches. Usually the churches invested time, energy, and prayer in new believers for several months, sometimes up to a year, before they were baptized. How could we keep up with that pace? Only by the power of God's Spirit!

How could we respond to all the open doors and new challenges he was giving? How could we speed up the effectiveness of our ministry and advance for the Lord? How could we find all the coworkers we needed? Only by God's help and many, many prayers.

HALFWAY POINT (1987)

Reports from around the world kept arriving, and hours were spent reviewing over a year's records from our Korea evangelistic teams. Thrilling as the statistics were, they gave only a small picture of the hours and hours spent in witnessing and all kinds of meetings. More than 144,000 people had been given gospel literature and a clear witness, and nearly nineteen thousand spiritual rebirths had been registered in heaven.

The Decade of Harvest was an opportunity to share in God's number-one priority—world evangelism. It was our prayer partners' chance to invest funds and intercession for eternal rewards. We urged our prayer warriors to not miss the crown God wanted them to receive (Rev 3:11). We pleaded with them to not sleep in the strategic time of harvest (Prov 10:5).

We constantly invited people to join in the spiritual warfare. It was their opportunity. Were we willing to invest significant prayer and funds? Often, we're moved by photos and stories of starving refugees, but even more tragic is people being eternally lost in hell because we failed to reach those who have never heard the good news of salvation in Jesus Christ! Five years of the Decade of Harvest had passed with five more to go. We continued to invest in those years daily, and we called everyone to invest in the harvest.

In early July, we held our annual mission retreat, and it was followed by our annual convention, where I had the joy of presenting the daily Bible studies, sharing an India update, and leading the healing service. God gave healing to physical, emotional, and spiritual needs. Afterward, a new group of missionaries attended two weeks of orientation at headquarters, where it was my privilege to speak to them on a number of timely subjects. The OMS board of trustees had an important session, and then we enjoyed one of our best annual conventions in several years. Attendance was up, and God was with us.

At the end of July, while lecturing at Trinity Evangelical Divinity School near Chicago, I was introduced to Dr. Gary Maxey, founder of the West Africa Theological Seminary in Lagos, Nigeria. He was among the more than a dozen candidates for the Doctor of Missiology degree. Most were professors of missions at colleges and seminaries in the USA, Canada, Guatemala, Hong Kong, Japan, Nigeria, and Colombia. My assigned subject was the role of the Holy Spirit and prayer in the life of a missionary. As a result of our time together, Gary purchased eleven thousand copies of *Touch the World through Prayer*, which he shipped to Nigeria. And later he was to open the way for even more ministry throughout Africa.

Remember the German Battleship, *Graf Spee*

From early to mid-September, I spoke at a youth camp, various worship services, a pastors' conference, and a Presbyterian seminary in Brazil. When I returned from Brazil, I stopped in Orlando, Florida, to attend the joint EFMA/IFMA retreat. At the hotel, I stood momentarily inside the front door, bowed my head, and prayed silently, "Lord, if You want me to meet someone here who can share

Battleship *Graf Spee*

information I need, or someone to whom I can be a blessing, help us get together."

I was just raising my head when a short, stocky man approached, then threw his arms around me, hugging me to his heart. "Brother," he exclaimed, "I believe I am here because of you!" He had me squeezed so tightly that I couldn't read his name on his convention badge! I asked, "Brother, who are you?"

He was Dr. Luis Bush, director of the "AD2000 & Beyond" Movement, which was coordinating, as far as possible, the ministry of Christian radio stations, missionary societies, and missionary work of evangelical denominations, seeking to reach all of earth's unreached people groups by the year 2000. He told me his grandfather was a British surgeon in Argentina, and when World War II came, he took his family back home to Britain. But he had a daughter who was in love with an Argentine young man, and after some time, she said to her father, "I want to go back to Brazil and marry my fiancé." She was returning to Brazil on a British passenger ship just outside the harbor of Montevideo, Uruguay, when one evening she was on the deck with some other passengers. The captain came out and told them there was a rumor that they were being pursued by the German battleship, *Graf Spee*—the very ship I had prayed to be stopped in 1939. "But you know, you can't believe wartime rumors," he said.

Dr. Bush continued the story. "I know you prayed. God stopped the *Graf Spee* that night, right at Montevideo. My mother reached Brazil, was reunited with her fiancé, and married, and in the course of time I was born. Brother," he almost shouted, "I'm in God's work today because of you!"

"Oh," I replied, "it is true God burdened me and I prayed. But there may have been a thousand others praying also."

"I don't know about the thousand," he said, "but I know about you!" The next morning, before he gave the main address, he took about five minutes to tell this story. He told the people, "I am in God's work today because of the prayers of Wesley Duewel!" How little we know how God sovereignly uses the prayers of his children to extend his kingdom.[1]

Writing Continues

God gave a new dimension to my writing ministry with the publication of *Touch the World through Prayer*. He was blessing the book in many lives and churches. Two nationally known evangelical speakers quoted from it in their retreats and messages. Translators were busily working to put it into Japanese and Korean. A Chinese publisher wanted a Mandarin edition for Mainland China, and a thousand dollars had already been donated to help with the costs. We were praying for more funds, as another publisher was considering editions in Russian and the languages of satellite Communist countries in Eastern Europe. Additional European languages were under consideration by other publishers.

Praise the Lord that another manuscript, *Let God Guide You Daily*, was finally sent to Zondervan. I had asked God to lead me and help me know when to decline requests for speaking and leading retreats, both in the USA and in other countries. I wanted his priority, as every engagement delayed my writing, but it still took longer to prepare the book than I had expected.

The first seventy-five thousand copies of *Touch the World through Prayer* were in distribution, and the sixth printing would be out the following April. The latest languages under consideration for translation included Spanish, Burmese, and Hindi. I asked for prayer, especially about Chinese and the languages of the Iron Curtain countries. *What a privilege to be used of God!*

THE POWER OF PRAYER (1988)

The Decade of Harvest ministry required special prayer focus in Indonesia, a majority Muslim country where ministry was slow to take root. Prayer targets for recurring intercession included daily anointing, guidance, and encouragement for the team. We asked

---

1   Editor's Note (David Dick): I heard Dr. Bush recount the same testimony on a separate occasion.

prayer for vision and courage in the face of opposition and discouragement, special answers to prove to the people that Christ is the living God, rapid growth in grace for new converts, unity in teams and in the congregations from diverse backgrounds, special help in the new congregations to become rapidly self-supporting, and courage for interested people to step out bravely for Christ. We asked for more prayer to see even more victories for Jesus.

God was giving victories—more than eighty baptisms were reported in the India prayer bulletin, but those results could be multiplied through more prayer. So, we encouraged more prayer and for people to believe for harvest. Wouldn't you have enjoyed spending December with our evangelistic teams and sharing in their Christmas witness? They were busy every month, but especially in December. Just try to picture the hours of work and the joy of Christmas, for the first time, for new converts and the first knowledge of Christmas for many Hindus and Muslims. No teams took Christmas vacation. It was too important a time for evangelism.

We praised God for daily harvest, interceding for him to restrain Satan's attacks on new contacts and new believers. Again and again, our people were threatened or attacked. We asked for intercession to restrain militant Hindu groups and transform them from Sauls to Pauls. The extent of our prayer support greatly influenced the extent of the harvest reaped in those days. We prayed that God would cover the more than 130 evangelistic church planting teams as they reaped the harvest around the world. We asked him to uphold all our teams so that they would be strong in faith and prevailing prayer. The teams were depending daily on our prayer, and we didn't dare fail them. In the last year, throughout OMS areas of ministry, God had given an average of four new churches organized per week. *To him be all the glory!*

There was no limit to what God would do unless we limited our praying and our obedience. We asked for people to stand with more than five hundred team members in daily prayer, for God to multiply the harvest and supply all needs. We asked people to cover the nearly

150 ECC teams with daily prayer. As we prayed, we shared the spiritual battles we faced, and our prayer and faith would bring the answers that led to the salvation of many. The Decade of Harvest marched forward on the prevailing prayers of God's people, and we prayed that the concluding months would be marked by greater harvest than ever before.

A MILESTONE YEAR (1989)

As we started the new year, I accepted some speaking engagements, a ministers' conference in North Dakota and an Asbury-Taylor college student retreat at OMS headquarters. One particular Friday, I felt the Lord's help as I spoke on prayer to the student body and faculty of Asbury College. Meanwhile, I was still trying to give priority to writing.

In April, I had three weeks of ministry in Canada, including the privilege of serving as the Bible teacher at the Prairie Bible Institute conference and the Briarcrest Bible College conference, with attendance ranging between three hundred and twelve hundred at the services. I was pleasantly surprised to renew fellowship with Prem Pradhan, one of my former ABS students, in whom we had invested ten years of our life. He had planted and organized the Evangelical Church of Nepal, then composed of eighty-five churches with thirty-five thousand members. He had also started a small Bible school with eight students, one of which was a Tibetan Christian who spoke many languages and served as the secretary to Dalai Lama. Prem had paid a steep price, such as the imprisonment I told you about, but like the apostle John, I was delighted to learn that one of my spiritual children was faithfully following the Lord.

As I continued full-time in writing and speaking, God led in writing my next book, *Mighty Prevailing Prayer*. In April, *Ablaze for God*, was scheduled to be published, and already we had received orders for about seven thousand copies. During those days, more contracts were signed for publishing *Touch the World through Prayer* in Italian, Lingala (Africa), Malayalam (India), and Serbo-Croatian (Croatia).

The contract for the British edition of *Let God Guide You Daily* had also been signed.

In early December, contracts were signed for two books to be printed in Nigeria, two in the Philippines, and for an Indonesian edition of *Touch the World through Prayer*. The Mandarin translation for Mainland China experienced repeated delays, but the Malayalam edition in India would be off the press that month, and the German edition would be the following month. A letter from Australia told how a copy was sent to Sri Lanka, resulting in a prayer group starting there.

To date, God had helped distribute nearly 230,000 books over the past three years. All the commissions, or royalties, were directed back into a special account for more overseas editions. *Praise the Lord!*

WRITING-MINISTRY MOMENTUM (1990)

From March through April 1990, I was in Japan for the graduation ceremonies of the Tokyo Bible Seminary and the Christian Academy of Japan, the Japan Holiness Church (JHC) pastors' prayer seminar, and the JHC ninetieth anniversary rally. Dr. Paul Rees and I alternated as speakers at the ninetieth anniversary celebration in the Hibiya Public Hall in Central Tokyo, where a massive 212-voice choir from forty-five of our Tokyo churches led in worship.

I had never heard a more thrilling rendition of the "Hallelujah Chorus" from Handel's *Messiah*. Such holy joy, anointing, and perfection caused me to almost unconsciously turn to see if Christ was standing beside our choir leader. God's presence was so real! Tears were in many eyes, and I wished we could have sung the "Hallelujah Chorus" again and again.

Working through my interpreter, God gave great liberty during the missionary message. At that event, donations were the largest single offering in JHC history. More importantly, more than a hundred people stood, indicating their desire to be saved or sanctified, and fifty-six youth yielded themselves for full-time service. Dr. Paul Rees led in an inspired prayer, and I was privileged to lay hands on all the youth who committed themselves for missionary service. Indeed, our ministry in Japan was anointed and blessed by God.

A leader from the former Yugoslavia, who had translated *Touch the World through Prayer* into his own Croatian language, wrote he wished he could place a copy in the hands of every pastor in Eastern Europe. The first edition of *Mighty Prevailing Prayer* sold well, helped by such friends as Leonard Ravenhill, Armin Gesswein, and OMS president, Dr. Ed Erny, who were so generous in their commendation of that book. *Praise the Lord!*

The Decade of Harvest reports from other OMS fields around the world told that God had given our churches twice as many new believers in the past year as the year before, and 162 new churches were organized. *Praise the Lord!*

Thank God the resurrected Christ is not only enthroned at the right hand of the Father but is also at work through our coworkers, and that more and more of the unsaved and unreached were coming to Jesus. How much God used these hundreds of evangelism team members who depended on their spiritual life and zeal but also upon others' prayer support. Unfortunately, by the time those reports were received, they were several months old. The need for prayer continued each day.

INDIA PRAYER CONFERENCES (1991)

As part of my responsibilities for the Decade of Harvest, the Lord gave me another opportunity to return to India and schedule two major events: India prayer conferences in 1991 and Bible-teaching conferences in 1993.

India had become our second largest field, and it was growing deeper and expanding wider every year. There is no way I can fully or adequately describe all that my teammates and I experienced, felt, and shared during this forty-day India trip for five major prayer conferences and related events in 1991. God did above and beyond our careful and prayerful plans and expectations.

He also greatly blessed those prayer conferences in deepening and unifying the spiritual life of the church. We were deeply aware that we were in his will, upheld by a great volume of prayer, and in a battle with Satan and the powers of darkness. We owed a deep debt of gratitude to everyone who supported that venture in prayer and through their sacrificial financial support. We thanked them for their vital involvement and real partnership with us to make this possible. In a very real sense, we were indebted to them for the results and God's great faithfulness.

Before we left India, testimonies of prayer lives being transformed and of pastors going back to their churches to put new emphasis on helping their people become a truly praying people were already coming in. The participants showed such love and appreciation that they requested a Bible-teaching conference two years later, in 1993. I returned to Greenwood, praising God that OMS's work in India was larger, stronger, better organized, advancing according to prayerful plans, and basically more spiritually grounded than I had realized. *To God be all the glory!*

A final miracle of protection happened on our flight home. You may be aware that there were (and still are) unusual tensions in India between members of the Hindu, Muslim, and Sikh religions. Daily, the newspapers reported shootings, killings, rioting, and threats. One week after we were in Varanasi, fifteen people were killed in the very section of the city where we had been. Air India did not take seriously three bomb warnings they received in Delhi.

When our plane reached London, however, the British did take them seriously. We were unloaded, and the plane was moved to the most remote corner of Heathrow Airport. Our luggage was spread out on the runway and, for hours, sniffing dogs and electronic devices searched the 747. A police representative gave this statement: "This was not just a threat. This was real." We were placed in a London hotel for a day, and then we flew one day later to New York. *Praise the Lord*, our bodies were not sunk to the bottom of the ocean. All lives were saved, and we carried on our ministry for the Lord.

We thanked God for his great faithfulness. We thanked those who made that ministry possible with their financial support and prayer and for being real partners in our work. My special thanks was due to Dr. Lareau Lindquist and to Rev. Charles Elkjer—my loving, praying, committed teammates in ministry. *To God be all the glory!*

DECADE OF HARVEST CULMINATION (1992)

Our final Decade of Harvest report was prepared and submitted in September 1992. We had a story to share to the glory of God! Because many prayed and gave, and because our ECC evangelists, pastors, Bible seminary students, lay brothers and sisters, and missionaries had faithfully proclaimed the gospel, God's kingdom strongly advanced. We reported more than 580,000 new brothers and sisters in Christ. Every nine minutes another person was saved. That meant nearly the equivalent of a new congregation of 160 believers had been added to our ministry every day over the past ten years. Those needed to be followed-up, shepherded, and baptized. *To God be all the glory!*

The figure of more than 580,000 conversions did not include revived members of our churches, nor were these just hands raised to accept Christ. We sought to do a thorough work and disciple, ground doctrinally, and baptize the converts. Only God knows the heart of each new person who confessed Christ as their Savior, but we had strong reasons to believe a large percentage of our converts were truly born again. It was generally understood that in many mass-evangelism crusades, if one in ten people who made a public commitment were followed up, baptized, and joined a church as a result of the effort, it was considered a healthy spiritual harvest.

Our churches in the past ten years had more than doubled in membership—from nearly 460,000 to more than 960,000. Most denominations would consider that amazing growth. Do you know of any church that has doubled in ten years? The number of our local churches increased 63 percent. We were planting an average of five new churches every two weeks throughout the ten-year period. An amazing 39 percent of those who accepted Christ were already followed-up, baptized, and serving as members in local churches. The number of our trained coworkers in our churches around the world increased 346 percent. Our national coworkers had numbered almost 2,500 ten years ago. Now, they numbered more than 8,500!

We didn't measure OMS merely by the number of its faithful missionaries, although we thanked God for each of those. The OMS vision and philosophy since our establishment in 1901 has been that we exist to train national leadership and help found national churches that will grow and carry on the vision till Jesus comes. As we think of our national coworkers, we say with Paul, "Now we really live, since you are standing firm in the Lord. How can we thank God enough for you in return for all the joy we have in the presence of God because of you?" (1 Thess 3:8–9).

Therefore, we urged people to measure OMS by the national workers it trains for the harvest and the churches it raises up to the glory of God. At that time, God gave us nineteen times as many trained national church leaders and pastors as we had missionaries. Indeed, he was raising up missionaries from the national churches we planted. And at that time, those churches had fifty-seven missionaries of their own sent out to twenty-three nations.

It was a great day to be alive and part of God's final missionary thrust before Jesus comes again. All those prayer investments in OMS over the years were not in vain. All the financial investment was not money sitting idle or going down the drain.

Do the churches God raises up through OMS really become self-supporting? Praise God, they do. Does God teach them to give? Yes, often sacrificially. The total giving of our national churches for their own ministry, outreach, and missionary endeavor, as we began the Decade of Harvest in 1981 was almost thirty-two million dollars. In the last year of the decade-long campaign, our national churches gave more than three times that much.

Training was always a priority with OMS. At the beginning of that decade, we had 828 students in training in our Bible schools and seminaries. After ten years, we had an increase of 339 percent; slightly over

2,800 were in training. We graduated nearly five thousand trained coworkers during that decade. They were the hope of the harvest—God-called, Spirit-filled laborers ablaze for God and hungry for harvest. If God could help us prepare that kind of laborer, who truly prevailed in prayer, we would reap his kind of harvest. *Praise God for a tremendous Decade of Harvest blessed by the Holy Spirit!*

The Decade of Harvest gave us a tremendous launching base for tomorrow. We needed to catch the new vision Jesus had for us and our world. We entered three new fields that decade—France, the Philippines, and Mexico. In 1992, OMS entered two more new fields—Hungary and Russia. Where else would God open the door for OMS before we celebrated our one-hundredth anniversary in 2001? Would he reopen China? That was our prayer.

In many ways, the major cities were the ripest harvest fields of the world. During the past decade, we had entered many new large cities—Bombay, Calcutta, Manila, Mexico City. Add those to Tokyo, Seoul, Hong Kong, Delhi, Madras, Madrid, and Bogotá, where God was already giving harvest. Would God now add the cities of China, Russia, and beyond?

If we could multiply prevailing prayer sufficiently, we could enter into a new decade of almost explosive growth. God would give the harvest. He foresees tremendous growth and advance as divinely possible. Would we catch his vision? Were we prepared to pray, sacrifice, and go forward as never before? Would our partners in ministry allow the victories of that decade to thrust us into a new day of fruitfulness for God?

6
The Duewel Literature Trust Years

ANOTHER TRANSITION YEAR (1992)

As I shared earlier, I began to seriously consider the advice to write when I stepped aside from the OMS presidency. Throughout my presidency, various papers I presented in non-OMS circles had been warmly received, and on one occasion became a book, *The Holy Spirit and Tongues*.[1] I prayed at some length and felt clear in my heart that the Lord was asking me to write about my deep, lifelong convictions on prayer and the Holy Spirit, but I continued accepting speaking engagements in such numbers that I did not have much opportunity to do serious writing.

Then, something significant happened during my public speaking ministry. Through the recurring affirmations of, and encouragement for, my books, I was inspired to consider establishing an organizational structure to provide solid, biblical, holiness-focused books beyond my own lifetime. From that point forward, I knew the Lord was leading me to write, publish, and distribute classic holiness literature. I placed my writing ministry before the Lord and followed his leading. Eventually, the Duewel Literature Trust (DLT) was established.[2]

---

[1] That book does not promote *glossolalia* as a legitimate gift of the Holy Spirit.

[2] The formation of the DLT is documented on page 264.

New President and New Assignment

In 1992, Dr. J. B. Crouse Jr. was elected the Society's eighth chief executive officer, and his new administration desired to capitalize on everyone's spiritual influence, ministry experience, and mission expertise. I was asked to rewrite my ministry description and submit it for approval, or revision, as necessary. It was accepted with appreciation and without alteration, and I prayed for God's continued blessing on my life and ministry. Continuing as "special assistant to the president for evangelism and intercession," my primary areas of responsibility were evangelism, intercession, writing and publishing, doctrinal assistance, and public relations.

Historically, OMS endeavored to minister spiritually to its staff and supporting constituency. That was accomplished in two primary ways: with spiritually nurturing messages delivered in OMS public gatherings and with printed literature. *Streams in the Desert* by Mrs. Lettie B. Cowman began that ministry, and my books were intended to serve the same kind of spiritual and inspirational function for OMS at large.

In order to produce as many books as possible and prepare for the Holy Spirit's fullest ministry through them, I restricted my reading of newspapers and periodicals, radio listening, and TV watching to prepare for a writing ministry. I also made use of travel time. Doing so also provided extra time to pray for God's blessing on our outreach, covering all fields of OMS, its leaders, and leaders of the national churches. I sought God's anointing and blessing in the messages of all my books. And chapter by chapter, as I wrote to bring the greatest glory to God and undergird the Society's ministry with prayer and fasting, I believed this work was effective and essential for OMS outreach and would yield his increased blessing on all of OMS.

I deliberately included mention of OMS at various places in all my writings, to testify as to how God was using it and/or to help the Christian public become more aware of and appreciative of OMS. I must have done fairly well at this, as a reviewer critiqued one title as being a propaganda book for OMS. Nevertheless, I did the same in prayer conferences.

I accepted public ministry opportunities to promote my books in as many denominations, missionary societies, and organizations as possible as well as to introduce OMS to the larger body of Christ. I advertised and promoted them in as wide a circle of evangelical organizations as possible for the same reason. I took copies wherever I visited among the OMS home-base countries, in order to increase the exposure and expand the impact of OMS. I also sought to arrange overseas book translations to bring greater blessing to the maximum number of people and nations. I considered my literature ministry part of the worldwide outreach of OMS, extending beyond our existing OMS fields.

EFMA and My First Book

In 1986, when I began to write *Touch the World through Prayer*, my hope was that God would use it to bless and multiply the work of all evangelical societies in the Evangelical Fellowship of Mission Agencies (EFMA). They had known me for a number of years, and they knew my burden for prayer. At the annual EFMA meeting, I requested prayer of all my fellow executives, asking that I be anointed by the Spirit in a way that the book would multiply prayer for all. I did not do this to help promote the book, but it did, as it resulted in orders for more than sixty-six thousand copies before it was even off the press. God helped me and gave gracious answers to prayer. *Touch the World through Prayer* was used by as many as sixty missionary organizations and denominations in its first year, and the number grew much larger after that.

Multiple reader testimonies were received, indicating that many, many of God's children around the world were blessed, spiritually helped, and guided by the books. The literature ministry proved to be one of the most fruitful times of ministry God gave me. OMS, too, benefited from the Duewel Literature Trust (DLT) ministry. OMS continued to provide office space for my secretary and me and warehouse space for the DLT inventory, for which I was very grateful. That support and service was deeply appreciated, and I often thanked God for it. In prayer and love, I was still very much a part of OMS, and I thanked God for the understanding, good will, prayer, and loving support of the OMS leadership and worldwide family.[3] *May God be pleased and glorified in it all!*

Zondervan's Role

Zondervan Publishing House (now a part of HarperCollins Christian Publishing) published nine major books and helped market the English-language editions, always asking what the books' primary purposes were and for whom they were written. The following information helps explain my motivation and promote the eleven major publications I have written.

Touch the World through Prayer (Zondervan, 1986) was written because prayer was always a passion of my life. I wanted others to share a prayer passion that could literally change the world.

Let God Guide You Daily (Zondervan, 1988) was written because, as I returned from India and began my ministry in the USA, I was repeatedly asked questions about knowing God's will on the campuses of Bible colleges, seminaries, and youth gatherings. People seemed to think there were only two areas in life where one needed God's guidance—marriage and vocation. So many people did not seem to understand that God loves us so much that he wants to guide us in the most ordinary activities in life. Isaiah 58:11 says, "The Lord will guide you always."

Ablaze for God (Zondervan, 1989) was written to encourage total commitment, all-out endeavor, and complete dependence on God for his presence, guidance, and power. God can give us divinely guided joy in daily living, in intercession, and in service and ministry—and a blazing Spirit-anointed, Spirit-empowered, Spirit-used leadership. He can give us not just a flickering flame but a constant white-hot flame.

---

3   The DLT continues to enjoy a three-office footprint in the OMS Research and Writing Center.

Mighty Prevailing Prayer (Zondervan, 1990) came out of my deep conviction that God's people need to enter into a deeper Spirit-enabled and empowered prayer life. Its message is for all Christians desirous of going deeper in prayer and especially for Christian workers and missionaries. The content became the basis for most of my prayer conferences and seminars. When I revisited India in 1991 for denomination-wide prayer conferences, copies of this book were provided for all our pastors in three major languages so each would have a copy they could understand.

So few people rarely seem to prevail in prayer. It seems almost as if they expect all prayer to be casual, and they don't know what it means to be burdened in prayer. Many situations with urgent needs do not yield to our ordinary, routine praying. Evil is often so deeply entrenched, and Satan is so determined to hold on to lives, that a more determined, more militant intercession is required before prayer prevails and God's will is brought to pass. God has predicated the advance of his kingdom on the Spirit's power and the cooperative intercession of Christ's prayer partners. I wrote this book, praying God would use it to motivate and guide praying people to a new level of effectiveness in prevailing intercession.

God's Great Salvation (DLT, 1991) was penned when I realized that, as I could not return to India again to live, I wanted to write a theological primer for our India pastors. I wanted to leave them clear doctrinal guidelines, particularly in the area of the Doctrine of Salvation (soteriology). Because some of our pastors were not highly educated, I knew I must not write with complexity but straightforwardly and simply.

When I revisited India in 1993 for denomination-wide Bible teaching and prayer conferences, copies of this book also were provided for all our pastors in three major languages so each possessed a copy they could understand. All pastors, seminary students, and teachers were invited to attend, and the Lord provided more than fifty thousand dollars to cover their cost of accommodation and transportation. Some of our coworkers had to travel five days to attend a conference, three days by foot, and then most of two days by train. We held five splendid conferences. While I didn't advertise or promote the book widely, especially among non-Wesleyan groups, it is still used in India by several Bible schools and colleges.

Measure Your Life (Zondervan, 1992) was written because one day I realized I had never heard a Christian minister preach an entire sermon describing when a Christian stands before the judgment throne of Christ (2 Cor 5:10). So, I felt led to write *Measure Your Life: 17 Ways to Evaluate Your Life from God's Perspective,* to suggest what I think God probably does every day, which will be important to us when our life is reviewed.

I had heard references to when sinners stand in judgment, but not an emphasis on Christians giving an account of their lives before God. Yet the Bible teaching is so clear, and the subject is so important to every Christian. I didn't want anyone to stand at the judgment seat, and have Christ point and say, "If you had been more faithful, you could have lived much more fully for Me."

Revival Fire (Zondervan, 1995) was written because, as a boy, I rejoiced to read accounts of "old-time" revivals. Then God gave me the privilege to minister in Wales among converts and friends of the great Welsh evangelist, Evan Roberts, and to count among my dear friends Rev. Duncan Campbell. Duncan was so used of God in the Hebrides revival, at which time he retold and described some of God's mighty workings in revival. How we need revival over and over in God's work! After receiving a number of requests from readers, I also prepared an eighteen-page, chapter-by-chapter study guide, which can be used in Bible study discussion groups.

God's Power Is for You (Zondervan, 1997) was the one exception in my writing experience. I can testify distinctly, that on June 13, 1995, God spoke to me through the words of Jeremiah 30:2, "Write in a book all the words I have spoken to you." Previously, I had contributed monthly editorials when I edited *Revival Magazine* in India. Of course, I prayed much over each editorial and always felt I had God's subject for that particular month. Those meditations and reflections were written over a twelve-year period, conceived and born out of much prayer. On this occasion, I felt it was God's instruction to write this book, and I felt such help of the Lord as I gave myself to that project all day. So the book was written at the Lord's guidance. It's a compilation of fifty-two editorials, arranged in chapters, one for each week of the year. My prayer was that God would make it a blessing to readers.

More God, More Power (Zondervan, 2000) originated out of a speaking appointment at the Holiness Emphasis Week at Asbury Theological Seminary during January 1959. God had given me a series of messages about holiness. Afterward, I prepared a forty-three-page booklet, "Be Filled with the Spirit." It was subsequently greatly revised and enlarged as the book, *More God, More Power: Filled and Transformed by the Holy Spirit*, thus identifying the spiritual growth after sanctification as "transfiguration," according to the meaning originating from the Greek biblical manuscripts.

My burden for people to be sanctified and filled with his Spirit led me to speak frequently on this subject. I realized so few people really preached clearly on sanctification—the Holy Spirit cleansing us from all sin. Then again, many who believed in God's cleansing seemed to forget, or overlook, the importance of continued spiritual growth even after sanctification.

Heroes of the Holy Life (Zondervan, 2002) was inspired because, from my youth onward, I read and re-read biographies of peoples' lives used by God in an outstanding way. This book contained fourteen biographical chapters on the lives of Savonarola and Madam Guyon of the Middle Ages; Frances Havergal and Amanda Smith—the ex-slave; Adoniram Judson and Praying Hyde, pioneer missionaries; John Smith, a mighty man of revival, with calloused knees; and well-known churchmen such as Francis Asbury and Bishop William Taylor; American evangelist Dwight L. Moody; evangelist Evan Roberts; and China missionary Jonathan Goforth, all used by God in revival and historic harvest. Then I included Oswald Chambers and Duncan Campbell of recent years. The example of their lives has blessed and inspired my soul again and again. I hoped they would do the same for others.

Christmas Is for You...and the World (DLT, 2010) was compiled as a short seasonal booklet composed of ten Advent devotionals from *Revival Magazine*. Initially it was sent out to all our personal donors and prayer partners, but eventually it was reprinted, used by other missionaries in OMS, and made available for general use from the DLT website, www.duewellliteraturetrust.org.

I started writing this autobiography only after considerable prayer and deliberation. As I prayed about writing an account of how God had worked in my life and ministry, I wondered why people kept mentioning it. Some said I should do it at least for the sake of my children and grandchildren. Was God trying to tell me something? I asked him to make his will clear to me. I'm a very ordinary person, just a brother-in-Christ. But I wanted to fulfill all he desired of me.

Occasionally I prayed about it, but I didn't have any clear sense of guidance. Each other book was undertaken only when I was convinced God was calling me to write it. I wasn't just trying to publish books for books' sake. As Solomon said, "Of making many books there is no end" (Eccl 12:12).

Over time, I came to believe that writing the story of God's gracious acts in my life was his assignment to me and could be of benefit to younger people trying to follow his will for their lives. I've always believed it's rewarding to obey God's call on one's life, and I wanted to underscore how rewarding it is. I prayed that my autobiography would demonstrate that very fact. God has been so good and gracious to me, and I pray that you, dear readers, will find this experience true in your own lives.

Other Publishers

In April 1972, I was serving on a panel addressing the topic of "Challenging Demonism and Occultism through the Holy Spirit" (aka CDO) at the annual convention of the Christian Holiness Association in Indianapolis. In December 1995, a pastor in Florida was given permission to reproduce CDO for a two-year period. His secretary reformatted it, with wider margins and larger font size, making it easily readable for his congregation. DLT received a 50 percent royalty from the sales.

In July 1996, during ministry in Brazil, I personally met Mr. Mauro W. Terrengui, executive director of Editora e Distribuidora Candeia, Sao Paulo, Brazil, and his wife, Marilene, who served as editorial director. They had previously published *Touch the World through Prayer*, and during that visit, Mr. Terrengui arranged speaking engagements for me and also asked me to write an article on fasting. Although that article, "Sanctify a Fast" (DLT, 1996) was never published in English, it was translated and published as a small booklet in Portuguese.

Mother's Answered Prayers for China

My special joy was to have three titles translated into Mandarin for China: *Touch the World through Prayer, Mighty Prevailing Prayer*, and *Ablaze for God*. Why did God give me a special burden for China? I think in his heavenly history, it dates back to my mother's prevailing prayers for that country from my childhood until she went to heaven. As I've mentioned before, as far back as I can remember, Mother prayed, often sobbing, as she wept for China during daily family prayer time. And years ago, when she suddenly became ill with appendicitis, prayed for healing, and—*praise God!*—was instantly healed, she was able to send her savings for treatment to OMS for ministry in China instead of using it for surgery. Therefore, because of my mother and God's gracious answers to her prayers, I've always carried a special heart-burden for the masses in China. After my mother's homegoing, I wrote a poem, "The Prayers of Saints Live On." I believe God continued to answer Mother's prayers for China through my books in Mandarin.

At first, the Chinese editions of *Touch the World through Prayer* were printed in Hong Kong on very thin paper and in a very small-sized type. The book could fit in a large coat pocket undetected. While Hong Kong was still a British "Crown colony," people carried small quantities of the books from Hong Kong into Mainland China. But this did not keep up with demand and I was told that, without authorization, three presses inside China reprinted someone's personally underlined copy. How many copies were clandestinely printed, God only knows, but a few thousand were obviously printed on these presses. I have sample copies with the underlinings. Eventually, however, God wonderfully opened the door for more copies to go into China.

When I reach heaven, I plan to tell Mother how more than one million DLT books were published and distributed in China in answer to her prayers. One of the government-recognized seminaries was also printing and distributing three DLT books in "official" editions. They printed smaller page "house church" style editions as well, thousands at a time. God continued to provide more funds to meet the demand. Our Chinese contacts sent photographs of the distribution, with people "standing in queues for hours gladly waiting" to get copies, groups of people thanking God with bowed heads before being given copies, and people weeping for joy after receiving copies.[4]

French and Spanish Editions

Several years ago, an African French edition of *Touch the World through Prayer* was published and distributed in two countries, the Democratic Republic of Congo and Cameroon. Rev. Joel Purcell, the SIM (formerly known as Sudan Interior Mission) literature coordinator, who directed this French project, gave me an update on the project. He explained the conferences were taking place all over French-speaking Africa. Some countries, like Mali, Guinea, and Burkina Faso, had totally finished the project, but others, like the Congo, had yet to receive their books. It has been a massive undertaking, made complex by the language and cultural hurdles.

---

4   In February 2020, the DLT signed a contract with Acclaim publishing in Hong Kong, who in turn contracted with *Kaimen* (Open Door) Digital Resources to convert and make available online all three of Dr. Duewel's books, *Ablaze for God*, *Mighty Prevailing Prayer*, and *Touch the World through Prayer*. But one month later, when Covid-19 became a worldwide phenomenon, both publishing houses were shut down.

During a six-year period, from 1995 through 2000, SIM reprinted *Ablaze for God, Mighty Prevailing Prayer,* and *Touch the World through Prayer* in English and Spanish for pastors' conferences in Ghana, Sudan, India, and Peru. More than fifty-one thousand SIM copies were distributed in "Pastors' Book Sets." *Praise the Lord!*

Readers' Letters

Even after all these years, testimony letters from many parts of the world are received, often from God's children in several different nations in the same week—at times, several per day. Often their English grammar is not the best, but I can usually understand their heartbeat and Christian love.

Hundreds of letters were from those who told how their lives and ministries have been "transformed" after reading my books. At times, they wrote to say they were preaching one DLT book, chapter by chapter, to their people. A number wrote that when we meet in heaven, they will tell me all about how they were blessed and used the books in their ministry.

Dear reader, you might ask how long it takes to write a book like *Heroes of the Holy Life.* I worked at it, among my other duties and assignments, over a period of several months. But actually, it was years in the making. I began to read about the lives of some of those great heroes of the faith, from books in my father's library, when I was in high school. Even then, I wept and prayed for the people and nations involved.

Unpublished Books

One or two other books were suggested to my mind during prayer, but only God knew if I would be given life and strength to write them. One book would probably be on God's healing power, and perhaps another on heaven. Another proposed book, which I titled *The Beauty of the Spirit-Filled Life*, based on Galatians 5:22–23 and the fruit of the Spirit, was in rough draft form, except for the final subtopic of "love." I worked on this book about four years, between 1994 and

1998. All that remains is to plunge the depth of the topic of "love," which seems almost incomprehensible.

Poetry

My interest in writing poetry began when I was a grade-school boy of nine. My first poem was about my father; after all, he was the one who first introduced me to the importance of communicating through poetry. It was not perfect in meter, but it rhymed. I remember the, now rather humorous, concluding line: "He gets my ball out of the gutter, and eats a lot of butter."

When I was in high school, I started two long poetic attempts. First, I tried to write the biography of David Livingstone in poetry, using poetic summary. I had enjoyed reading a biography about him so much that I composed several typewriter pages about his time in Africa, in the style of Henry Wadsworth Longfellow's "Hiawatha." Obviously, I got busy and never finished the poem.

I made another ambitious start on a poem in high school, this one about the second coming of Christ, beginning with chapter 4 in the book of Revelation. This also thrilled me, because I was enamored with the premillennial second coming of Christ, and I purchased several paperback books on the second coming. For years, I saved those early, over-ambitious attempts to write poetry.

The Role and Impact of Divine Inspiration

Most of my poems were "given" to me during prayer times, while reading God's Word, or when in meditation during our years in India, and when I began writing books. Over the years, God gave me about a thousand poems, many of which were related to prayer, missionary passion, soul-winning, and other related topics. Almost all were written during times of personal prayer, when I was alone in my office, or in my bedroom during the night, or when I was traveling by plane. Most were inspired at ordinary times. But some were inspired at special times and places, such as when I was in John Wesley's Prayer Room, kneeling on the floor where John Knox wrestled in prayer for Scotland, and once when I was at the spot where the Hebrides revival broke out in Wales off the west coast of Scotland. Some of my poems had been set to music by composers in the United States and Australia. Sadly, only a few were published.

At times, I wrote comparatively little, but at other times, it seemed as if the anointing and guidance for poetry came upon me with tremendous force. One time, during a day of prayer alone with God in Northern Ireland, the Lord inspired twenty-six poems, the most I ever wrote in one sitting. Even before I got up in the morning, as I was just dedicating the day to the Lord, the first poem began to come. I read God's Word and prayed all that day, with poems just springing up in my soul. That night after a prayer meeting, I was already in bed, when another poem began in my soul. While in ministry in Colombia, I began a series on the first two chapters of the Song of Solomon, writing twelve poems in one day.

Those moments were always the result of the overflow of my heart; it was never a willful intention, like, "Now let me see if I can write a poem." They were all the old-fashioned poems, with rhythm and rhyme. I would have inserted more of them in my books, but publishers were not encouraging, saying people usually don't like to read poetry.

Public Speaking and the Literature Ministry

What wonderful days of ministry in prayer conferences God gave! He kept opening new doors of opportunities with new groups. The first of many repeated open doors was in Florida, then another in Virginia, and more in southern Ohio, Kentucky, and Indiana.

What a joy it was also to engage in international ministry to Costa Rica with hundreds of missionaries and teachers from many denominations. I was asked to hold prayer conferences in three centers in Nigeria the coming year, and they planned to print twenty thousand more books in preparation. God gave a very blessed time of ministry in Barbados, West Indies, to pastors and Christian workers from various islands in the Caribbean.

In Georgia, one Saturday afternoon there was a half-mile-long prayer parade to remind people of the National Day of Prayer. And Sunday night, the final prayer rally filled the Trade Center to overflowing with more than a thousand people present, plus a 250-voice united choir. *Praise the Lord!*

It wasn't long before I realized God was opening doors, both domestically and internationally, as a way to further introduce and distribute the books he had guided me in writing. Hundreds of books were sold in those meetings and shipped to various parts of our nation and overseas. We received many rewarding testimonies from people, as they told how God had used the books to change their lives. In one gathering I was introduced by a minister who said, "This is the author of the book that changed my life."

Those were wonderful experiences. One service was so blessed that though three speakers were scheduled, we had no sermon—just prayer, praise, testimony, and confession. It was almost like authentic revival. I never had a happier time of ministry nor a time with so many visible results.

When I was preparing for ministry in South Carolina, Louisiana, and Indiana, before I departed for India in 1993, what thrilled me most after such busy months was that I was extremely blessed preparing the material. I trusted that God would make it a real blessing to others. Before long, translations of my existing books were in sixteen nations, and five others were soon to be off the printing presses.

Official OMS Materials

Over the years, God helped me write more than two dozen "position papers" related to OMS theology and doctrine. Among the many papers, the "OMS Articles of Faith," as contained in the "OMS manual," are still the primary theological foundation by which the mission operates today.[5] God also gave me the privilege and responsibility of editing *The Missionary Standard*, the official magazine

---

5   Dr. Duewel was the primary author for all official OMS theological and doctrinal materials from 1967 through 1993.

of OMS, until it was replaced by the *OMS Outreach,* edited by Mrs. Eleanor Burr.

INDIA DOCTRINE AND REVIVAL CONFERENCES (1993)

God guided and directed during the India doctrine and revival conferences. "This is of God!" my interpreter said, as he explained why he was not worn-out from hours of interpretation. Others said, "My life and ministry will never be the same again," and "My life was completely changed by the prayer conference two years ago, and now God is working again." I wish you could have been there to sense God's presence, again and again, and to have heard the prayers and comments from our Indian coworkers.

Every conference delegate was provided a book. They brought them to the services as we taught the clear truths written about in *God's Great Salvation.* The books had been translated during the preceding months, and they were off the press in time! The Hindi edition arrived only hours before the conference began. During the coming months and years, they would be able to revisit those truths again and again.[6]

After half a century, what a privilege to minister to nearly all our coworkers! I was deeply impressed by the spirit of prayer, more than in most churches around the world. I repeatedly told them it was probably my last visit. The interpreter choked with tears and could hardly repeat what I'd said to the people. Our India leader, Bishop Sargunam, announced that he wanted me back. When he put it to the people, all hands were raised, saying they wanted me to return. I made no promise. It was all in God's hands. I did my best. *To God be all the praise and glory!*[7]

---

6   In May 2019, the *ECI Church Planter,* the official monthly newsletter, reported 8,330 permanent churches and 14,410 house churches for a total of 22,740, well on the way toward the 2056 goal of one hundred thousand churches with ten million members.

7   The dates of the doctrine and revival conferences were October 14–November 13, 1993.

DUEWEL LITERATURE TRUST MINISTRY (1994)

Early in this new phase of ministry for me, OMS's Executive Vice President Dick Capin and I had many conversations about research, writing, and publication. It was my understanding that I was following his official advice and counsel, and that the best way to expedite, develop, and cultivate my calling to writing and publication, to further God's kingdom interests in a legitimate and legal manner, was to incorporate as a separate publishing trust. I was confident that writing, publishing, and distribution of solid Wesleyan holiness literature was something to which God was leading me—so much so that I started taking the serious, practical steps to establish a legally separate 501c(3) not-for-profit organization, which would be called the Duewel Literature Trust (DLT).

Incorporating a separate trust would require a separate board. I stayed within the existing OMS board and invited members who were available or had been recommended to me by OMS. I approached members of the OMS board who had suggested I incorporate a new registered and legal organization. Dr. Dennis F. Kinlaw was the OMS board chairman at the time, and he and Dr. Harold Burgess had recently launched the Francis Asbury Society (FAS), a legally registered and incorporated tax-exempt organization. I asked Dr. Burgess to assist, and he readily agreed. We began the complex application and registration process.

To ensure and safeguard the identity of the DLT as a separate and legally incorporated organization, it was registered with the government and approved to accept donations, gifts, or other monetary compensation for income tax purposes. In June 1993, we rejoiced to learn the state of Indiana had formally approved the legal incorporation of the Duewel Literature Trust, Inc. Harold served as DLT chairman, beginning with the inaugural organizational meeting on August 13, 1993, until his death on March 30, 2011. It was through the kindness of those gracious and generous OMS board members that we were able to apply, register, and comply with not-for-profit rules and regulations and operate in full compliance with the law with minimal overhead.[8]

The DLT was launched strictly as a faith enterprise. There were no grant monies, endowment funds, legacies, or inheritance money from any family members or friends. Total funding up to that point amounting to $685,000 had come as a result of prayer, gifts from interested friends, profits from the sale of English-language books, and what I had saved from my OMS monthly allowance to reinvest in the ministry.

Operating the DLT was much more time-consuming than anyone realized, requiring negotiating the printing of books, securing copyrights, maintaining and storing inventory, reprinting books, arranging for displays, negotiating overseas editions, considerable correspondence, phone conversations, and filling orders, which were often urgent, as a result of phone requests. Many letters requesting free copies of the books were received. Most such letters were in poor English, asking for English-language copies, telling of how they would use the books.

Only Hilda Johnecheck and I gave consistent follow-through to the DLT ministry. But ultimately, the Lord helped us publish and distribute ten major books, through correspondence, personal promotion, and providing subsidy assistance. We received many readers' letters, repeatedly testifying of blessings and requests for complimentary copies.

Each book was written, not because I wanted to write another book, but because I felt a divine compulsion—clear guidance that God wanted me to write on a given subject. It became, in effect, his call or commission to me to write on specific subjects. I had such joy in

---

8   Some OMS board members wanted the DLT to remain under OMS. Finally, on January 28, 2008, fourteen years after the state of Indiana's formal incorporation, the OMS board of trustees formally recognized the DLT as a legally separate, tax-exempt, not-for-profit organization. Because the status of DLT was a recurring topic of debate and discussion at the OMS board level, on August 14, 2008, the OMS board of trustees documented the DLT status in their formal records, and the matter was finally closed for discussion.

writing and receiving reports about how God was using the books that writing became a new phase of God's call on my life.

I gave very little thought to marketing. The proliferation into multiple languages was God's doing more than mine. Except for the book on doctrine for our India field, I did not seek to accommodate multiple languages. It all unfolded as requests came for translations. Eventually, books in print surpassed the half-million mark. And I didn't believe God was finished using and blessing DLT books, since I was continuing to receive letters asking for copies and testifying how God was using them.

God was so good. All the sales commissions and royalties were credited into a designated OMS book fund account and used specifically to print more copies of majority world editions. When the DLT was incorporated, and all my books were copyrighted under the DLT, this designated account remained active for the convenience of the OMS bookstore and for DLT financial transactions. *All praise to God!*

Korea Ministry

Late in September, I flew to Denver, then to San Francisco, and then on to Seoul. I thanked God for our prayer partners who upheld my ministry while I was in Korea through mid-October. Again, the faithfulness of God blessed the entire time.

Throughout my time in Korea, the people's eyes and ears were really glued on the speakers and interpreters. There were hour-long times of testimony and multiple messages, accompanied by beautiful singing. The Korean people really poured out their hearts in prayer. I spoke many times, and I learned that my books were selling well.

After concluding that ministry trip, I started the long flight back to the States, and, because of crossing the International Date Line, I reached home before noon the same day!

Nigeria Ministry

Late in October, I was off again for New York, headed for Lagos, Nigeria, albeit in a somewhat circuitous route through Brussels, Belgium; Kano, Nigeria; and Yaoundé, Cameroon. God truly answered our prayers during the five weeks, from late October through early December.

My hosts in Nigeria, Dr. Gary and Emma Lou Maxey, founders and leaders of Wesley International Bible College (later West Africa Theological Seminary), lived very simply, economically, and sacrificially. They arranged for thousands of my books to be available throughout our speaking itinerary, including the cities of Lagos, Owerri, Calabar, Aba, Makurdi, Kaduna.

There were many indications that Satan was attacking the whole time I was there. Right from the outset, in particular, the electricity service was so uncertain that public address systems repeatedly ceased to function. That whole section of the city was without electricity for a time. I had to strain my voice for all to hear, and people crowded to the front to hear me more adequately. The electric company came to fix the lights, but within three to four minutes power was off again. They brought a generator, and in two to three minutes it shorted out. They brought a second generator, and it also shorted out.

Except during the English-language hymns, the people clapped and swayed in time to the music. After services, people surrounded me, and asked me to put my hand on their heads and pray for them. God was truly working despite many evidences of Satan's opposition, and I'm sure there will be eternal results. God strongly anointed the services.

Everywhere we went, the Lord was faithful to anoint, and the younger people introduced me as "Papa." Tremendous love and great respect for me as an elder were constantly shown. Imagine having eighteen hundred people all praying aloud at the same time for several minutes for "Papa" and his ministry!

Many messages were preached, with hundreds present. God continued to anoint, especially on the topic of a "prayer burden" to more than a thousand people one afternoon. He gave great, prolonged prayer times, praying for revival, while people were walking back and forth, praying and gesturing. Then I asked permission to share my personal heavy burden for my unsaved children. My burden became so heavy that I would have been willing to die if that would lead to their salvation. The people went to prayer, and we had a tremendous time of intercession.

Dozens of denominations were involved in the meetings. On the one hand, it's sad that so many Nigerians wanted to start their own faith group; this individualization fragments the body of Christ. You can't believe the wide variety of names used by the multiple denominations, even "the Cherubim and Seraphim," who distinguished themselves by wearing all white. Most any pastor seemed able to get himself named "bishop," "overseer," "apostle," or some other awe-inspiring title, even if he had almost no formal training. On the other hand, adjusting to the African style of worship, with everyone moving and swaying in time to the music as they sang, was quite exhilarating. After my messages, the leader would give a prayer request related to the message, and instantly all would pray aloud. After two or three minutes of thunderous prayer, he would call out, "In the name of Jesus" three times, and that seemed to serve as the sign for all to be silent. Then he would give the next request, born out of the message, and everyone prayed for it instantly. Such prayer seasons would go on for up to a half-hour or even longer. What a volume of united prayer!

Overall, attendance was not as large as they expected with prayer conferences held by TV evangelists. However, conferences with seven hundred, a thousand, and eighteen hundred in attendance were worthwhile. At the third conference, a pastor came to me and said he had attended the first conference, too, and already his life and ministry had been permanently changed. He said he had read *Ablaze for God* through twenty-nine times. Many said, "Our prayer lives are going to be changed from now on."

After each meeting, we always had great prayer times—with hundreds of people—and I was given many handwritten prayer requests. The Lord truly anointed in all services. As we wound down our time in Nigeria, my hosts told me we had ministered to a grand total of 6,700 at the prayer conference. On my last day, I was driven back to Lagos International Airport and spent the night in an airline lounge. For the next two days, I flew from Lagos to Brussels by Sabena Airlines. The airline put me up overnight in a hotel, where I was able to rest some prior to my transatlantic flight. Then I flew back to New York and Indianapolis.

COMMONWEALTH COUNTRIES (1995)

We thanked our prayer partners for upholding us in such faithful prayer and support while we were busy for the Lord in New Zealand and Indonesia. I don't know if I have ever felt such constant prayer support and such a constant awareness of the anointing of the Lord so strongly upon my ministry. How we thanked the Lord for their partnership!

Traveling on Malaysian Airlines, I accompanied Betty to the Kuala Lumpur airport and helped her on to her flight for Indonesia before my plane left for Brisbane, Australia, and Auckland, New Zealand. John met Betty when she landed in Jakarta, and Darlene and Terry, now serving with OMS in Indonesia, met her when she got to Surabaya. That way, she enjoyed a much longer time with each of our two children and their families.

OMS New Zealand had invited me to another opportunity for ministry. Their home director and his wife, Denis and Joan Shuker, had a well-planned schedule across the North Island to Tauranga, and then we crossed by ferry from Wellington to Picton. We went to Christchurch on the South Island, and then from church to church from the east coast to the west coast.

On one occasion, as I followed my host into his garage, he inadvertently touched the button of the garage door opener, and the door came down on my head, knocking me to the floor. It split my scalp open for more than two inches, and blood came streaming down my skull. I went back into the bathroom and tried to wash the blood away, but from my youth, I have been a "bleeder," so the flow did not stop quickly. I held a wet washcloth to my head as we started our trip.

My host drove along the coast past surfers, kayakers, container ships, and small foreign ships taking on loads of fish. We drove past homes that appeared to be just "hanging" on the cliffs, with some built-on concrete columns "driven deep" into the island. We passed botanical gardens and flower houses. Upon our return, his wife saw me (I must have looked dreadful) and insisted her husband take me to the "emergency care." The doctor immediately laid me down, gave me six numbing shots, cleaned out the cut, and put in seven stitches. He gave me an anti-tetanus injection and told me to have the stitches removed after a week. When I sat up, there was an eight-inch pool of blood where my head had laid. I'm sure it was God's loving miracle that I hadn't bled all afternoon, while sightseeing. Instead, I had only a slight headache and felt a slight drawing of my scalp. Does not God take care of us? *Praise his name!*

From the very first prayer seminar and, over the next five weeks, there was such a constant and strong anointing of the Spirit wherever I went that, in complete confidence, I just knew untold intercession was upholding me. Almost regardless of the church—Methodist, Baptist, Presbyterian, Anglican, or Christian and Missionary Alliance—hearts seemed so prepared, open, hungry, and eager to obey the Lord. So often the anointing hand of God was felt very strongly. Whoever was upholding our ministry in prayer, thank you so much, and thank the Lord!

What choice Christian friends we met. Person after person said, "My prayer life is going to be different from now on," or "My prayer life will never be the same," or "My ministry will never be the same." One of the first ministers greeted me by saying, "Next to the Bible, your book *Ablaze for God* has been the greatest spiritual influence in my life."

Leaving New Zealand, I departed by Malaysian Airlines to Brisbane, Australia, and then to Kuala Lumpur, Malaysia, where I enjoyed getting horizontal in an airport terminal overnight hotel. After a refreshing shower the next morning, I proceeded on to Surabaya and Malang, Indonesia.

Indonesia Ministry

When I arrived in Indonesia mid-April, it was nice to see Betty and John and family waiting at the Jakarta International Airport. At the time, John worked with fifteen employees and four printers, and he held a very nice formal reception for us, with about forty people present.

We drove to Salatiga, in Central Java, to escort my grandson David to his school dorm. I spoke fifteen minutes to the "juniors" and "seniors" on the "Privilege of Hunger." Santi, I was told, was the best Bible student. We were also told that, at a school retreat, Santi sat quietly for an hour, wrote a poem on commitment to Christ, and then stood and gave a clear testimony of her commitment to Jesus before all the school.

The next day, we flew to Surabaya, East Java, where Terry met us and escorted us to Malang, where they lived in a lovely home with tile floors. At the evening OMS prayer meeting, I reported on my recent New Zealand visit and the literature ministry. I don't believe I have ever arrived on a field as ready for my ministry as I was in Indonesia. Our missionaries, churches, and seminary students had been praying. The students had had several all-nights of prayer as well as prayer chains.

We held a joint worship service at the OMS office that evening for four or five mission organizations. The next day, we held four services on the OMS seminary campus, which was so beautiful. The chapel accommodated as many as 850 people. We began the prayer conference with two hundred to three hundred in attendance—missionaries, pastors and wives, laypeople, and seminary students. I became obviously sick while giving the first message, but I finished, and the remainder of our visit there, I spoke four times. In service after service, it was such a blessing to see Darlene and Terry sitting near the front with their eyes closed as they prayed for me throughout a message. Often, they ran one-and-a-half hours long, and these two were truly my prayer partners.

All in all, we praised God for the beautiful prayer times, new commitments, and the testimonies of the victories He'd given. One lay leader in one of our churches came to me hesitatingly. He had been a secret police interrogator and was a strong, stern man. He said, "I don't know if I'm losing my manliness, or what! In these services I just want to weep." I explained that Jesus was revealing his love to him. The next Sunday in his local church, he began to testify, then burst into tears. Almost the entire church was moved to tears. In another city, an ex-military interrogator came to me with almost the same testimony of how God was now melting his heart with the love of Jesus. He was amazed when I told him he was the second interrogator within a few days to give that testimony.

I was able to complete my entire schedule for that conference, the Bible-teaching conference that followed, and another prayer conference to a group of three hundred to five hundred at a nearby seminary. Despite some continued physical weakness, the Lord helped me to complete the ninety-nine speaking engagements over two months. *Praise the Lord!*

Betty's Perspective

Betty was so thrilled to be with our two children and their families for two months. She reported, "What a treat for me to enjoy the loving hospitality and fun with our children and grandchildren. I kept well; thanks so much for your prayers."

Some of the highlights were: a reception given by our son, John, and wife, Retno, to meet some forty friends, expatriates and Indonesians, meeting more friends at a hiking club, attending an Easter program at our grandchildren's school, and other happy family times together.

Dr. and Mrs. Duewel and Darlene

A mosque is located very near Darlene and Terry's house, so one was awakened at 4:30 a.m. by the loud mournful "call to prayer." It's a reminder that our missionaries are in a non-Christian land and need our prayers.

It was interesting to see how Terry and Darlene juggle their schedules at Wesley International School (aka WIS, a missionary children's day school), the seminary, and the OMS office, answering phone calls, delivering faxes, giving hospitality, running errands, attending meetings and committees, etc. But we also found time for happy family times together. I attended the Spring Festival musical of WIS in which my grandsons Jonathan and Jason sang.

The missionary retreat at Junggo, high in a nearby mountain, cool and comfortable, like a paradise, was a time of blessed fellowship with our devoted missionaries. We were given a very warm welcome by the pastors and students, too. How beautifully the students sing!

There was much more to tell, like about the beautiful Indonesian singing, the committed leaders God was raising up in our churches, and the mini-revival blessings God gave. *To God be all the glory!*

The first week in May, Betty and I flew back through Kuala Lumpur, Malaysia, and Taipei, Taiwan, then on to L.A., finally arriving in Indianapolis. I still felt weak from my illness in Indonesia, and I lacked any real appetite or physical strength. But God was good and once again had sustained me throughout an intensive series of ministry meetings!

Literature Ministry

Praise God for thousands of Chinese scripts of *Touch the World through Prayer* printed in the area where Jonathan Goforth experienced the revival at the beginning of the century![9] That was all they dared print at one time for fear that a larger purchase of paper would attract the government's attention. Nor did they have safe storage for larger amounts.

---

9   Jonathan Goforth, with his wife, Rosalind, were Canadian Presbyterian missionaries to China. He became the foremost missionary revivalist in early twentieth-century China (1906–1910) and helped to establish revivalism as a major element in Protestant China missions.

We were also informed that SIM International planned to include thousands of Spanish-language copies of *Touch the World through Prayer* in their "Pastors' Book Sets" in South America.

In June, Rev. Joseph Tson, from Hungary, visited the OMS office, informing us there were thousands of Hungarian copies of *Touch the World through Prayer*. He felt *God's Great Salvation* was also very important for Hungary.

We had just sent nearly two dozen books to each of more than a dozen nations, and we received a constant stream of appreciation and thanksgiving letters. We also sent multiple books to, and subsequently received letters from, people in the Philippines, India, and Sierra Leone.

At the end of June, our annual retreat was held in Wilmore, Kentucky, where Dr. Steve Harper, vice president of the Asbury Theological Seminary campus in Orlando, Florida, was a featured speaker.

In early July, OMS held our annual conference, and the registered attendance was eight hundred. On the occasion of Betty's and my fifty-sixth wedding anniversary, OMS president, Dr. J. B. Crouse Jr., called us to the speakers' platform and gave us a beautiful plaque in honor of "fifty-three years of devoted service," counting up to my "official" retirement, two years previously.

After the conference in July, we sent subsidy funds to print thousands of Kuki-language copies of *Touch the World through Prayer* in India. We also received and signed the contract for the Portuguese-language edition of *God's Great Salvation*. Then the first week in August, very surprisingly and pleasingly, we learned that Mrs. Harold (aka "Peaches") French had composed some beautiful music for my poem, "There's a Gap Awaiting You." It was another one of those rare, but delightful times when others put my poetry to music.

At the end of July, J. B. stopped by my office and informed me that the OMS board had unanimously approved my designation as "president emeritus." Again, this was an honor I had neither requested nor sought but for which I praise God.

Precious Prayer Time

In early August, I experienced another blessed time of loving the Lord, yearning for him to use me and my writings, offering myself to him. I asked him to use my words, anoint my words, and help me to express his heartbeat. The Lord was so preciously near that I didn't want to stop my meditation time. I regularly prayed each evening, as I briskly walked around the OMS headquarters hallways. Thank the Lord, I was allocated an office in the building, where there was such liberty to roam the halls and pray. *Praise the Lord!*

Korea Ministry

Soon thereafter, I left for Seoul, Korea, where four-hour traffic jams in and around the city are commonplace. The next day, I spoke at the third service of one of our churches with a membership of more than two thousand people. Then I went on to another of our Korean churches.

Dr. John and Mrs. Elizabeth Hong took me to a retreat center rented by his newly formed organization, the World Evangelization Research Center. There, 265 people were registered, including Korean Evangelistic Holiness Church prospective missionary candidate couples. God strongly anointed each session, with over an hour of tremendous blessed prayer times that followed till the end of our time there. We drove back to Seoul. John Hong, my wonderful interpreter, and I were very tired, but God gave us a good night of rest.

We visited a large, rural church tent, with eight hundred people filling it on a weeknight! One young man insisted on carrying my bag, and whispered, "I have no grandfather, so you are my grandfather." A woman, carrying a small child in one arm, tried to lift my arm as she walked beside me. I felt respect and love from everyone everywhere. Upon our departure, four men and two ladies gave me a jar of honey and flowers, which I carried as we flew by Korean Airlines to Chicago and then returned to Indianapolis.

While in Korea, I learned the manager of Ye Chen Press had printed thousands of copies of *Measure Your Life, God's Great Salvation,* and

Let God Guide You Daily. Word of Life Press also printed some other titles. Also, we learned a press in India would print another couple thousand copies of *Touch the World through Prayer*. The literature ministry kept growing by God's good hand.

One evening in November, I was sitting thinking of all those who had faithfully prayed for and given to our ministry. How can I thank the Lord enough for their faithful love and prayer for so many years, and for their faithful partnership in our financial support! The older Betty and I got, the more we realized how important their role was in our lives. In heaven, we'll talk it all over, and our partners will discover how important their love was to us and to God's work.

How many more Christmases would we have before we all met around Christ's throne and in one another's homes in heaven? Yes, we were getting older, but God was still answering prayers and giving us health and strength. My blood pressure, however, did become increasingly difficult to control strictly through diet and exercise, when I was in so many homes, with so many styles of food, and spoke up to four and five times on many days. Therefore, it became a special prayer request item. Also, I asked prayer for Betty when I was absent so often in ministry. But throughout 1995, God gave me opportunities and anointing to speak 172 times for the cause of his kingdom. *Praise his holy name!*

The next year's travel schedule was also suggested as a priority prayer matter. I planned to go again to Korea in January; to Regina, Canada, in February; to the British Isles, also in February through April; then on to Peru, South America, for a large conference in the remaining part of April. Continually, I leaned on God and our prayer partners' intercession for travel mercies, anointing in ministry, and the ever-widening literature ministry.

AN AFFIRMING YEAR (1996)

The Lord led me back to Seoul, Korea, for a prayer retreat at Kwang Lin Retreat Conference in central Korea, where several hundred participants registered, and then one in our largest church in Pusan at the very southern tip of Korea. Ministering in our lovely churches in Pusan and Inchon was a wonderful privilege. We felt an unusual anointing throughout the services. There was also a four-day lecture series at the graduate school of our Seoul Theological Seminary.

On another occasion, I had just gotten to my room, after an evening service when a woman of about thirty years of age knocked on the door. When she stepped in, she handed me a piece of cake, then immediately fell to her knees, and prayed silently. Arising, she looked up to heaven and burst into joyous song, singing "How Great Thou Art" in Korean. It was as if she didn't see me, but her face was radiant, as she looked up to Jesus and sang. She was lost in communion and thanks to God for the services. Her joy was absolutely beautiful and thrilling. Then, she stepped out of my room.

I was so impressed by the genuineness and quality of spiritual life of Korea's people. They just drank in the messages and were so instantly ready to call on God in prayer. Dr. Hong translated for me several times, and he said he was unusually blessed during our time together.

It was the praying that blessed above all. Before and during each service I prayed, "Lord, let there be results from this service in eternity." When five or six hundred Koreans are all pouring out their hearts in prayer at the same time (the Korean way), you feel they are really prevailing. At times, their corporate prayer went on for at least twenty minutes, especially as they prayed for revival and for God to tear down the invisible, yet impenetrable, political curtain that separated them from North Korea and burst open the gates for the gospel. Thousands of believers were ready, at almost a day's notice, to rush north with the gospel, when God opens the door. I believe they still are. Upon departure, I was given a gallon of honey and three large apples.

Then I left Seoul and flew to Portland, Oregon, then to Cincinnati and on to Indianapolis, finally arriving home.

British Isles Ministry

Facing the next stretch of meetings, prayer was requested for missionary services in England, Scotland, Northern Ireland, and Wales; and for a large pastors' conference in Peru with pastors from five nations.

In Northern Ireland, we spent the "OMS Weekend" in Portrush, at a Christian guesthouse in Castle Erin that overlooked the Atlantic, on the northern shore of Ulster. Over a hundred OMS coworkers and supporters prayed and praised the Lord together. A good percentage of younger people, as well as the faithful older "OMS family" members, listened devoutly to the message, and as a result, the young people who spent summers on OMS fields banded together and held OMS promotional meetings from place to place.

For the next several days, we spoke many times each day at various locations. It seemed God was gripping people at every meeting. On one occasion, a man burst out in prayer, and then a woman. What a tremendous time of prayer was in store for those who were willing to wait.

There were several services at Londonderry in the Independent Methodist Church, where great liberty overflowed while speaking. We enjoyed another good service at Ballymena, and the next day at First Presbyterian Church in Portadown, and at the Mission Hall in Dungannon.

We also drove to Ahoghill, to the home of Pastor Derek McMeekin of First Presbyterian Church. When God sent revival in the mid-1800s, there were such crowds that a second church was built, and then a third. Thousands gathered and hundreds were saved. It was thrilling to pray in the old stone Kells schoolhouse where four young Irish men prayed throughout the winter of 1857–1858, leading to great revival in 1859. Pastor McMeekin had researched and written a book on the revival and gave me a video and cassette tapes of his own lecture on it.

During that revival, more than three thousand people crowded into the church one night, up into its "U-shaped" balcony, until the pillars began to sink into the ground. The balcony began to sag, and it seemed the building was about to collapse. Evidence of that occasion still shows to this day. People rushed outside and stood in the pouring rain for several hours, until hundreds of them became so convicted of their sins that they fell on their knees in the mud, repented, and were saved.

After flying from Belfast to Manchester, we attended the British Isles OMS board meeting. Bill and Kathleen Burnett were approved as executive directors, replacing Billy and Jeanne Campbell, who were leaving for Hong Kong. There were also meetings in Liverpool, England, and an OMS staff and regional men's retreat. On OMS's Founders' Day, we held multiple meetings in Liverpool, Bootle, Preston, and other places.

While at the evening service in Chester, a retired conference superintendent of the Free Methodist Church came to tell me how a girl, who was saved during my meeting in his church twenty-four years ago, was now the leader of the women's work in his denomination. Each weekend we had a prayer conference, and on weeknights, we continued to speak on prayer at the Fulwood Free Methodist Church and the Morecambe Free Methodist Church.

We drove to the OMS Scottish headquarters in Kilsyth, where in 1839, God also sent mighty revival. The next day, we drove all the way to Northern Scotland and across the new bridge to the island of Skye. It was an intense week in the Hebrides islands and in Scotland.

From Skye, we took a ferry to Tarbert, Isle of Harris, at Lewis. There were two services in Lewis, the area where God so graciously used Rev. Duncan Campbell in the 1948–1953 Hebrides revival. We enjoyed a good service in the High Church of Scotland, and then went on to Barvas. What a blessed time we had in the Barvas church, where the Hebrides revival began, sharing fellowship and stories of the revival with the godly local pastor and his wife!

We returned to the mainland by ferry, then drove back to Glasgow and to Cambuslang, where John Wesley and George Whitefield once preached. We had nightly services in Glasgow churches, and in Cambuslang, in the natural amphitheater there, where in 1742, George Whitefield preached to over twenty thousand people, and God sent a mighty revival. Rev. D. MacFarland gave me a rare book on the revivals of the eighteenth century, particularly at Cambuslang, with three Whitefield sermons taken down in shorthand.

We visited the Kilsyth Congregational Church, packed in the front, and into the "U-shaped" balcony. We remembered the Shotts revival in 1630 as dozens of people spent the whole night in prayer. A young man from Kilsyth, compelled by God after an all-night of prayer on his own, had timidly begun to preach. On that occasion, God came mightily, and more than five hundred people found Christ.

While in Scotland, I visited the John Knox home in Edinburgh. His house is about halfway between the castle and the fort on the "Royal Mile." I went to the third floor and knelt on the wooden floor where John Knox spent hours wrestling with God, repeatedly praying, "Oh God, give me Scotland or I die!" Then we flew to London, where there was a prayer seminar for more than 130 staff and students of the Worldwide Evangelism Crusade and Operation Mobilization, and a prayer emphasis in Baptist and Methodist churches. Then we drove to our headquarters in Wales, where ministry was scheduled in a number of churches.

When in London, I always endeavored to visit the John Wesley home, explaining to the custodian that there was no need for his kind offer to "show" me around. I preferred to go alone to John Wesley's small prayer room, and into the bedroom where he died, after whispering his last words, "The best of all, God is with us." I wrote several poems while on my knees in his prayer room.

There was another service in Launston, in the middle of Cornwall, and we went to the Plymouth area and enjoyed good services. The next day, we went to Wales, then to Gorseinon, where we met Rev. David Shepherd, the son of Thomas Shepherd, who was one of the first five converts under the great Welsh evangelist, Evan Roberts.

Once more I flew back to Northern Ireland and ministered several times in the great annual Easter convention of the Faith Mission, a British home missionary organization. Rev. Duncan Campbell was their best-known leader, but then the mission was led by Rev. Dr.

Colin Peckham and Dr. and Mrs. Ted Randall. Some three thousand people were in attendance, but no church could hold that many, so there were simultaneous services in three Presbyterian churches.

In Northern Ireland, I was privileged to speak several times at both the Worldwide Missionary Conference held in Wellington Hall in Belfast, and at the Worldwide Missionary Conference, held in Bangor.

Thank God for the wonderful praying friends I found in Northern Ireland! Never will I forget the day of prayer spent at the Mulligan home in Armagh. During that day of fellowship with Jesus, God led me to write twenty-six poems—the first before I got out of bed in the morning, and the last after I was already in bed that evening. I got up, turned on the light, and wrote the twenty-first poem!

God gave me another six wonderful weeks of ministry in the British Isles, including a week or more in Northern Ireland, the Hebrides, Scotland, central England, and Wales. God was so faithful in repeatedly anointing me and keeping me in good health. God's people also purchased hundreds of DLT books. My prayer was that God would continue to use all greatly.

Returning home for four days, I discovered how six weeks of correspondence and mail really piles up! Those days were largely consumed by committee meetings and a conference. Mid-April, the Southern Baptist Mission board ordered several hundred copies of *Revival Fire*. God then sent me to Peru, also in mid-April, for another week of international ministry.

Peru Ministry

I flew to Lima, Peru, where it was a special privilege to have been invited by SIM International to conduct a major prayer conference. I was met by my host, Brother Joel Purcell, coordinator of SIM literature ministries. The conference was hosted by a large Christian and Missionary Alliance church that could accommodate a thousand people at a time. Joel's father-in-law, Rev. Ed Robb, shared conference speaking responsibilities. He spoke on holiness, and my preaching topic was prayer. Brother Joel later wrote, "The Lord is using these conferences beyond our greatest vision. All praise to him!"

Back in the States

We continued shipping hundreds of DLT books, sending free copies to those requesting in Ghana, Nigeria, the Philippines, Zambia, and Jordan. More than 6,600 books were sent.

In early May, OMS headquarters celebrated the National Day of Prayer. Our staff met for prayer in the chapel, and then at noon, we moved to the front lawn to dedicate our newly erected "flags of the nations" centered on the parking lot. The Greenwood mayor spoke briefly.

Near the end of May, delegates from our Korea church came to headquarters for a conference. As the invocation was lifted before the Lord, mentioning the South Koreans' burden to return to North Korea and reach their family members, I was again moved to tears as we prayed with and for them.

At the end of May, Betty and I had the joy of welcoming Darlene and her family home for furlough from Indonesia, where Terry had been serving as the acting OMS field leader. Their boys, Jonathan and Jason, had really grown. They planned to stay with us until God provided more permanent housing and revealed his plans for them.

Shockingly and unexpectedly, Dr. Ev Hunt Jr., former OMS Korea missionary, my immediate successor and the sixth OMS president, experienced a heart attack in early June and suddenly died. A few days later, after the cremation, a victorious memorial service was held.

In the afternoon of June 3, my birthday, Dr. J. B. Crouse Jr., our eighth OMS president, graciously arranged for a staff birthday celebration for Betty and me. Betty would turn eighty-one on June 11, and I was now eighty. For a few minutes Betty reminisced about our first years in India, thanking God for his goodness and mercies. Then we enjoyed birthday cake.

OMS Ninety-Fifth Anniversary Conference

Late in June, we held our OMS annual conference, in Wilmore, Kentucky, celebrating our ninety-fifth anniversary with 840 people registered. Dr. Kinlaw, board chairman, preached a series on "Thinking the Way God Thinks." We also enjoyed splendid field reports by Dr. Ben Hur Lee, representing China; Dr. Yugo Matsuki, representing Japan; and Bishop Ezra Sargunam, representing India.

At the healing service on Friday afternoon, we anointed forty-five people for various forms of healing. Later we celebrated with an anniversary banquet. On Saturday night, my message was on "The Revival We Need," and I poured out my heart. Perhaps 150 people came forward to pray for revival, and different ones called out their request for revival.

Shortly thereafter, on June 29, Betty and I celebrated our fifty-seventh wedding anniversary.

Brazil Ministry

Ten days later, I began nearly a month of busy ministry in Brazil and requested prayer for an upcoming three weeks of demanding ministry, including six prayer conferences, four organized by our OMS-related church workers and two by godly friends. I felt so constantly in God's will, and despite a brief health problem, God was continuously at work.

The Lord anointed and gave a real liberty as he carried me through fifty-two speaking engagements. Teaching-preaching is a joy when you believe in the urgency of the message, when the Lord keeps anointing, and when the people are receptive and loving. The longer I minister, the more I realize what a wonderful people God's children are. How rich in love we are in Christ! While in Brazil, I met with our Portuguese publisher, Marilene Terrengui, and her husband, Mauro. We enjoyed a blessed fellowship together, and they purchased the rights to publish all DLT books in Portuguese. Their bestsellers were books by Josh McDowell and my books. They requested me to prepare a shorter book on the role of fasting and prayer, intended for all denominations, which they wanted to supply to the Christians all across Brazil, as they prepared for a national day of prayer and fasting. Thousands of copies of *Sanctify a Fast* (*Santificai O Jejum*, DLT, 1996) were then distributed.

No time in my ministry was more fruitful, more joyful, more extensive, or more appreciated. God is so good! My prayer was for the literature ministry to live on and produce fruit that would last for eternity. *To him be all the praise!*

Europe Ministry

We responded to more ministry invitations from the Czech Republic in mid-November, then on to Germany and Hungary at the end of November. I planned to return to Greenwood the first week of December, after conducting prayer conferences from country to country.

I departed for Detroit, then flew by KLM 747 to Amsterdam, and finally to Prague. I was welcomed by Dr. David L. Kjosa (pronounced *Chosa*), president of Harvest International Ministries, and the prayer seminars were scheduled for afternoons and evenings. Each night the chapel was full, and God continued to give a good spirit of prayer.

Again providentially, Brother Peter Kuzmic discussed translating and publishing Czech editions of *Revival Fire* and *Touch the World through Prayer*. An opportunity in a Bible college near Prague was opened by an old pastor-friend from New Zealand who was also in the Czech Republic. Once again, it seemed God brought these two men involved in publishing to the services, and they assured me there would be Czech editions of those two books the next year. It was obvious that God helped wonderfully. *Praise the Lord!*

In Germany, missionaries from several nations attended the prayer conference in Wesel. DLT books sold well to English-speaking Christian workers, and more orders were received afterward. Friends were working on arrangements that might also expand my literature ministry in German.

The Lord gave a blessed serendipity experience, when one day, while crossing a German river, I saw the area where my forefathers had lived. My mind tried to recall some of our ancestors' history and imagine what life must have been like for them.

Duewel House in Egge, Germany, 2014

Taking off on KLM from Prague, I landed in Dusseldorf, where Brad Thurston of Globe Europe met me. We drove to the missions conference banquet at Steigenberger Duisburger Hof, a five-star hotel, with about 150 people in attendance. Later, we drove to the Neukirchener Mission head-quarters at Neukirchen-Uloyn for a missionary retreat, where I had full liberty and felt the Lord's sure anointing. At the second session, the Lord helped again, and we had a good period of prayer following. There, too, I met Rev. Gunter Krallmann from England, who had served with Youth With A Mission (YWAM) since 1978 in discipleship and leadership development. We visited and talked about prayer and publishing.

People all seemed very appreciative, and a good number of books were purchased. Upon departure, because of snow, Brad and I went to the train station, and I caught a train to Amsterdam, then took another train to the airport, for my flight to Budapest. Praise the Lord for his help throughout the whole conference!

In Hungary, coworkers David and Carol Cosby were there to greet and host me. We met with OMS coworkers, Free Methodist Church members, and Hungarian Evangelical Fellowship in beautiful Budapest and other parts of the nation. The last two days there, I spoke multiple times each, plus traveled several hundred kilometers. There were so many of God's providences and special touches of his goodness, mercy, and love. *Praise the Lord!*

God so faithfully blessed during my ministry in the Czech Republic, Germany, and Hungary. I had opportunities to speak at least fifty times and, many of those times, the Lord guided so that key leaders picked up the burden to translate and publish DLT books. Praise God for testimonies like: "My prayer life will never be the same again" and "I am going to put a new emphasis upon prayer in my ministry."

CONTINUED LITERATURE MINISTRY DEVELOPMENT (1997)

Every public ministry opportunity opened the door for promoting DLT books and selling the inventory. These opportunities enabled us to use profits to reprint more for the majority world nations. *Praise God for his enabling!*

Family News

At the beginning of the year, God gave me the honor and privilege of conducting the ordination service for our son-in-law, Terry Rueger, at their community church in Lawrenceburg, Indiana.

Another Sunday morning, in our local worship service, God touched me so that I had tears in my eyes as I prayed for unsaved loved ones. I was so caught up in prayer during the worship service that I was unaware when our pew row went forward for Communion. Someone gently touched my shoulder to get my attention. I asked myself, what more I could do to see my loved ones truly committed to the Lord.

Early in July, I was scheduled to have surgery to remove several polyps and "extensive infection" in the nasal area, extending up to near my eyes and brain. The congestion I'd been experiencing had affected my breathing and overall health. God was merciful and sustained me throughout the operation, where the surgeon removed the infection, polyps, and part of the septum. Praise the Lord there was no trace of malignancy. They found that one nostril was 100 percent blocked and the other was 75 percent blocked. I rejoiced to be able to breathe better and easier afterward.

Literature Ministry

God provided funding for publishing twenty thousand DLT books inside China, and they were personally delivered into the hands of Christians. No sooner had the first ten thousand copies been delivered than the Chinese publisher began receiving letters begging for more. So, God enabled us to send funds for more copies. *Praise the Lord!*

Within a ten-day period, four letters arrived from Northeast India, each telling of another language edition being held up due to tribal fighting. Satan was trying to slow down the ministry, but God was intervening, because we also received correspondence about progress on the Mizo, Paite, and Vaiphei language India editions. *God's Power Is for You* had undergone its first printing of 14,660 copies.

SIM International asked for subsidies for twenty thousand Spanish-language copies for South American pastors. Each pastor received two books, *Ablaze for God* and *Mighty Prevailing Prayer. Praise the Lord!*

Our copyright was received for *Sanctify a Fast,* and five thousand Brazilian Portuguese copies were printed.

We were also notified of 2,500 printed copies of the Philippine edition of *God's Great Salvation*, and also *Revival Fire* was sublicensed for printing in the Philippines. Also, the Ethiopian, Amharic edition of *Touch the World through Prayer* was off the press. More editions, more languages, meant more people were gaining exposure to God's principles and promises. It was also a joy to attend the Romanian Missionary Society's annual conference at the Billy Graham Evangelism Center in Wheaton, Illinois, where they had just printed five thousand copies of *Touch the World through Prayer* and presented me with four author's copies of the Romanian edition.

The Korean edition of *God's Power Is for You* was off the press, contracted by Word of Life, who published *Revival Fire* in February. And three author's copies of the Korean *Revival Fire* were received. The book was printed none too soon, it seemed, because one denomination requested a copy for every one of their pastors.

Zondervan completed the twentieth printing of *Touch the World through Prayer*, the tenth printing of *Ablaze for God*, and the seventh printing of *Mighty Prevailing Prayer*.

Touch the World through Prayer was translated into the Nepali language, and Operation Mobilization distributed the book in Nepal. *Praise the Lord!*

Every advance was made in faith. The DLT literature ministry was assured to continue even after the Lord called me to heaven. Nearly nine hundred thousand books were already in circulation. It was, perhaps, the most fruitful time of my life! *Praise the Lord!*

Africa and Asia Ministry

Near the end of August, I departed for ministry in five nations of Africa and Asia. I started a prayer conference in Burkina Faso for Wycliffe Bible Translators, then traveled from nation to nation, in prayer conferences and local church challenges, in South Africa, Mozambique, Philippines, and even a brief stop in Hong Kong. I asked prayer that God would give me strength, and I spoke more than eighty times in two months. *God was good and merciful!* It was great to be back in South Africa after some thirty years. How I thanked God for the prayer commitment of our OMS friends there! It was also good to see the beginnings of our OMS work in Mozambique, a nation with tremendous need. My prayer was for the Lord to help us become quickly and deeply involved in a fruitful harvest.

I must tell you what a great day God gave in Manila. Four groups cooperated in sponsoring an all-day prayer seminar. *Praise the Lord*, 1,359 people registered! They stopped the registrations, but people kept coming. Chairs were placed in the aisles and along the sides. People sat on the floor in front, and others stood in the balconies. The total attendance was well over fifteen hundred, and more than a thousand books were sold. *Praise God!*

My blood pressure got "scary" in the Philippines during the two days we were in a prayer conference among the Igorot tribal people at a Bible college and academy in Northern Luzon at an altitude of

7,300 feet. It soared dangerously high (208/130), and there was no telephone to call anyone in the outside world, asking them to pray, so I asked the Lord to alert people to pray for me.

At the same time, I felt such a sweet awareness of the Lord, and I knew I was in the center of his will, so I didn't worry. I sensed his anointing on me, and the people showed so much love. I can still see tears coming down the cheeks of a man in his seventies as he repeatedly thanked me for coming to them, and the about a hundred people lining the mountain road to wave their loving goodbye as we left. God had melded our hearts together in love. Spending a few days in Hong Kong, then a part of China, gave such inspiration and renewed burden. Oh, how China needs prayer! Tremendous ripe harvest was evident in many places, but persecution was also strong across the Mainland. Hong Kong itself seemed little changed. Twenty-five thousand DLT books were in circulation inside China, and we believed the door might open for many more. I was trusting for God's arrangements to be perfected soon, so that the ministry could be multiplied. I asked for people to please stand with us in prevailing prayer.

It was a very full year, a blessed year, and a year of many answers to prayer. God gave more than 175 opportunities to share his Word, ministering in many churches of various denominations, leading in prayer conferences, and providing prayer ministry in a half-dozen nations.

ECI'S ONE-THOUSANDTH CHURCH DEDICATION (1998)

Betty and I had first sailed for India in December 1940. What a joy to be back! What wonderful answers to prayer over those fifty-eight years! It was our privilege to be there at the earliest beginning, and here I was, returning to speak several times at the dedication of the one-thousandth Evangelical Church of India (ECI) church, rejoicing in the harvest.

According to the ECI plan, I was to address our India coworkers—almost all in attendance—and attend the special International Church

Missions Consultation of our OMS fields and homeland-sending nations. How did God want us to advance in the new millennium, which was only two years away? The motto was, "Holy Nation—Global Proclamation." Yes, we were called to be God's holy people proclaiming the gospel to the whole world.

About a thousand of our pastors from all across India attended, commemorating twenty-five years of our Every Community for Christ (ECC) church planting teams, especially supported by Dr. Stanley Tam. For years, he was the vice chairman of our board, and he served as a major speaker at this glorious event.[10]

We had prayed for God to raise up our first church, and when Betty and I left India, there were twenty-five churches. Bishop-President Ezra Sargunam challenged India coworkers in the Madras area to believe for one hundred churches. When that goal was reached, it was increased to two hundred, and then three hundred, and eventually a thousand. Here we were witnessing the vision fulfilled with the one-thousandth church dedicated, and the work launched years ago continuing to grow. We started to pray for the day there would be two thousand churches! *To God be the glory!*

Another great event was a mass baptismal service. Over 2,200 new believers were accepted as candidates for baptism by their local churches and had registered their names with the intention to be baptized on that occasion. A large swimming pool at the college facilities was used, and a number of pastors climbed in and baptized simultaneously in the presence of several thousand Christian witnesses. The final event was the dedication of another church in honor of Byron and Ailene Crouse, the parents of our president, Dr. J. B. Crouse Jr. How fitting that he and his wife, Bette, could be there for that occasion.

Hundreds and hundreds of Christians were in the processions, including OMS overseas guests, who were visiting for these special dedications and celebrations. Usually, one or two drummers and six

---

10   Stanley and Juanita Tam founded U.S. Plastic Corp. and channeled their profits into the "Stanita Foundation" to support OMS evangelism worldwide, subsequently gifting the foundation to OMS for the same purpose. See Kevin Kempton, *God Still Owns This Business* (Francis Asbury Press, 2020).

or eight trumpet and trombone players led the procession. Along one of the main routes, there were fluorescent light tubes, about thirty inches in length, and dozens and dozens of these stretching for at least a half-mile, all set up for the occasion. They were hung end to end on each side of the road and made a lovely sight throughout the nights of the occasion.

Processions of hundreds of people, with all the related activities, cannot but help diminish prejudice and help non-Christians be more open-minded to the gospel. During my years in India, I never dreamed that one day I would be part of such a Jesus-glorifying procession. *Praise the Lord!*

International Church-Missions Consultation

After all the events in the Chennai area, selected church leaders and theological educators from our fields around the world gathered several hundred miles away in Bangalore, to attend our International Church-Missions Consultation (ICMC) meeting. We enjoyed helpful messages, lectures, and discussions led by internationally known speakers. There were plenary sessions, and then the group was divided into task-alike groups for discussions, focused on their respective ministries, such as evangelism, training, church planting, and church growth and development. In some small-group sessions, we were grouped by the part of the world we represented, such as East Asia, Asia, South America, the Caribbean, and Europe. It really helped unite us as a worldwide family as we shared our means, methods, challenges, problems, and solutions.

Following the ICMC event, I returned home through Great Britain, stopping briefly in England to minister in a prayer conference for the staff of British, German, and American Christian workers serving with YWAM.

A Few Health Challenges

Following my return, all that recent air travel flared up some infection in my ear and nose. Praise God for modern medicines because antibiotics corrected that problem in short order. Betty, however, was experiencing some back pain, and was diagnosed as having severe osteoporosis, mild compression of three disks, and one broken bone in her back! After reviewing the bone density test, the doctor discovered that she'd had two broken bones earlier. For two weeks, she had to sleep in a recliner chair, but eventually she was able to sleep in bed. Doctors hoped she would heal properly within six weeks, but until then, she was able to do only light housework and limited shopping.

Mexico Ministry

What a challenge to minister for ten days in Mexico City! Can you believe it? Thirty million people in one city! One night after the service, my hosts, Leroy and Kay Lindsey, drove me to near the top of one of the mountains on which the city is built. Of course, there was no one place where one could see the entire city, but what a prayer burden came on my heart for it!

Nineveh had 120,000 people, and God said, "Should I not be concerned about that great city?" (Jonah 4:11). Think of what overwhelming concern, love, longing, and prayer burden must be paining Jesus today, as he sits on heaven's throne beside God the Father, ever interceding for us and our world, and especially for Mexico City!

There must be tears of love again and again in Jesus's eyes, as he prays for our broken, lost world. I told our Mexican coworkers, "We dare not ask the Lord for less than one hundred churches in Mexico City!" Afterward, I learned that our field director was asking God for three hundred in Mexico. Was that too much? No, God gave us the burden and passion to pray for this, if Jesus tarries. We then had seven churches in Mexico City and Acapulco. *Lord, multiply our ministry!*

Prayers for Harvest

God gave us another good international conference on the Asbury College and Seminary campuses. Some eight hundred of us, counting locals who walked in, enjoyed rich fellowship together. We shared thrilling reports from all our fields. At every conference, the need was so great that we prayed for God to give us laborers for the harvest, more harvest, and more churches.

We knew God had answered prayer in China, where there were several hundred "underground" house churches related to us! Some of the believers suffered imprisonment for Jesus. Their family members suffered the confiscation of personal property. Even now, think of the harvest waiting in China, the world's most populous nation. Pray for the people there. *Lord, give us a prayer burden for China!*

God had increased our outreach. OMS was then laboring in seventeen countries around the world, and our Korean churches had sent missionaries to thirty-six nations! Any time you pray, day or night, somewhere in the OMS worldwide network, someone is laboring for the Lord. Pray and believe. Their reward is sure, and every prayer and gift given makes their heavenly reward even greater.

REMAINING ACTIVE (1999)

It was the first time for years that our family was all together at the same time. John's daughter, Santi, our only granddaughter, was a junior at Yale University. Oh, we prayed so much for her and all of our grandchildren. Two of our grandsons would be ready for college the following year. God had kept all of us safe. We had so much for which to be grateful. My prayer was for God to help all of our family to fully commit their lives to Jesus and live for him.

In addition, appointments for me were coming, and I needed prayer for God's anointing and blessing. God continued to sustain a busy speaking and writing schedule in my eighty-second year. How I felt the need for prayer, especially for my time in Haiti.

Haiti Ministry

Some years earlier, there had been a division in our churches in Haiti, and now there were two groups of churches. But all were joining together for the conference at our center in Cap-Haitien. I prayed for God's guidance and anointing, for each message and in all the sessions. How wonderful if he would give renewal, reconciliation, and blessed unity! I couldn't bring it about; only the Lord could do that. *Praise God!*

We thanked God for my time in Haiti, and the real joy to minister there again. Pastors and leaders numbering 216 registered for the services. When the manager of our radio station heard the first service, he canceled regular programming and put the entire conference on the radio. Thus, it was heard in most of Haiti and the surrounding islands. The Lord was with us, and the Haitian church was greatly encouraged. This was the first time they had all been together for such a conference. God worked to bless and unify many hearts.

Our 60th Wedding Anniversary

Despite our best efforts to stay healthy, Betty and I were still getting older. We quietly celebrated our sixtieth wedding anniversary in June with a lovely, decorated cake that read: "Congratulations/60 years together/ Wesley and Betty."

For one week we were eight-three, the same age, but then Betty had her eighty-fourth birthday. She had a hernia operation, which went well, and after thirty-four years with the same partial lower denture, I had it replaced. It also looked like I may need to do something about my hearing.

Wesley and Betty, 60th Anniversary, June 1999

Betty and I visited Ed and Chris in West Virginia and joined them in celebrating Justin's graduation from high school. We always enjoyed being with family, especially as the years went by so rapidly, and our times together were so few and far between.

Literature Ministry

We often received interesting letters, as well as many requests for prayer, in the mail from the countries where DLT books had been translated and published. A pastor of sixteen churches in Ethiopia walked three to four hours a day to reach his churches. About *Ablaze for God*, he said, "[It] not only strengthened my spiritual life; it also strengthened my muscles." He explained he got so weary, walking from church to church for long hours, but God had strengthened him in his weariness through the book. *Praise the Lord!*

He also wrote that he was sharing the message of the book by means of teaching and preaching. You see, that's just a part of what God was doing through people's prayer and support of our literature ministry. *Praise the Lord!* Again, what a story we will learn when we get to heaven! That pastor also wrote, "May God bless your writing ministry and use your mind and your hand to write other books before you go to your eternal home! And pray for my difficult ministries."

So many of God's children expressed deep prayer hunger and prayer burdens for his answer in personal problems and for loved ones. Deeply moving letters touched my heart, as people in various countries wrote for prayer. Many phone calls were also received requesting prayer. Some of those who read my books on prayer tended to expect God to answer my prayers. My prayer was that God would be faithful to them all. Certainly, he was giving real answers to prayer and real harvest. My prayer was also that he would have mercy on our nation and send real revival here as well as around the world.

LITERATURE MINISTRY EXPANDED IN EUROPE (2000)

God continued to give me opportunities to travel abroad. Due to our age, however, I asked people to pray for both Betty and me while I was traveling. My plan was to leave for an important time of ministry in Russia, Finland, and Estonia from mid-April through mid-May. I would hold a series of prayer seminars for the dozen OMS church planting teams in Russia, the five in Estonia, the Salvation Army training center in Finland, and in St. Petersburg and Vyborg, Russia. At each seminar, I would speak multiple times (with equal time for interpretation), plus lead corporate closing prayer after many of the sessions. I would be on my feet much of the time on most days. Also, there was still snow and ice on the ground most of the time, so moving about outside could be treacherous.

I requested prayer for the Lord's anointing each time I spoke, his guidance each day, and for health, strength, and freshness hour after hour. I also asked prayer for the Holy Spirit to transform hearers, to bring people from local churches to attend also, and for God to bless my books to their hearts. Three DLT books were already in Russian, one was in Finnish, and many of the Estonians could read Russian.

My only problem throughout the entire nearly 24-hour trip was losing my handbag at the Moscow airport. I had two Bibles, correspondence, family pictures, and a camera in it. As I stopped to take my book-filled suitcase off the carousel, I put the handbag right behind me so I could lift the suitcase with both hands. When I turned around, someone had snatched my bag. My heart sank, as I reported the loss. A day later, the airport called, saying they had found my bag. When we went to claim it, everything was in it except the camera. So, my ministry did not suffer, and one of the missionaries loaned me his camera. *Praise the Lord!*

From my room in Moscow's Hotel Rossiya, I looked right down on the Kremlin, just across the street. A church planting team member came and escorted me to Yaroslavl, four hours by train. Randy Marshall was our leader in that part of Russia. We used the local Baptist church, and God gave a responsive group of about 150 people, including eight of our church planting teams. There was good liberty in the prayer times, and people were eager for a chance to pray. The pastor was so moved by the Holy Spirit that he asked me to take both services the next morning. The Lord especially blessed in those Sunday services.

Back in Moscow, I stayed three nights at our OMS seminary, and I had a precious time of sharing with Dr. Alexi Bychkov and his staff. He served as both host and interpreter. I spoke at the seminary chapel on the important role of prayer. The seminary was filling a real spiritual vacuum, and each of the students was given one of my books, in Russian or English. I also placed a set of nine DLT books in the library.

Brother Austin Sullivan was in ministry in the Vladimir area. He was a former assistant to my coworker, Rev. Bruce Hess, in the eastern region of the USA. He escorted me on the Moscow underground metro trains that accommodated more than ten million passengers daily at a very reasonable rate. For less than three dollars, one could purchase monthly passes to 176 underground stations in the Moscow area. At some places, the metro is more than 240 feet below ground.

Austin also escorted me to the airport, and we flew to Rostov-on-Don in southern Russia for the second prayer seminar. The Salvation Army commander for the entire Baltic area and the second highest Salvation Army officer in London traveled on the plane with us.

We had five church planting teams in the Rostov area. About thirty people attended, mainly team members, plus some believers from our new church there. Sunday was Russian Easter (one week later than most of the rest of the world), at which I brought my Easter message, "The Upper Room Commission."

John Creech, our OMS Russia field director, left for three days of committee meetings, and my escort became Brother Viktor, a bi-lingual speaker. We traveled on the famous Red Arrow electric express train overnight from Moscow to St. Petersburg. It was a comparatively quiet, clean, and comfortable overnight trip. It was wonderful to have such good train service throughout my travels in Russia. What a contrast to my India days!

My book suitcase was becoming lighter all the time, as I handed out copies to our team members and students at every stop. I gave a set of DLT books to the St. Petersburg Christian University library, a splendid Bible college operated by the Missionary Church. We also visited the press where Russian editions of DLT books as well as many Russian Bibles were printed.

Brother Richard Grout, a missionary representing FEA Ministries who was serving at the Christian Center in Vyborg, arrived to drive me to Vyborg. He was the one who had arranged the publication of DLT books in the Russian language. God also blessed in the services at the Vyborg Baptist Church on Sunday. In the afternoon, I spent more than an hour answering questions on prayer. The pastor was deeply moved and said if he had his life to live over, he would put more emphasis on prayer.

Brother Grout and I drove to Finland along a forest-lined road to the capital, Helsinki. God helped us cross the border in remarkably quick time. We were hosted at the Salvation Army headquarters and their beautiful training campus for their officers in Moldova, Ukraine, Georgia, Finland, Estonia, and Russia. I was thrilled to bring them greetings from General Paul Rader, the worldwide general of the Salvation Army. I gave them a set of DLT books for their library as well.

Brother Heldur Kajaste, leader of our five Estonian church planting teams, came by ferry to Helsinki to take me to Tallinn, Estonia, on the fast express SuperSeaCat ferry. It was a two-hour journey across the Gulf of Finland, an extension of the Baltic Sea. Our hearts were quickly knit together as Heldur served as my interpreter, prayer partner, chauffeur, and guide. We had multiple services in Tallinn with the ECC teams; visited a seminary and an historic Lutheran church, where we had a precious time of prayer with the pastor; and had four interviews, three on the radio and one for a newspaper. It was God's perfect closure and seal on the month of ministry in the Baltic area.

In Russian churches, the women seem to outnumber the men and the old to outnumber the young, but the fellowship with the believers was precious and wonderful. What thrilled me, especially, was that in the prayer seminars, whenever I opened up time for prayer, there was no waiting on one another. Person after person immediately led out in prayer. I felt they were a praying people.

Heldur and I had a wonderful conversation for three hours on my last night. I knew I was in God's will, I knew he had planned all the details, and I knew many were praying for me. What a joy it is to serve the Lord, and what a joy it is to meet his people! *To him be all the glory!*

Early the next morning, I took a flight back to the States. I don't know when I had gone on such a prolonged time of ministry feeling my need of prayer more, and I don't know when I returned home from such a period of ministry feeling so conscious of God's hand upon me all the way. I felt the whole trip and ministry had been planned by the Lord. *Praise his name!*

Back in the States

At the OMS annual conference in Wilmore, Kentucky, I had to have all my wits about me to present a morning session with a lively Pals group (youngsters from six to ten years old) before a prayer seminar for the entire conference with my coworkers, Phil and Lorna Chandler, formerly from Taiwan. In the late afternoon, we held our regular healing service, where people with all sorts of prayer burdens gathered together. Afterward, I met with our coworker from Hong Kong, Dr. Tony Kwan, and we prayed together about China.

Earlier that year, the total circulation of *Touch the World through Prayer* inside China had reached 115,000 copies, distributed primarily among "house churches" (aka "underground churches"), and we had already received a request for twenty thousand more books! Then, a special request for ten thousand copies came from the "official three-self churches" (the government-recognized churches) and eighteen seminaries inside China. So, we sent the funds for that printing. In greater freedom, the "official" churches were multiplying rapidly. We received so many testimonies of transformed lives and ministries through that book from pastors in other parts of the world. It was thrilling! *Praise the Lord!*

Also, a letter arrived urging a printing of a Russian edition of *Ablaze for God.* When I wrote them that I would send the funds as soon as I prayed them in, they responded that the door was open, but it could swing shut again if I waited too long. Oh, that I had the faith of a George Müller!

Orient Ministry

What a blessed time of fellowship and ministry God gave in Japan and Korea in October. Wherever you find committed Christians, you find loving people. Many of the churches that invited me for ministry were spiritually eager to pray and obey God. Afterward, the Japan Holiness Association (JHA) coordinator, Dr. Saoshiro, wrote:

> Thank you indeed for the Spirit-anointed, powerful, and fruitful ministry at our JHA Conventions in four places. The

Lord's message, through your life and being, will ever remain with us. We shall seek for a richer, deeper walk with the Lord, being filled with the Spirit.

I flew to Korea, where Dr. John Cho and the Korea Holiness Association took over. Oh, what rich fellowship again, with the presence of the Lord in every service, including church and seminary services! The conference was held in the large new chapel at the OMS-related Seoul Theological University. They had four hundred seminary students, four hundred music students, and about two thousand other students. My, what a joy to be backed by a chorus of "amens" from the student body! One of several one-hundred-voice choirs led the chapel services.

One night as I closed with prayer, a Korean leader took over, and soon more than fifty people were kneeling all around me on the platform, seeking the fullness of the Spirit. Praise God for the ministry of our more than three thousand Korean churches! *To God be all the glory!*

The literature ministry and its related correspondence continued to provide great joy as I received numerous testimonies of blessing by letter, as well as in person. I knew our statistics were always conservatively reported, but at least nineteen language editions of DLT books were printed that year, and the first editions in Finnish, Gujarati, Hausa, Kannada, Khasi, and Norwegian came from the press. Thousands of copies were printed inside China, as we relied on three to five presses to provide *Touch the World through Prayer* and *Ablaze for God* to the leaders of the "house church" movement, who were largely untrained.

Praise God that the eleventh printing of *Ablaze for God* was published by Zondervan! Praise God that three editions of *More God, More Power* came off the press that year and were being used by the Lord! The Free Methodist Church gave a copy to every pastor and missionary who could read English. So, the grand total of books off the presses to date was more than 1.1 million in fifty-one languages, plus we didn't have the statistics from four presses inside Nigeria, and three inside China, that had printed unauthorized editions. So far that year, God had provided nearly ninety-two thousand dollars in publication subsidies. He provided every dollar through prayer and fasting.

Family News

It was a good year for both our ministry and our health. We were beginning to realize that we really were older, but God had given good health to Betty and me in our sixty-one years together, sixty of them with OMS. With osteoporosis, Betty took ibuprofen for her backache, but she kept busy shopping, baking, and preparing for a happy family time together during the holidays.

In late November, I mowed our yard, to mulch leaves that had been raked previously, and I even used the ladder to clean leaves out of all the gutters on all sides of the house. Then I had to get the lawnmower repaired, and as the repairman helped me remove it from the car, he said, "You ought not to do that!"

"Why not?" I asked.

"You're eighty-two, aren't you?"

"No," I said, "I'm eighty-four!"

Truly I thanked the Lord for his goodness and mercy extended to both Betty and me.

OMS CENTENNIAL YEAR (2001)

Starting our OMS centennial year, God gave me nearly a dozen opportunities to share in Vancouver, BC, Canada. It was a multi-ethnic event with people from Japan, China, Vietnam, India, Indonesia, the Philippines, Sweden, Africa—even a missionary from Tibet. The denominations represented were Mennonite, Baptist, Christian and Missionary Alliance, Anglican, Christian Reformed, Episcopalian, and Pentecostal. They were mainly from Canada, but a few were from the USA. The prayer times were wonderful, and the Lord drew near.

On Easter Sunday, I wondered how many of God's children routinely read from one or more DLT books. With about 1.2 million copies now in circulation in various countries, there must have been many. And because many of those people possessed so few Christian (or other) books, no TV, and little Christian radio, some might even be reading my books on Easter Day. Based on the number of thankful letters we received from people who knew enough English to write, many had been blessed.

Peru Ministry

In early June, I flew to Atlanta, headed for Peru. When I arrived in Lima, Brother Joel Purcell took me to the Wycliffe guesthouse. SIM had already purchased ten thousand copies for the series of pastors' conferences called, "Ablaze for God." Each pastor received a set of fourteen books, which included *Ablaze for God* and *Mighty Prevailing Prayer*.

The next day, we flew to Tumbes, near the Ecuador border. On the street, we met a typical Roman Catholic procession displaying a huge picture of Christ, and all the marchers were chanting one-to-two-sentence prayers to Mary nonstop. On June 3, I turned eighty-five. In Peru, it was Election Day, so no public gatherings were permitted.

The next day, forty pastors, including ten from Ecuador, registered for the conference. The Lord gave us a time almost too precious for words. Praise God for a good interpreter!

Then, we drove five hours to Piura, with much of the trip along the coast. During the message, God was speaking to people. It was almost like revival, with the whole front of the church filled with fifty to sixty people earnestly praying at the same time.

The last day, I opened my heart with two dozen teens from the States also in attendance and spent hours praying with them afterward. The final count showed 124 people registered for the series. I prayed for each pastor personally, and many were very responsive. Afterward, we returned to Lima by taxi.

At the end of the first week, we met at an Assembly of God church in Lima, where people swayed and sang in tempo with the music, like the Africans did. I recognized people calling out the name of Jesus and shouting "Hallelujah," but not much else.

For two weeks, I poured out my soul in multiple services with multiple congregations in multiple venues, illustrating each message with Scripture and stories of William Taylor's life; Miss Jacobsz from South Africa's experiences; of John Hyde, known as the apostle of prayer; and of evangelist Evan Roberts. The final day, God gave revival to those new churches, with a total attendance of 450 people. Many asked me to lay hands on their heads and pray.

Those SIM International-sponsored interdenominational pastors' conferences were blessed by the Lord, and God gave opportunities to share multiple times at three conference centers—in Tumbes, Puira, and Lima. His anointing was so strong in some of the services, and the people were so receptive, that I knew there was much prayer lifted to the throne of grace on my behalf. They were still using the 1996 videos in pastors' conferences and said that practically every one of the Protestant pastors, regardless of denomination, had attended the five-message series. When we're together in heaven, I will introduce you to them.

Centennial Retreat and Conference

We had two wonderful and historic events in relation to OMS's one-hundredth anniversary. We met on the campus at Taylor University in Upland, Indiana, for our centennial staff retreat, where 550 OMS staff and children attended. We then moved twelve miles to Indiana Wesleyan University in Marion, Indiana, for our centenary OMS conference, where we had more than 1,700 OMS staff and constituents. We also had leaders and missionaries from all nineteen of our OMS-related mission fields and from all six "sending countries," namely countries where OMS had offices and representatives who actively mobilized to gather three key resources: prayer, people, and finances.

People from twenty-nine nations were present. It was the most comprehensive OMS gathering we had ever had, the only time in our one-hundred-year history that we had tried to gather all members of the Society together in one location. It was also the largest group of OMS retirees we ever had together, and probably the largest group of OMS missionaries! There were singing groups from Korea, India,

Russia, Mexico, and the USA. On Saturday night, we had a special concert by Steve Green, celebrated Christian songwriter and singer, backed by the 100-voice choir from the Community Church of Greenwood.

OMS Family 100th Anniversary Retreat and Reunion, July 2001

We were blessed with many wonderful speakers—OMS missionaries, leaders from some of the national churches on our fields, and then some well-known outside speakers, such as Dr. Jay Kesler; Miss Nancy DeMoss; General Paul Rader, retired general of the Salvation Army; and Dr. Dennis F. Kinlaw, retired president of Asbury College, and for thirty years the chairman of our OMS board of trustees. The closing services were marked with many kneeling at the altar for prayer. God is always available to meet hungry hearts. Praise God for a worldwide international fellowship of loving commitment that keeps growing in the number of nations where our witness is shared, and our mutual obedience and fellowship is experienced!

The largest overseas international delegation was from the British Isles. Some I had known for fifty-three years. Groups from Korea, India, and Mexico had also come. The loving fellowship that bound us together as one family made us members of each other's groups regardless of denomination, race, or nationality.

It was a blessed foretaste of heaven! And again and again, I was reminded of what a blessed fellowship and reunion we will have there. One of the nationals said, "This is not like other organizations; OMS is a family." *Praise God*! Think of the ultimate reunion we'll have in heaven! Spanning more than a century of ministry and love, the full OMS record is with God alone. But undoubtedly there will be millions rejoicing in the OMS-related praise celebrations of heaven.

Literature Ministry

The literature ministry had reached a dimension I never dreamed possible, and the letters kept flowing in, telling how God was using them. We continued to reinvest all the proceeds, and almost all the love offerings received, for printing more books for the majority world countries, including China, where another edition would soon go into circulation. Each weekend, I prayed for millions of homes around the world that had DLT books, asking the Holy Spirit to apply the contents to their hearts.

That year, twenty-nine new language editions came off the press, including: Hakha Chin in Myanmar, and Gujarati, Nepali, Simte, Thadou-Kuki, and Zou in India. The first Chinese Mandarin edition of *Ablaze for God* had been printed and distributed inside China the previous year. Multiple printings of *Touch the World through Prayer* in Chinese had been distributed there during the past few years, and by the end of the year, worldwide circulation of nine titles totaled more than 1.4 million copies—in fifty-five national languages.

LOOKING TOWARD HEAVEN (2002)

In 2002, I was blessed to minister in so many places and with so many opportunities: with the Free Methodists on the Gulf Coast; with the Baptists in the Chicago area; through two radio interviews in Ohio; at the central yearly meeting of the Friends in Indiana; at the Southern District Conference of the Evangelical Methodist Church in Georgia; with the Christian and Missionary Alliance in Florida, at Wesley Biblical Seminary in Jackson, Mississippi; and through a radio broadcast in Mississippi. There were also workshops at the Free Methodist national conference on urban ministries in Indianapolis and with the North Arkansas Baptist Association. What a joy to speak again and again on prayer and revival! God gave a spiritual hunger to his people.

We needed to revise or update our book statistics. Our distribution statistics were constantly changing, and requests for more subsidy funds to translate and reproduce DLT books were constantly reaching our desk. I was praying for God's miraculous provision to make it possible. In Romans 1:15, Paul said, "As much as is in me, I am ready to preach the gospel" (NKJV). To the fullest extent of my ability, I, too, was ready for whatever ministry the Lord continued to open before me.

I received a letter from a born-again university professor in Tanzania, Africa. He thanked me and told me how God had blessed his life through my book *Measure Your Life*. He begged me to permit him to translate it into Swahili. I told him to go ahead with the translation, but that I would not be able to help with funds until I was first able to fund a hundred thousand copies of *Ablaze for God* for China. I did, however, assure him I expected God to supply the funds in his time. He told me there were eighty million Swahili readers in Tanzania, Congo, and Kenya, but he didn't know how many Swahili believers there were.

During my nightly prayer in the office, I had for some time been feeling that God wanted DLT books in at least one more language. That would be our fifty-sixth foreign language. I asked him to find and call the translator and publisher, for whatever that language was. Perhaps it was Swahili? God would still have to find the publisher and funds. What a huge additional challenge!

God kept enlarging my horizon and ministry. Once more, I believed this was the most fruitful time of my life. Who was I that God should keep opening doors like that? All continued to be possible because of our partners' Christian love, prayer, and financial support of the ministry. I thanked God again for their partnership in his great harvest. And again, what rejoicing we will all enjoy when we get to heaven! Many new believers will meet our partners in heaven and thank them. How wonderful is the fellowship of God's family wherever found! Our fellowship begins on earth and will be continued in heaven. *To him be all the glory!*

THIS IS YOUR LIFE (2003)

At headquarters, OMS continued to allocate office space for me and my secretary, Hilda, who extended her missionary service beyond her official retirement. Hilda sensed the DLT literature ministry had become her life's ministry.

In late February, our home church surprised Betty and me by making the morning worship a "This Is Your Life" service. After the beginning part of the service, the pastor announced, "This service will be a little different. Today we honor two faithful servants, Dr. Wesley and Mrs. Betty Duewel." Everything was a complete surprise to us. Two ushers came and led us to the platform. Then a side door opened, and twenty OMS missionaries came in and took reserved seats at the front. Ed and Chris and Darlene and Terry, with their son Jason, had been waiting in a separate room, and now they came from a side door and greeted us on the platform. We had no idea any of our family or OMS personnel would be there!

A twenty-minute video by Dave Stotts was shown. They had prepared an overview of our life, in five parts, illustrated from family photographs. It included brief scenes from our youth, our marriage, our service in India, and then at OMS headquarters.

Our Free Methodist Conference superintendent, Rev. Chet Martin; our OMS executive director of international ministries, Dr. David Dick, on behalf of the OMS president, Dr. J. B. Crouse Jr.; and our former pastor, Dr. Donald Riggs, all spoke. We were given a lovely plaque, presented by Chuck Ball, and a scrapbook from friends, family, and fellow OMS missionaries.

Afterward, an international dinner was served. Many Indianapolis churches were closed that morning because of a terrific snow and ice storm, but about two hundred people attended and enjoyed the meal with us. I'm sorry all our faithful friends and donors could not enjoy the surprise. It was a very happy occasion for us. Several people remarked at the sacredness and joy of the whole event.

Family News

That was our sixty-fourth year with OMS, in extended missionary service, and undoubtedly, we had slowed down. Betty didn't want me to drive long distances, so at times Hilda drove for us. I still enjoyed the ministry of the Word and especially holding prayer conferences. Soon, Betty would be eighty-eight and I'd be eighty-seven.

Betty had been experiencing health problems the past several months, so she stayed with Darlene and her family in Lawrenceburg for about two months. A physician and a nurse in their church, both women, took a special interest in Betty's case and arranged various tests at their hospital. They found her weight was down to 110 pounds, caused by what turned out to be a severe case of diverticulosis. By God's grace, I kept quite well.

DLT books continued to open doors for public speaking, which I did on weekend prayer retreats. In September, the heaviest series of all was the most blessed of all. The church had been praying for several months, and just before the retreat, they prayed around the clock for forty-eight hours. They were hungry and expectant. In a very real way, the DLT literature ministry was extending the worldwide ministry of OMS. What a privilege! My life's motto continued to be *All for Jesus*.

By the time she turned eighty-eight, Betty was somewhat better physically than she'd been for several months. We expected to have all three of our children and their spouses, and all but one of our six grandchildren, with us that Christmas. How quickly the years pass by! Eventually, we will no longer be able to show our love to Jesus here on earth. Prayer is still one of the greatest ways to demonstrate our love to him, and we still needed prayers for some unanswered prayers in our lives.

YEAR OF GOD'S BLESSING (2004)

Betty still had a variety of health problems that somewhat limited her activities in 2004. I was continuing to slow down as well. But in June, my spirit picked up on my eighty-eighth birthday, when I received a package from China. In it were four copies of *Mighty*

Prevailing Prayer, printed in the lovely, but difficult to write, Chinese script. The package included a letter and seven color photographs of *Ablaze for God* being used in China. Instantly, my eyes filled with tears of joy. God was so good! It was a birthday present from Jesus to me.

Three DLT books were printed in China in two editions—one for the "house churches" and the other for the "government-recognized churches." God had opened the door so wonderfully. The translations of two DLT books, into Vietnamese and Korean, also arrived that week. So, the work continued. *Praise the Lord!*

DIMINISHED SPEAKING, INCREASED PRAYER (2005)

God continued to give me fairly good health and strength, even at the age of eighty-nine. Betty, despite several health concerns, continued to do her own grocery shopping and driving. God was very good to us.

We celebrated Betty's ninetieth birthday on June 11 with a party at Darlene and Terry's home in Lawrenceburg. She was crowned "Queen Elizabeth" for a day, replete with a crown and cape.

Haiti

In August, I revisited Haiti, the very first field I visited as OMS president. On the occasion of the fifteenth anniversary conference of our Emmaus Fellowship of Churches, I was invited to share the Word of God in a series of six weekday messages, enjoyed attending two local churches and the seminary groundbreaking service, and then participated in a precious time of fellowship as an OMS family at the home of David and Marilyn Shaferly the evening before I left Cap-Haitien.

We knew it would be hot in Haiti, and there had been concern about how an eighty-nine-year-old visitor would stand the heat. I asked God to sustain and protect me, and praise the Lord, I hardly noticed the heat at all! In fact, I kept saying how pleasant the weather was until several stared at me, because they thought it was so hot. It had been many years since I'd experienced India's heat, and I thought

I would feel it a lot more, but God took care of it completely. I thanked him for my eight or nine previous ministry visits to Haiti, and this fourteen-day trip was wonderful! *Praise his name!*

Prayer Bulletins—EFMA and CHA

On several occasions in times past, I had been asked to present special topics for EFMA conference sessions, which became short "white papers" but were never published. I had suggested to my fellow executives in the EFMA, now Missio Nexus, that it would be good to have a monthly confidential prayer letter, which would include requests that were urgent. I desired fellow executives of EFMA to share the prayer burden with us. I had a deep burden and conviction that if we really shared and lifted our brothers' and sisters' prayer requests to the Lord, God would greatly bless us as others began to similarly pray for us.

The suggestion seemed appealing, and the next thing I knew, I was asked to begin and edit such a bulletin. For almost twenty-nine years, my office produced the monthly EFMA Fellowship of Prayer bulletin. Over time, the types of requests changed, perhaps because the original suggestion had been forgotten or never passed on to successors. At the beginning, the bulletin consisted of urgent needs, three or four from each organization. In later years, though, some agencies sent their own monthly general prayer bulletin and asked me to select three or four items.

We continued to serve the EFMA in a wide variety of ways, including writing various articles, position papers, and prayer bulletins. Some asked if they could share these prayer items with their coworkers, which we trusted them to do, for the items were genuine prayer concerns and not necessarily confidential. For nineteen years, the CHA bulletin was produced and sent out of our office to the executives of this smaller member group. I prayed the Lord would use our efforts in producing these two prayer bulletins to multiply appreciation of one another, deepen love for one another, multiply prayer for one another, and multiply the kingdom of God and prayer rewards in heaven—for all who sincerely shared in the prayer undoubtedly received heavenly rewards.[11] How widely each respective executive shared the bulletin with his or her fellow executives or staff members was up to each organization. As we began to take the prayer burdens of the other agencies upon our hearts, we believed God multiplied the number of those who prayed for us.

My whole intention was to unite us closer together in prayer for each other. God certainly multiplied the prayer for us. My office was reimbursed each year for the printing and postage, and we donated our time and services to our dear fellow-workers in God's vineyard. We rejoiced in one another's victories and wept over one another's burdens, fulfilling the law of Christ (Gal 6:2).

A YEAR OF SPECIAL JOYS (2006)

The year 2006 was another year of special joys, beginning in mid-April when Allahabad Bible Seminary dedicated the "Wesley and Betty Duewel" faculty apartments. *Thank the Lord!* On June 3, I rejoiced in my ninetieth birthday, and eight days later Betty celebrated her ninety-first. OMS commemorated our birthdays during our OMS World Outreach Celebration in Marion, Indiana.

Betty's health was not the best, but she carried on, "keeping the home fires burning"! The children and grandchildren were safe and well. God was so good to us. I walked more slowly and cautiously, because I didn't want to fall, and I had recently started using a cane. I could do without it, yet it helped to ambulate a little faster.

God had given me sixty-seven years of full-time ministry. Although I had slowed down, I was privileged to serve him in Arkansas, Indiana, and Ohio that year, and in the coming days, I was scheduled to be in Michigan. In between ministry appointments, there was continuing correspondence, email reports, letters to read, and prayer requests to go through each day, plus welcoming occasional guests who visited

---

11   Dr. Duewel compiled and distributed the prayer bulletin for the EFMA from January 1983 through June 2012. He compiled and distributed the prayer bulletin for the Christian Holiness Association, now Christian Holiness Partnership, from January 1988 through December 2006.

the office, or talking with people asking for prayer on the phone. *Praise the Lord!*

I spent more than an hour on my prayer list every day. If you don't use a prayer list, I urge you to do so. You may not remember all the needs—and all the people for whom you really want to pray—unless you do. God keeps record of every prayer of intercession you invest. Those acts of love are a major basis of our eternal rewards. You will thank God throughout eternity that you invested through prayer.

Increased Health Concerns

One brother-in-law and one sister-in-law of Betty's had joined the saints in heaven recently. Two sisters were also in poor health. Though walking with a cane, I was still working more than full-time each day at my office at OMS headquarters. Betty's health, however, needed the Lord's touch in several ways.

Literature Ministry

I continued to speak in meetings, averaging about once a week. I was also still interceding for OMS and its leaders every day. I prayed for many people and organizations, but I always started with my OMS prayer list.

Hilda and I continued to produce and distribute monthly issues of prayer bulletins with requests gathered from the EFMA and CHA. They paid for the paper and postage and sent lists of requests, and we supplied the editing, publishing, and mailing.

We still received letters, usually several each day, from overseas readers of DLT books, often asking for free copies. And still, there were phone calls asking for prayer and visits by OMS personnel and other guests, often involving prayer with them.

One or more of our ten major DLT books were now published in fifty-seven languages, and world circulation was now more than 1.8 million. Our main publisher, OM Books India, continued to translate and publish in at least twenty-three of the languages of India. In addition, reprints of their English-language editions were published for people who could read English. From north to south and from east to west, more than 227,000 copies were in circulation, and God was using the messages of the books to bless believers in many parts of India.

EFMA "LIFETIME OF SERVICE AWARD" (2007)

My, how time flies! There I was, ninety-one years of age, with Betty, soon to be ninety-two! I had recently preached in Frankfort in central Indiana, and after preaching for forty-five minutes, I didn't even feel tired! The local congregation hosted a birthday dinner before someone chauffeured me back to Greenwood. *Praise the Lord!*

That September, the Evangelical Fellowship of Mission Agencies (EFMA) flew me to Dallas, Texas, for a special occasion at their annual convention. The theme was "Engaging the Next Generation" in missions. My coworker, Rev. Donald Saum, who served in our international ministries department, accompanied me to the conference. In recognition of my contribution to the Great Commission, they presented me with the inaugural EFMA Lifetime of Service Award. The closing session included a six-minute video, highlighting sixty-eight years of my missionary ministry.

After a special presentation of two meaningful gifts—a hand-painted, wood-framed portrait of me and a bronzed set of praying hands—I was invited to participate in a brief commissioning exhortation and prayer for about thirty "young leaders" in the closing minutes. EFMA also asked me to autograph copies of *Touch the World through Prayer*, which were given to everyone in attendance. What a precious surprise to receive that award! It was a joy to be with that group of mission leaders again. *To God be all the glory!*

EFMA/The Mission Exchange First Lifetime Service Award, Sept 2007

Betty's Declining Health

When I returned home from the office on October 3, I found Betty had fainted and fallen while washing dishes. An overturned chair told the story of how she had dragged herself across the room and then draped herself over the arm of the recliner chair. I knew I couldn't lift her alone, so without family nearby, I dialed 911. Soon an ambulance and police arrived and took her to the hospital. Hilda came and drove me there, and we stayed with Betty until early morning. Betty could not remember exactly what happened, but it seemed she'd had a mini-stroke.

After three days, Betty was transferred to Greenwood Village South, an excellent rehabilitation center, for several weeks of therapy. I spent several hours each day with her, and Darlene came to assist us. Mid-November, Retno arrived from Indonesia, and John came ten days later. They were all a wonderful help to us.

On November 17, Betty was moved by ambulance to Hearth at Stones Crossing, a graduated health care center, as I could not care for her on my own at home. She adjusted well to living alone in a new studio apartment only six miles from our home, which made it easier for me to spend several hours with her each day.

A YEAR OF SIGNIFICANT EVENTS (2008)

As we entered another year, I reflected on God's gracious work in Betty's life. He continued to answer our prayers. Betty's room at the Hearth was quite pleasant, and she was able to move to the bathroom and to meals, with some limited assistance using her walker.

Betty's Homegoing

On April 3—suddenly, shockingly, and unexpectedly—Betty was taken home to heaven. The love and support of our friends during those days upheld me and meant so much. At times, I felt almost in a whirlwind at the rapidity of events occurring in connection with her homegoing.

Little did I realize when I shared hours at Betty's side that last day that it would be our final time together on earth. Early the next morning, I was awakened by a phone call informing me that God had called her to her heavenly home during the night. Truly, our nearly sixty-nine years together had proved God's faithfulness in so many ways, and I vowed to keep serving him heart and soul until he called me home as well.

Elizabeth Dolly Duewel
June 11, 1915 – April 3, 2008

Memorial Service
April 11, 2008

A spirit of quiet triumph prevailed as some three hundred family, friends, and Christian leaders attended Betty's memorial celebration service at the nearby Center Grove Presbyterian Church on April 11. OMS leaders and Free Methodist pastors shared with solos, Scripture reading, and a biographical sketch. We sang hymns with assurance, and our hearts were led to God in prayer. OMS president Dr. David Long gave a gracious tribute to Betty's sixty-seven years serving with OMS, and John, Chris, and Darlene each shared tributes to their mother. Our dear friend and former pastor, the Rev. Dr. Donald E. Riggs, officiated and urged us all to serve the Lord as Betty had and to join her in heaven someday.

I received expressions of concern and promises of prayer support through many phone calls (even international calls), a multitude of cards and notes of love and appreciation, and many beautiful flowers. The Betty Duewel Memorial Fund gifts were designated to print and distribute more of my books in China.

My annual reports to the OMS board were submitted with real joy, constant gratitude, and daily hunger to know of more and more working of the Holy Spirit throughout OMS and our needy world. There were prayer moments before I arose in the morning and throughout the day, but OMS was routinely first in my prayers. *To God be all the glory!*

Literary Milestone

On May 20, 2008, at the OMS world headquarters, OMS celebrated with me for more than two million DLT books in circulation! Ten major books had been translated into fifty-eight different languages, including Chinese, Indian, Korean, Russian, Portuguese, Spanish, and various tribal languages. I continued to pray daily for the Lord to use the DLT books around the world to his glory. And I continued to receive letters from pastors telling me they were preaching chapter by chapter to their people. Oh, that God would continue to greatly bless the literature ministry!

That year, I received a copy of the new Japanese translation of *More God, More Power.* I prayed that God would make it a great blessing to many readers. We also granted permission for a reprint of the Romanian edition of *Touch the World through Prayer.* And we issued a contract to a church in Germany for an Amharic edition in Africa. *It is always a blessing to serve the Lord!*

God's Special Christmas Gift

In my January 2009 prayer letter to our ministry partners, I shared how God had given Betty and me to each other in 1939, and how we had shared nearly sixty-nine years together. As the months passed after God took Betty to himself and, at the age of ninety-two, I proved the truth of Genesis 2:18: "It is not good for the man to be alone."

Betty and my long-time office secretary, Hilda Johnecheck, were close friends, and Hilda knew our family quite well. We attended Sunday school class and church services together, and in more recent years, she had assisted us by driving us to my speaking engagements, to our medical appointments, and so on. In the office, there was always beautiful harmony, and I realized more than ever this harmonious working relationship was God's provision.

After Betty's graduation to Glory, my relationship with Hilda unfolded in a new and uniquely special manner. No other person, besides Betty, knew the details of my life and ministry like Hilda. I soon realized God began planning for us before we were even aware of it, and I asked her to be my wife for the rest of our lives. She accepted and made me the happiest person possible.

I knew that she, too, would continue to carry the burden for the purpose of my literature ministry, if God should call me home before her. I knew she would do all within her power to ensure the DLT books were kept in print and distributed to those places in the world where we, and my family, had invested so much prayer and intercession effort throughout our lives.

My deep desire was for my children to welcome Hilda warmly into our family. When John and Retno arrived from Indonesia for Christmas, that first evening I introduced the topic and asked for John's permission and blessing on our wedding plans.[12] He expressed his total agreement to both Hilda and me. Next, I placed phone calls to Chris in West Virginia and to Darlene in southern Indiana, and they both happily gave their consent and loving support.

So it was through God's guidance, while John and Retno were home from Indonesia for Christmas, and all the family could gather (except for one grandson and his family) that the Lord gave me the joy of marrying my long-time coworker and trusted secretary, Hilda Mae Johnecheck. Ours was a beautiful but simple "family only" wedding on Saturday morning, December 27, in the Duewel Memorial Prayer Chapel at our OMS headquarters, with the Rev. Dr.

Wesley, Hilda, John, Chris, Darlene and families Dec 27, 2008

---

12 When Dr. Duewel's father, Louis Duewel, was making plans for his second marriage, he wrote to Wesley in India, asking for his permission/ blessing. Dr. Duewel chose to follow the same courtesy with John, his son and first child.

Donald Riggs officiating, witnessed by Dr. and Mrs. David C. Long, OMS president and first lady. They committed us to the Lord in prayer as Hilda was now my loving bride, faithful companion, and helper.

HAPPY ADJUSTMENTS (2009)

During the first quarter of 2009, Hilda and I continued normal office work, handling incoming correspondence, receiving phone calls, and participating in OMS headquarters chapels, staff meetings, prayer rallies, and other special prayer times.

In our literature ministry, two Indian editions of *Touch the World through Prayer*, Hindi and Malayalam, were published, and distribution began immediately at a large festival in South India. Zondervan had just sent a copy of the eighth printing of *Revival Fire*, which indicated God was continuing to use it rather widely.

At that time, there were three major projects for overseas editions of DLT books. Requests came for Chinese reprints of two DLT titles needed for distribution during the Christmas-Chinese New Year season. We sought to pray in the funds for those two printings of thirty thousand copies each. Translation work was completed for the French edition of *Ablaze for God* for francophone Africa. SIM International arranged for the books to be distributed personally to each pastor who attended pastors' conferences during the spring of 2010. The challenge was to trust God for the twenty-five thousand dollars needed to print sixteen thousand books that would be distributed to pastors in about a dozen African nations.

OM Books India continued to reprint and distribute DLT books through their bookshops across the country. We regularly received requests from Brother K. C. Joseph, publisher-director, for the next book he planned to translate and publish.

At the request of a publisher in the Czech Republic, I granted permission for the Czech edition of *Touch the World through Prayer* to be formatted into a digital version for the Internet. Praise God for making that book available to people who otherwise would not have access to its message!

Evangelical Fellowship of India "Lifetime Service Award"

The EFI asked me to travel back to India to receive an award. I replied that at age ninety-three, I felt it would not be wise for me to do so. Therefore, they sent me a beautiful bronze plaque with the following inscription:

> Presented to Dr. Wesley L. Duewel in recognition of your servant leadership exemplified to the Body of Christ and faithful contribution to the Church and Mission in India, on the occasion of the 5th All India Congress on Church in Mission, this day of October 14, 2009; "Well done, good and faithful servant! Come and share your master's happiness" (Matt 25:21–23).

Married Life

Hilda and I were very happy together, and we continued to serve Christ with much joy. I thought I knew her after she had been my secretary for some forty years, but I was getting to know her delightfully better now. She was so thoughtful in constantly watching for how she could help me. I walked with my cane on short distances and steadied myself by taking her arm, but for longer distances, I used a walker, on which I could sit and rest, if necessary. She was careful to park as close as possible to the exact places we were going.

CHANGES AT OMS (2010)

Two major changes occurred within OMS in 2010. First, in January, our society formerly known as OMS International changed its name to One Mission Society, with the tagline, "One Lord. One Life. One Calling," based on Ephesians 4:4–6. After an intensive study, our leaders felt this new name clearly conveyed that we all have only "One Lord to Serve, One Life to Live, and One Calling to Fulfill." Our passion was still the same—reaching the nations for Christ!

Second, OMS underwent a tremendous period of reconstruction and reorganization of our main headquarters building. Our DLT office was on the lower ground floor for several years, and President David Long thoughtfully and generously arranged for it to be relocated to another office building, formerly the U.S. ministries department, several hundred feet from the main, or central, building. In February, several of our coworkers and volunteers worked very hard to enable our move to the new building, renamed the Research and Writing Center.

Hilda and I occupied four smaller offices, as part of the DLT office suite, facing Duewel Drive, renamed four years earlier on the occasion of my ninetieth birthday. We thanked God for providing the office space to accommodate my extensive library, plus storage for archival copies of DLT books, related manuscripts, and research materials. *To God be all the glory*!

I was very grateful for many reports telling how God continued to use our ten major DLT books in many areas of the world. Email and phone orders for the books came into the office regularly. As reported previously, we never kept one dollar from the sale of the books. All proceeds, above costs, went into a fund to print more books for distribution in poorer majority world nations. Final printing arrangements for the French edition of *Ablaze for God* were scheduled for September, so we were expecting to soon hear it was off the press. That printing would be distributed during pastors' conferences in about fourteen nations of Africa. We asked for prayer that the printing process would be on schedule and that the books would arrive safely in Africa in due time.

In preparation for the Advent season, the Lord led me to compile a small booklet, *Christmas Is for You...and the World*, which was our Christmas love gift to Jesus that year. It was our prayer that the nine Christmas editorials, written when I served as editor of *Revival Magazine* in India in the 1950s and 1960s, as well as the brief article and poem at the end, would be a blessing and challenge at that Christmas season.

HEARTFELT PRAYER (2011)

Recognizing that every year brought me closer to heaven, I wanted to make sure that my family had every opportunity to know, understand, and make a volitional choice to accept the salvation available in Jesus Christ. So, at Easter that year, I wrote a personal letter to each one of them, the contents of which follow, so that if you, my dear reader, have not made that decision, God, in his mercy, will give you another chance through reading my life's story.

Dear Children and Grandchildren,

Happy Easter to you! I trust this finds you well and that things are going well with you. In a few weeks I will be ninety-five. God is so good to keep me well.

I just want to send you and all our family Easter greetings at this special time of the year. Easter reminds us of how much Jesus loved us and continues to do so, and it reminds us of the awesome price he paid in order to make it possible for us to become children of God, and to be sure when we die, we are ready for heaven.

Any sins we have committed, and of which we have not repented to God and asked his forgiveness, disqualify us from entering heaven when we die. That means we are blocked from heaven forever. I so much want to spend eternity with you, as we all share everlasting life in the place God has prepared for us.

Heaven opens to us a whole new dimension of everlasting life, fulfillment, and joy. The alternative to heaven is eternal separation from God and all the wonderful plans he has prepared for us in heaven. Satan controls whatever is outside of God's sphere and plan. That is neither good nor pleasant to anticipate.

So Easter assures us that God has wonderful plans for us if we welcome and accept his transforming love. His heaven is more wonderful and blessed than we can fully imagine or anticipate. I hope you are making full preparation.

What better way to observe and celebrate Easter than to pray to Jesus and ask his forgiveness for any and all the sins of our past! And ask him to accept us as his followers, forgiving anything in our past that is contrary to his love and plan for us, and asking him to help us live from now on, in a way pleasing and acceptable to him.

You are part of my family, and I want to keep you in that good fellowship! The only time we can give our life to God the Father and his wonderful and loving Son, Jesus, is while we are alive. And the only time we can qualify for the joys of his eternity, which he is planning for us, is now. By accepting his will in our life now, we can qualify for the wonderful life and plans he has prepared for us.

Please accept my love for you and accept the love and place Jesus is preparing for you. Your Father and Grandfather.

Something we seemed to be doing with increasing regularity, was attending funerals and memorial services. In late March, we attended the memorial service for Betty's niece in Cincinnati. In early April, we participated in a life celebration service for Dr. Harold Burgess, former OMS board member, in Wilmore, Kentucky. Dr. Burgess also served as the inaugural DLT chairman from its incorporation in 1993, until he entered heaven.

In June, we enjoyed attending the "OMS family reunion," a special time of celebration and thanksgiving as we recounted God's great faithfulness during the past 110 years of OMS's worldwide ministry. Dr. John Oswalt, our special speaker from Asbury Theological and Wesley Biblical seminaries, challenged us with messages on the necessity of holy living as we seek to reach nations for Christ. It was thrilling to hear scriptural holiness preached in such a relevant and contemporary fashion!

I celebrated my ninety-fifth birthday the first week of June on three special occasions: Darlene and Terry joined us for the OMS birthday gathering; Senior Christians Are Marvelous People (SCAMPS), the senior group at our home church, honored me at their monthly breakfast, called "Biscuit Therapy"; and Hilda and I had enjoyable fellowship at a lunch with two of our very dear friends and loyal prayer partners. *God was so good!*

The promise I so often claimed and quoted was Psalm 91:16, "With long life will I satisfy him and show him my salvation" (KJV). And again I claimed these words in Romans 1:15, "As much as in me, I am ready to preach the gospel" (NKJV). I was ready to continue *all for Jesus*.

We had so much for which to thank God. He gave me comparatively good health, and though I now depended on a wheelchair for longer distances, daily Hilda and I went to the office so kindly provided by OMS. We were very blessed as we worked and prayed together. God enabled Hilda to take such good care of me, and I thanked him for her several times each day.

A LOOK BACK (2012)

At ninety-six years of age, I looked back at the faithfulness of God. *How I praised him!* I prayed daily for God to keep blessing the DLT ministry. By then, one or more DLT books were still in fifty-eight languages, with a world circulation of more than 2.5 million books. *To God be all the glory!*

OMS graciously gave me opportunities to share life experiences with our missionary candidates during orientation sessions, with other groups attending training seminars, and one-on-one with prospective candidates and others visiting headquarters.

In June, Hilda and I attended the Wabash Annual Conference of the Free Methodist Church, held at its retreat center in Clay City, Indiana. My history with the Free Methodist Church started shortly after Betty and I moved from Los Angeles to Greenwood in late 1965. I began teaching an adult Sunday school class at West Morris Street Church, which later became the senior adult class. Over the years, God also gave me the privilege of speaking at dozens of Free Methodist gatherings, including, but not limited to, the Wabash camp, pastors' conferences, and prayer retreats in Alabama, England, Florida, Illinois, Indiana, Michigan, and Oregon, also teaching during the "J-Term" for pastors and local churches.

At the conference, what a surprise it was to be presented a "certificate of appreciation" in recognition of my forty-five years of ordained ministry! Dr. Donald E. Riggs, our former pastor at West Morris Street Church (who had also officiated at my and Hilda's wedding four years earlier), was also honored for sixty years of ordained ministry in the conference.

In September, I authorized OM Books India to reprint twelve editions, and to begin translation work on eight new editions, in major Indian languages: Bengali, Hindi, Gujarati, Kannada, Marathi (two titles), Tamil, and Telugu.

In October, we were blessed by the visit of Bonnie Tsai, a dear Chinese lady who translated my book *Touch the World through Prayer* into Mandarin. By then, at least 350,000 copies of *Touch the World through Prayer* had been printed and distributed to Chinese readers, mostly inside China. *To God be all the glory!*

Bonnie Tsai with Valetta Crumley and Wesley

Our friends in Hong Kong informed us of the need for another reprint of three DLT books in the Chinese language. With God's provision of funds, we authorized those reprints, which came off the presses in time for distribution in strategic places during the Chinese New Year season, mid-February 2013. *Praise God!*

In Brazil, the current publisher of Portuguese-language editions requested permission to publish new editions of five DLT books, making revisions, as necessary, considering the new Portuguese grammar.

MY NINETY-SEVENTH YEAR (2013)

What a joy to submit my annual report to the OMS board of trustees as I celebrated my ninety-seventh birthday on June 3! God alone was worthy of praise for the ministry he gave me, even at my advanced age. Daily, I feasted on God's Word, and in extended prayer times, I asked God to help OMS accomplish his goals. I rejoiced to receive reports from many areas of the world, but especially from India, telling of God's blessing upon the efforts of our OMS coworkers. Oh, for God to pour out a mighty revival on all our work in many nations! *Praise his name!*

During the previous months, I had continued to enjoy the opportunities to meet and share with OMS candidates, local church youth, and others while they were in Greenwood for orientation, training, mission awareness, and spiritual challenges. *To God be all the glory*!

Zondervan—HarperCollins Christian Publishing

In the previous year, Zondervan and Thomas Nelson had begun collaborative efforts to form HarperCollins Christian Publishing. They had also created a new Author Concierge Services team, and we would now relate to that department when placing book orders. Now under the name of HarperCollins Christian Publishing, our American publisher continued to reprint five DLT titles: *Ablaze for God, Heroes of the Holy Life, Mighty Prevailing Prayer, Revival Fire,* and *Touch the World through Prayer*. In the spring, they'd designed a new cover design for *Mighty Prevailing Prayer*, and that new edition was now off the press.

Three of those titles—*Heroes of the Holy Life, Mighty Prevailing Prayer,* and *Revival Fire*—were available in eBook format. In addition, we authorized eBook editions of *Ablaze for God* and *Touch the World through Prayer*, although royalty statements didn't yet reflect that those titles were available. I looked back at the faithfulness of God, and my heart overflowed with gratitude to him for our faithful partners in ministry. Hilda and I were very grateful to serve together, fulfilling all the Lord intended to accomplish through our united lives. Our lives and our futures are in God's wonderful hands. *Praise God from whom all blessings flow!*

We deeply appreciated our prayer partners, and our prayer was that God would bless every one of them. Letters kept coming to my desk, telling how God was making DLT books a blessing to readers. *To God be all the glory!* God alone is worthy of praise for the ministry he continued to give me, even at my advanced age. Psalm 146:1–2 says, "Praise the Lord. Praise the Lord, O my soul. I will praise the Lord all my life; I will sing praise to my God as long as I live." *How I praise him!*

God was so good! Throughout the year, we enjoyed a good measure of health and strength for each day's opportunities to serve him. Just as our partners' prayers and support were a vital part of our ministry, we faithfully prayed for them—and God's blessing upon them!

NEW OMS PRESIDENT (2014)
DLT Contributions to ECI Bible Libraries

At the beginning of 2014, my heart overflowed with gratitude to God for his blessings and mercies extended over the previous twelve months. It was thrilling to send English-language editions of DLT books and other writings, to each of the thirteen ECI Bible libraries in India. It was a special joy, particularly because I helped to found the Allahabad Bible Seminary, the first OMS Bible training institution in India. In October, we packed two each of ten DLT books, plus some other writings over the years, for each of the thirteen libraries, a total of 491 books in ten boxes.

Those DLT books were loaded onto two shipping pallets—containing one hundred boxes with 4,627 books—OMS was sending to the seaport of Chennai, India, along with a container of books sent by Christian Book Distributors. Dr. Samuel Jayakumar of the Evangelical Theological Academy of the ECI, was in turn responsible for redistribution to the thirteen theological training institutions of the ECI. We prayed for the shipment to arrive safely in India in early 2015.

To celebrate my ninety-eighth birthday on June 3, Hilda planned another party at OMS headquarters. Some sixty OMS staff, our pastor, and Darlene and Terry joined us in thanking God for his great faithfulness. We had also enjoyed precious fellowship with many OMS friends and colleagues, our church family, and our families on several other occasions those past months.

Dr. Robert Fetherlin's Inauguration

It was an honor and privilege to attend the late June inauguration service of our tenth OMS president, Dr. Robert Fetherlin. Dr. Fetherlin and his wife, Esther, served previously with the Christian and Missionary Alliance Church as missionaries to Mali, West Africa, and eventually, as the CMA's vice president of international ministries. Dr. David Long, our outgoing, ninth OMS president for the past ten years, along with his wife, Lori, continued his service with OMS as vice president of theological education.

Sadly, late afternoon the same day, we joined OMS staff in our fellowship hall, to say farewell to our eighth OMS president, Dr. J. B. Crouse Jr. He was taken to glory suddenly, and those who could not travel to Wilmore were able to view the celebration of his life through live streaming from Hughes Auditorium at Asbury University. Dr. Crouse and his wife, Bette, served in Korea for many years prior to his term as OMS president. God used him as a great man of faith and action to accomplish so much in the Society during his thirteen years as OMS president.

Dr. Fetherlin started his first official day as OMS president by leading our monthly staff prayer rally the first of July. We were thankful for the strong emphasis OMS continued to place on prayer and intercession for the OMS work worldwide. Our annual conference was held on the beautiful campus of Indiana Wesleyan University in Marion, Indiana, where we enjoyed wonderful days of inspiration, challenge, and fellowship with OMS missionaries and friends we hadn't seen for several years. With deep thanksgiving to God for his great faithfulness, and with deep appreciation to OMS, my future was in God's wonderful hands. *Praise God from whom all blessings flow!*

By now, OMS was engaged in outreach ministry in about seventy-two nations around the world, with a strong emphasis on evangelism, church planting, training, and partnership. In India, God had grown the Evangelical Church of India, with those thirteen Bible training seminaries, into 4,500 local churches and more than a million believers. My prayer was for God to help all of us sense anew the urgency of praying for and sharing the love of Jesus with those who need our Savior. We invited everyone to join us in prayer.

MY NINETY-NINTH YEAR (2015)

As we entered 2015, Hilda and I thanked God for the way he continued to enlarge and bless the DLT ministry. I had done my best to remain steadfast and faithful in my efforts to provide the evangelical world with quality Wesleyan-Armenian theological materials. As executive secretary of DLT, Hilda's invaluable contribution merited special acknowledgment and deep appreciation.

As I approached my ninety-ninth birthday on June 3, I could truly say along with Paul, "I thank Christ Jesus our Lord, who has given me strength, that he considered me faithful, appointing me to his service" (1 Tim 1:12). OMS celebrated my June birthday during our monthly prayer rally, focusing on OMS India ministry for that special occasion. Bishop Ezra Sargunam, bishop-president of the Evangelical Church of India, one of my early students in India, presented an encouraging update of current OMS ministry in India by way of a live video conference call. He shared words of appreciation for my twenty-five years of missionary service in India and that the ECI had a goal of establishing ten thousand churches with one hundred million believers by the year 2020! I'm confident that through mighty prevailing prayer, these goals, too, shall be reached. My heart rejoiced as I reflected on God's faithfulness to me throughout my life.

My ministerial credentials were with the Wabash Annual Conference of the Free Methodist Church. In mid-June, we drove to Clay City, about an hour and thirty minutes southwest of Greenwood, for one day of the 130th FMC annual conference. Conference officials honored me with a "certificate of appreciation" for faithful service in recognition of forty-eight years of pastoral ministry in the conference. We rejoiced in the encouraging reports of God's blessing throughout the conference, and we thanked God for the opportunity to fellowship with pastors and conference leaders throughout the year. Each year, we attended the annual conference and Christmas gatherings of the FMC Wabash Conference.

On October 31, about twenty OMS missionaries showed up at our home, unannounced, to celebrate Hilda's eightieth birthday! Dr.

Robert Fetherlin pulled off this surprise by in advance arranging to visit me before noon. For Hilda, it was a very pleasant surprise, you can be sure! Numbers 6:25 says, "The Lord make his face shine upon you and be gracious to you."

Perhaps my greatest ministry at that stage of my life was intercessory prayer, especially for OMS work worldwide and God's continued blessing on my writings, local church, and family. Over and over again, I thanked him for calling me to India when I was just a five-year-old boy. I praised him for the privilege of helping to found the OMS work in India and investing twenty-five years in that spiritually needy land. How I rejoiced to read such encouraging reports of how God was expanding the OMS work across that nation!

I thanked God for the privilege of being in my office each day. My custom was to begin the day by reading my Bible and praying, and then handling incoming mail, phone calls, and greeting visitors. Hilda and I sought to be a blessing as we participated in the chapel services, monthly prayer rallies, and other special prayer times scheduled at headquarters. *To God be all the glory!*

With deep thanksgiving to God for his great faithfulness for more than ninety-nine years and with deep appreciation to the members of the board of directors of Duewel Literature Trust, Inc., I again expressed deep gratitude to God for my brothers and sisters in Christ, and his constant blessing on the literature ministry. *To God be all the glory*!

THE WORK GOES ON (2016)

For seventy-five years, since 1939, it has been my joy, challenge, and privilege to be a member of a missionary organization God continued to use greatly. OMS was founded by a soul-winning layman, who, in the first six months after his conversion, personally led seventy-five of his fellow employees in Western Union to receive the new birth.

When God called Charles Cowman to go out into the world, by faith in his provision and without a human society behind him, his coworkers closed in around their former boss in a fellowship of love, faith, and obedience. OMS was initially called to Japan, the first OMS field, where the first converts were primarily telegraph operators, who together formed the "Telegraphers' Missionary Prayer Band." In their mission hall in 1901 in Tokyo, Charles said about their first year, "Every night without exception, we have seen souls coming to Christ; sometimes one, often five and ten, and not infrequently on Sabbath evenings there have been twenty or more seekers. What a glorious record for one year!"[13]

In the book about her husband, Mrs. Lettie Cowman wrote:

> The winning of a soul was to him what the winning of a battle is to a soldier; what the winning of a bride is to a lover; what the winning of a race is to an athlete. Charles Cowman lived for just one thing—to win souls for Christ. This was his sole passion.

IN MEMORIAM

Dr. David E. Dick

On Saturday, March 5, 2016, at 11:50 p.m., God called Dr. Wesley L. Duewel home. The Lord had given him a rich and full life, which he in turn gave totally for the cause of Christ around the world. As in all his earthly endeavors, Wesley Duewel prepared well in advance for his memorial service. Therefore, it brought glory to God, reflecting his lifelong ministry in this world.

As a younger missionary, I asked him, "How do you know God's will for your life?"

He replied, "God's will is dynamic, but he always leads through his Word and prayer. Stay in his Word and ask God to show you. I'm sure he will."

In that little capsule of counseling, he underscored the very experience of his own life. God's will was dynamic throughout his life, but his call was never uncertain, and he followed it throughout his life on the field, in administration, and to the very end of his time on this earth. Dr. Duewel's ministry continued through his writing and

---

13   Cowman, *Charles E. Cowman, Missionary-Warrior*, 155.

publication ministry under the auspices of the DLT. He left a virtual treasure trove of poems and manuscripts never published, but he always included copies of his poetry in his routine correspondence and annual letters, selected for the purpose at hand. How he managed to compose such depth and quality in the context of the unpaved, dusty, dirty roads of rural India, and produce draft after draft of lectures, devotionals, and poems, never ceased to amaze all those who realized what a nonstop, Spirit-energized person he was during his prime. He continued to pray for the literature ministry on a regular basis. If you stopped by his office throughout the week in the early morning, you'd find him faithfully reading God's Word. He had a tremendous love for the Word and had read it daily since childhood. He read the entire Bible 209 times and the New Testament 354 times. And he continued to carry a constant burden for the unevangelized millions of the world, his constant emphasis upon prayer as the key to harvest and revival.

As an individual, few have ministered with less defect and reached similar glowing heights of sanctification without arrogance while doing so. The primary and prominent feature of Dr. Duewel's life was his devotion to the Word of God and prayer. Like many who have gone before him, and from whom he no doubt learned, his underlying message was, "When I pray and meditate the most, I accomplish the most." This was the guiding principle of his actions, both public and private. He was always diligent, eager to do the right thing, be humble, demonstrate patience, and serve zealously, always motivated with love for God, his adored Redeemer and Friend, and his fellow man.

In planning his own funeral, Dr. Duewel wrote:

I have loved and prayed for my family members and loved ones for years. I want us all to love Jesus, serve him here on earth, and be a blessing to others. I want to spend the endless years of eternity with all of you in heaven. I chose the song, "I Dreamed I Searched Heaven for You," for any of my dear ones who may have thus far failed to make their clear-cut, total commitment to Jesus. Please don't delay—the longer you delay, the more rewards that Jesus longs to give you will be missed by your delay. I love you. I want to spend eternity with you. I want to rejoice eternally over your abundant eternal reward. —Wesley.[14]

Mrs. Hilda Duewel

Our loving Lord very graciously fulfilled his promise to Wesley, my precious companion: "With long life will I satisfy him and show him my salvation" (Ps 91:16). At ninety-nine years of age, only three months short of reaching his one-hundredth birthday, Wesley completed his earthly journey and entered the joys of heaven.

My sincere appreciation to our friend and colleague, Dr. David E. Dick, vice president at large of One Mission Society, for carefully honoring Wesley's preplanned instructions and officiating at a victorious celebration of life and ministry service on Tuesday, March 15, 2016, hosted by our home church, West Morris Free Methodist Church in Indianapolis. Family and friends came from Indonesia, London, and eleven USA states, including Wesley's three children— John, Chris, and Darlene—their spouses, Wesley's six grandchildren, and one of his three great-grandchildren, as well as several extended family members.

Nearly three hundred friends and family gathered for the sacred, triumphant service. Our OMS family and Free Methodist friends joined in the singing of hymns, prayer, and reading of Scripture and Wesley's poem "Tis Jesus! Heaven Has Begun!" Some sang solos. Heartfelt tributes were given by Dr. Robert L. Fetherlin, president, One Mission Society; Dr. Mike E. Conkle, former pastor and Free Methodist Church representative; and Wesley's children—John, Christine, and Darlene. This victorious service closed with a majestic rendition of "The Hallelujah Chorus."

Wesley was laid to rest with Betty, and next to Eugene and Esther Erny, at Forest Lawn Cemetery in Greenwood. Again, I thank God for our dear friends and OMS coworkers who assisted our family in numerous ways during those days.

---

14 "I Dreamed I Searched Heaven for You," James D. Vaughan, Lawrenceburg, TN, 1932.

Although Wesley had four brief hospital stays between July and December 2015, his severe stroke and homegoing within a period of five hours was a tremendous shock to me. Throughout the previous seven months, we experienced God's faithfulness repeatedly as our OMS and church friends surrounded us with loving prayer, encouraging visits, phone calls, and practical help. Medical doctors and hospital staff were considerate and attentive to Wesley's health issues. We were very grateful!

OMS established a Memorial Fund Project in Dr. Duewel's honor, designated for Christ the King Diamond Jubilee Church in Minjur (Chennai area), India, which was completed in 2018.

Often during our seven years of marriage, and especially at mealtimes and evening prayer together, Wesley and I thanked God for you, our partners in ministry. Thank you for every expression of your love for us and for the Lord. With deep gratitude to God, through many years, with the psalmist I can say, "The boundary lines have fallen for me in pleasant places; surely I have a delightful inheritance" (Ps 16:6).

DLT Succession

At Dr. Duewel's invitation, Dr. David E. Dick began serving on the board of directors of Duewel Literature Trust, Inc., in 2011. After Dr. Duewel's entrance into heaven, in its annual meeting in November 2016, the board elected Dr. Dick to succeed Wesley as president. At that time, Dr. Dick shared this statement with the board:

> When Dr. Duewel invited me to serve as a board member of the DLT, he expressly asked me if I had a burden to continue the translation, publication, and distribution of his books after his passing, and I said, "Yes, because I see no reason why your books will not continue to meet a need in the world at large and in the Wesleyan world in particular."

In October 2016, our Evangelical Church of India (ECI) leaders gladly accepted our offer of Dr. Duewel's personal library. On this second occasion, a tractor trailer truck picked up another fifty-nine boxes of 1,933 books to transport to Christian Book Distributors, in

Boston, Massachusetts, for a shipping container going to Chennai, India. On January 14, 2017, Rev. Samuel Duraiswamy, our ECI international partnership liaison, communicated that the shipment had arrived and would be distributed to the three major seminaries, in Allahabad, Calcutta, and Chennai.

The OMS Memorial Fund Project to honor Dr. Duewel was designated for the Christ the King Diamond Jubilee Church in Minjur (Chennai area), India. The Rev. Dr. D. Sundar Singh wrote:

> The dedication of reconstruction and renovation of the ECI Diamond Jubilee Church at Minjur held on the seventeenth June 2018 went well. The Minjur church has so far established five branch churches. The church is now doing outreach ministry at a nearby village called Uranampet, where a seminary graduate has been appointed as pastor. The church has started thirty-five house churches and conducts Sunday school for non-Christian children at four other locations. . . . The last Sunday of every month is observed as Mission Sunday, and through this emphasis, the congregation is supporting twenty-two Malto tribal children and five indigenous missionaries monthly.[15]

ECI Christ the King Diamond Jubilee Church, Minjur, Chennai Diocese, June 2018

In late 2016, One Mission Society and the DLT compiled a collection of tributes to Dr. Duewel, *All for Jesus: A Celebration of the Life and Ministry of Dr. Wesley L. Duewel (1916–2016)*, Dr. David E. Dick, editor, with the assistance of Mr. George F. Allen, author and freelance consultant, and the professional publishing services of Mrs. Susan McCarty and Mr. James Bova at Spotlight-Strategies of Franklin, Indiana.[16]

---

15   David E. Dick prayer letter extracted from Dr. D. Sundar Singh's report.

16   Dick, unabridged *All for Jesus*, iii.

We are very grateful to everyone joining their prayers with ours in the preparation of Dr. Duewel's life story and testimony and for the ongoing literature ministry worldwide.

Only one life 'twill soon be past.
Only what's done for Christ will last.[17]

---

17   "Only One Life, 'Twill Soon Be Past" poem by C. T. Studd, the famous British cricketer turned missionary, based on the Scripture verse that says, "So we make it our goal to please him, whether we are at home in the body or away from it" (2 Cor 5:9–10).

Bibliography

Cowman, Lettie B. *Missionary Warrior: Charles E. Cowman.* Greenville: One Mission Society, 2019 (originally published in 1928).

_____. *Missionaries Prayed—He Answered.* Los Angeles: The Oriental Missionary Society, 1955.

Dick, David E. *All for Jesus: A Celebration of the Life and Ministry of Dr. Wesley L. Duewel (June 3, 1916–March 5, 2016).* Franklin: Spotlight Strategies, 2016.

Douglas, Cecelia Luelf, and Ruth Smith Taylor. *The History of the Bible Holiness Church.* Shoals: Whispering Pines, 2011.

Duewel, Wesley L. *More God, More Power: Filled and Transformed by the Holy Spirit.* Grand Rapids: Zondervan, 2000.

_____. *Touch the World through Prayer.* Grand Rapids: Zondervan, 1986.

Erny, Ed. *This One Thing: The Story of Missionary Leader Eugene Erny.* Greenwood: OMS International, 1991.

Knapp, Martin Wells. *God's Revivalist and Bible Advocate.* Cincinnati: Revivalist, n.d.

Moser, Kevin M., and Larry D. Smith. *God's Clock Keeps Perfect Time, God's Bible School's First 100 Years (1900–2000).* Cincinnati: Revivalist, 2000.

McCasland, David. *Oswald Chambers: Abandoned To God.* Grand Rapids: Discovery, 1993.

Shelhamer, E. E. *How To Get Healed and Keep Healed.* Cincinnati: God's Bible School and Revivalist, 1929.

Smith, Larry D. *A Century on the Mount of Blessings*: *The Story of God's Bible School*. Cincinnati: God's Bible School and Revivalist, 2016.

Pradhan, Prem. *Apostle to Nepal: The Man as Great as the Himalayans*. Jacksonville: SeedSowers, 2008.

Wood, Robert D. *In These Mortal Hands*. Greenwood: OMS International, 1983.

Wikipedia. "Lamsa Bible." *Wikipedia*. Accessed September 20, 2019. https://en.wikipedia.org/wiki/Lamsa_Bible

DUEWEL LITERATURE TRUST LIBRARY

Coffee Break News, 13 October 1967; 31 January 1970; September 1971; 15 February 1973; 1 May 1974; 15 May 1974; 15 August 1974; 15 January 1978; 15 February 1978; 1 August 1978; 1 December 1979; 1 May 1979; 15 June 1979; 15 June 1980; 1 May 1981; 1 April 1981; 1 April 1976; 15 August 1978; 1 June 1978; 15 August 1978; 15 February 1978.

Duewel, Louis J. "One Hundred Years of Duewel History (1852–1952)." Duewel Literature Trust, 1952.

Duewel, Wesley L. "Challenging Demonism and Occultism through the Holy Spirit." Duewel Literature Trust, August 1972. Revised, September 1973.

_____. July–August 1944. "Evangelism at the Mela Festival." *The Flaming Sword*. The Bible Holiness Church.

Duraiswamy, Samuel, ed. May and December, 2019. *Evangelical Church of India: Church Planter*. Chennai, Tamil Nadu, India.

Forward Together, July 1969; October 1969; February 1970; 16 March 1970; August 1970; December 1970; January 1971; February 1971; May 1971; June 1971; September 1971; November 1971; February 1972; 18 July 1972; June 1973; July 1973; September 1973; December 1973; September 1974; January 1975; June 1975; April 1976; June 1976; July

1976; May 1978; December 1978; May 1980; July 1980;
15 April 1981; December 1981; September 1981; January
1982; October 1969.

Outreach, January 1970; January 1974; February 1974; March
1974; November/December 1974; May 1976; June
1976; September 1976; October 1976; November 1976;
March 1977; June 1977; September 1977; April 1978;
May 1978; April 1979; September 1979; June 1982;
January–December 1987; May–June 1987; July–August
1987; September–October 1987; March–December
1988; September–October 1989; January–March 1990;
November–December 1987 through January–March 1992;
April–May 1992; January–March 1993.

The Missionary Standard, April 1954; November 1964; April 1965;
February 1965; July 1967; November 1969.

The righteous are held in everlasting remembrance.

Endorsements

Late one evening in the summer of 1966 as I was transitioning from the business world to OMS as staff artist, Wesley came into my newly assigned office space and passionately commissioned it, me, and my tools of the trade to God's new and eternal purpose. A couple of years later, as I committed to systematically read completely through the Bible at least once a year, I discovered that Wesley had done so hundreds of times. Two decades later, when I determined to pray around the world through a world atlas, I was profoundly encouraged and affirmed by Wesley's new book, *Touch the World through Prayer*. Early in 2000, as I assumed leadership of a team of warfare prayer intercessors, I determined to hinder the president of Haiti from rededicating to Satan the nation for another 200 years. As I sought Wesley's counsel, he said, "You're in uncharted territory. I will faithfully pray for you and the team." And he did. But he also gave me copies of *Mighty Prevailing Prayer*, which I shared with the team. That book became our warfare prayer manual, inspiration, and guide to sustained faith. Prayer did in fact prevail; Haiti was not rededicated to Satan, and the president was exiled to Africa.

In an age of disappointing failure of far too many evangelical leaders, writers, and speakers, *All for Jesus* is a refreshing reminder that God has indeed graciously sustained a uniquely authentic voice. For countless thousands around the world, Wesley L. Duewel is known primarily as a prolific author of deeply spiritual books and periodicals. Among those are a multitude who have actually been in attendance at his many decades of preaching and teaching venues. And amongst that multitude are those who enjoyed a personal relationship with this man of profound faith and prayer. For more than half of Wesley Duewel's ninety-nine year sojourn on this earth, I was privileged to be numbered with that truly blessed group. For me, *All for Jesus* adds context, texture, and fresh color to cherished memories that were beginning to fade.

> Eugene Robert Bertolet, Graphic Artist
> One Mission Society

I had the privilege to serve with Wesley Duewel for forty years. I knew him as a man with unwavering integrity and love for Jesus. Dr. Duewel had a consuming passion to serve the Lord and tell everyone how to know Jesus and be His disciple. Dr. Duewel was very intelligent. His love for the Lord, his knowledge of God's Word, and his willingness to give himself away to countless thousands around the world may have made him the greatest disciple-maker in the twentieth century.

> Warren Hardig, Former Executive Director
> Men for Missions International

It is indeed an honor to have been asked to write something about this inspiring book. I hope it is read by the multitudes who have been blessed by his writings. Dr. Duewel's autobiography demonstrates a life that was *All for Jesus*—his life's motto. Although known for his effective missionary service and his inspiring books, it was his hours and days of prayer that explain the success of all he did. To read this book is to be challenged to live a life that flows out of prayer.

> Aletha Hinthorn, Founder/Leader
> Women Alive (aka, Come to the Fire)

If you're after a so-so prayer life, a watered-down faith, and lackadaisical commitment to Jesus—this book is *not* for you. Halfhearted *anything* wasn't Wesley's way. But, if you're longing for more of Jesus and a real-life example of what a prayer-soaked, faith-full, and Spirit-led life with Jesus can become, *All for Jesus* belongs on your shelf and in your heart and mind.

All for Jesus is a riveting and inspiring life-story of the internal fire God lit in Wesley Duewel's heart that set ablaze a life of white-hot love and action for God's Kingdom. The world is blessed that God ordained Wesley to live just shy of a century. His life-changing prayers, powerful messages, purposeful engagements, and scores of books written and translated worldwide enabled so many people globally (my wife and me included) to run the race of faith with greater passion, purpose, and speed. I'm all-in with *All for Jesus*. I encourage you to read this book and allow God to ignite a unique *heart on fire, life on purpose* passion in you through Wesley's story.

Dr. Dwight Robertson, Founding President and CEO
Forge Forward

"Every time I read Wesley Duewel, my heart is lit on fire." That's what I tell people when I introduce them to the written ministry of Dr. Wesley Duewel. For over 40 years, he has been one of my heroes of the holy life. In every one of his books, starting with *Touch the World through Prayer,* Wesley called me to a greater love for Jesus, a greater hunger to see the world come to know Jesus, and a deeper yearning to spend more time in prayer interceding for spiritual harvest and revival fire. *All for Jesus* is Dr. Duewel's remarkable story of how he *Let God guide him Daily* through nearly 100 years of life sharing the great salvation the Lord lived through him. His love for Jesus and his life of *Mighty Prevailing Prayer,* shines through in every page—contagious and inspiring!

My wife and I had the great honor of getting to know Dr. Duewel in his final years. Every time I talked to him or introduced someone to him, he always had the unmistakable glow of the joy of the Lord on his face. His love for Jesus was always fresh and vibrant. One day I asked him what he would want me to share with younger leaders as they served the Lord. He looked at me, eyes shining and face radiating joy, and replied, *"Go for it! All for Jesus!"*

That face and those words summed it all up for me. The reason my heart was lit up when I read Wesley's writings is because he wrote from a heart *Ablaze for God.* May his story set your heart on fire for Jesus, too!

Dr. Tim Roehl, author, *TransforMissional Coaching*
The Fit & Flourish Network

Reading the book was like taking a personal journey with someone I genuinely wanted to be with and know. Repeatedly I was brought to tears of praise and adoration for Dr. Duewel's work in God's great world Kingdom.

As I read Dr. Duewel's acceptance speech when he became president of OMS, my heart beat faster, because I wanted every Christian worker, whether lay, ministerial, or missionary, to be challenged anew by his earnest call. He wanted each one of us to be alarmed, challenged, and more dedicated.

I believe the enormity of his ministry, which is detailed toward the end of the book, helps to see what one person can accomplish. I am reminded of what the founder of OMS, Charles Cowman, said, "The world is yet to see what God can do through a consecrated soul . . . providing he [or she] does not touch the glory." Without a doubt, Dr. Duewel did beyond what was humanly possible and did not touch the glory. I was mesmerized in worship and adoration as I read the manuscript—truly captivated and inspired.

Mrs. Iris Riggs, pastor's wife
Free Methodist Church

Made in the USA
Monee, IL
17 June 2023

35801284R10193